Teaching and Learning
for Wholeness

Teaching and Learning for Wholeness

The Role of Archetypes in Educational Processes

Clifford Mayes

ROWMAN & LITTLEFIELD
Lanham • Boulder • New York • London

Published by Rowman & Littlefield
A wholly owned subsidiary of The Rowman & Littlefield Publishing Group, Inc.
4501 Forbes Boulevard, Suite 200, Lanham, Maryland 20706
www.rowman.com

Unit A, Whitacre Mews, 26-34 Stannary Street, London SE11 4AB

British Library Cataloguing in Publication Information Available

Library of Congress Cataloging-in-Publication Data

Names: Mayes, Clifford, author.
Title: Teaching and learning for wholeness : the role of archetypes in educational
  processes / Clifford Mayes.
Description: Lanham : Rowman & Littlefield, A wholly owned subsidiary of
  The Rowman & Littlefield Publishing Group, Inc., [2017] | Includes bibliographical
  references and index.
Identifiers: LCCN 2016027263 (print) | LCCN 2016039842 (ebook) |
  ISBN 9781475826685 (cloth : alk. paper) | ISBN 9781475826692 (pbk. : alk. paper) |
  ISBN 9781475826708 (Electronic)
Subjects: LCSH: Holistic education. | Jung, C. G. (Carl Gustav), 1875–1961.
Classification: LCC LC990.M393 2017 (print) | LCC LC990 (ebook) |
  DDC 370.11/2—dc23
LC record available at https://lccn.loc.gov/2016027263

Printed in the United States of America

Contents

Introduction   1

1 The Psychodynamics of Educational Processes   19

2 Jung's Archetypal Epistemology   39

3 The Archetypes of Teaching, the Politics of the Classroom,
       and the Case for Archetypal Reflectivity   55

4 Training In the Sign, Education in the Symbol   81

5 In the Light of the Shadow Curriculum   93

6 The Hermetic Teacher   129

Conclusion   145

Bibliography   159

Index   171

About the Author   175

Introduction

Approaching the Archetypes of Education

BASIC ELEMENTS OF JUNGIAN PSYCHOLOGY

Jung's Two Claims

In the opening decades of the 20th century, the Swiss psychiatrist Carl Jung made two claims that radically challenged the two major schools of psychology of his day—Behaviorism and Psychoanalysis.

The first claim was epistemological, dealing with *how* we know *what* we know—or rather, what we *think* we know.

Jung asserted that human beings are born with certain fundamental means and modes of experiencing their lives and then interpreting that experience. These innately fundamental means and modes of experience and interpretation are what Jung called "the archetypes" (1969a). The idea that the human being is born with archetypes already inscribed in his being at its very core was a scandal to Behaviorism.

What Behaviorism offered was, unlike the idea of the archetypes, simple enough. Indeed, it was so simple that it was simplistic. Behaviorism forwarded a model of the human being as just a behavior mechanism, a value-free organic machine, entirely a product of different types and schedules of externally administered, positive-or-negative reinforcements.

Jung's notion of the archetypes stands in the starkest possible contrast to the Behaviorists' denial of anything "mental," especially as innately mental and generative of meaning as the archetypes. For through the archetypes, and *only* through them, Jung asserted, are we able to experience the world, others, and ourselves—and then try to make meaning of it all. Without the archetypes, there would not even be the possibility of experience. There would simply be a creature that was not *experiencing* things but simply *responding* to them from moment to moment, in which case the Behaviorists would be right: a person would be nothing more than a stimulus-response mechanism. But that is not what a human being is.

The first thing to note about the archetypes is what they are not. They are not the cognitive categories and terms of either our daily speech or even our specialized academic discourses. The archetypes go both higher and deeper than that. They are more than those ordinary forms of consciousness and language. True, we *also* organize our experiences with those ordinary forms but not *nearly* as profoundly as happens at the archetypal level. Indeed, it is out of the archetypal realm that those other, secondary forms of practical and rational thought arise in the first place.

Therefore, Jung characterized the archetypes as both "primal" and "transcendental" in the sense that they exist both before and after our usual ways of comprehension and expression (Jung, 1978, p. 30). This is why Jung preferred the word *psyche* to *mind* in trying to imagine how and "where" the archetypes worked. Mind was too suggestive of mere rationality, which the archetypes contained but to which they must not be reduced.

The archetypes that structure psyche operate not only at the conscious level of mind but also beneath and above it, picturing psyche metaphorically in spatial terms, as if it were also a kind of "structure." But in using spatial metaphors of "structuring" to talk about the archetypes, we must be careful while we do, remembering that the archetypes are the source of all mental structures and so, by definition, could not themselves *be* a structure. If they were, then we would then have to now look behind *that* structure to find *its* source, and so on, in an infinite regression.

The archetypes, then, as what *structures structure*, cannot themselves *be* a structure. Although it is tempting, and possibly necessary, to "image" the archetypes in that manner, we must do so fully understanding that whatever terms we use are necessarily metaphors of a mystery.

With those caveats, let us picture the archetypes as *lenses* that psyche must "put on" to "see" and to make sense out of things.

It is in the nature of these archetypal lenses that they allow us—indeed, *require* us—to understand our existence as an ever-evolving *narrative*. Our narrative of our lives at any given moment is our present "best guess" about our lives—about where we have come from, where we stand, where it all might be leading, and what it all might *mean*. We are beings who forge our stories *sub specie eternitatis*—as self-aware creatures of eternity. Without a sense of meaning, we feel abandoned, lost, and await only death.

Without such a narrative, one's life is disoriented. With such a narrative, one intuitively apprehends *significance* in one's life. The archetypes as the infrastructures of our narratives are *significance-making*. And they accomplish this largely through the production of those foundational *symbols* and *stories* around which our life narratives form and by means of which our life narratives are moved forward, whether we are aware of this or not. The psyche is meaning-making and narrative-making—ultimately the same things.

For it is simply a matter of existential fact that every person *has been born into*, or later, in a fundamental exercise of one's existential free agency, *has bought into*, certain symbol systems that direct his life. These symbol systems exist as cultural and spiritual traditions. In them, the archetypes are most radically and impressively active. In these cultural and spiritual traditions, the archetypes manifest themselves as sacred stories, or "myths." These are the foundation of all culture and religion—culture and religion being, at the archetypal level, impossible to separate. As the great 20th-century Existentialist Theologian Paul Tillich famously put it, "Religion is the substance of culture, and culture is the form of religion" (1956, p. 103).

In another of their more compelling manifestations, the archetypes are the driving force behind the production of dreams and art. And to the extent that a dream or a piece of art approaches the source of its energy in the archetypal realm, it is an important dream or great art (Jung, 1966).

It is in such "incarnations of meaning" as sacred narratives and symbols, dreams and art that the presence of the archetypes is most compelling. For, culture, religion, art, and dreams provide us with what Jung called the *archetypal images* that body forth the otherwise unknowable *archetypes*. Without these archetypal images and narratives, we would have no way of either organizing our lives or finding any significance in them, for without archetypal images and narratives, we would have no means of accessing our archetypal core, our own very nature.

In fact, however, the archetypes are *always* operating—shaping how we see the world, ourselves, and others at *every* level and in *every* situation, although the clarity and intensity of our awareness of an archetype's presence will vary.

But when, for whatever reason, we *are* intensely aware of the presence and operation of the archetypes, we feel that they are what Jung, borrowing from Rudolf Otto (1958), called a *mysterium tremendum et fascinans,* a "tremendous and fascinating mystery." Feeling the primal and transcendental pull and tug of the archetypal realm creates in us a sense of what Jung, borrowing from the Greek, characterized as the *numinous*, "the spiritual." Our evaluation of something, someone, or an experience as "significant" varies to the degree that it has brought us to the realm of the absolute archetype.

Even science is no exception to the invisible but omnipresent sway of the archetype, Jung declared. For science is ultimately just another symbol system that has emerged from the archetypal realm, another "narrative," another "best guess" about where we come from, are standing, and are headed (Jung, 1978, p. 105).

The sciences are also organized around certain cherished images and privileged narratives of "how things are" and "how things operate." Those images and narratives can, and will, change from time to time in their historical evolution, such as the shift in imagery of the universe as a black box to a set of infinite, parallel strings. Such a symbolic and narratival change at a cultural level is what constitutes a "scientific revolution" and its "paradigm shifts," much more than "evidence" within the old paradigm does. For, "evidence," no matter how seemingly radical, is allowed *as* evidence only to the degree that it is fundamentally consistent with the old paradigm's parameters but is rejected as not "counting" as evidence if it does not (Kuhn, 1970).

These ideas make up Jung's first challenge to academic and clinical psychology as its major schools existed in his time and pretty much continue to exist in ours.

Jung's Ontological-Ethical Claim

Jung's second controversial idea was not an epistemological one but an ontological and ethical one—one, that is, that involves our status as *existential beings* for whom *the value of things* is crucial.

For based upon his studies and clinical experience, Jung concluded that at the core of all psychic functioning[1] is the need for a spiritually sustaining sense of contact with the Divine, whatever or whoever an individual might feel that to be. In this sense, God is the archetype of archetypes as Jung put it in a psychological rendering of Plato's metaphysics.

Of course, psychology should never try to prove, as did Plato, that the Divine actually exists. That is beyond psychology's scope. It could only assert that the need to commune with the Divine is the central psychological impulse, and that "God" is the most powerful archetype and therefore the core around which all the other archetypes revolved, like planets around a sun. This was all that psychology could say on the matter of God's existence, and this is precisely what Jung *did* say (1977, p. 706).

There is good reason to believe, as I argue elsewhere (Mayes, in press, 2016), that Jung did believe—in his own highly unique, Gnostic way—in the existence of Divinity (Jung, 1977, p. 667). However, for our purposes here, it is enough to say at this point that, according to Jung, the human *need* to touch the Divine and to *feel* that it has in some way and to some degree done so is the central thing to grasp in understanding psyche's many states and endless transformations.

This "archetype of the Divine" would necessarily be felt by the individual to be greater than himself; broader, deeper, and higher than the mere "ego" of his ordinary consciousness. Yet, in his experience of the Divine *within*, the individual would come to know himself *as* the Divine or at least as being in the most intimate possible communion *with* the Divine.

Around this psycho-*spiritual* center, the individual could now organize his life, in the world and for the world yet also *beyond* the world, in satisfying and creative ways. Living one's life as both a *temporal ego* and, simultaneously, a *timeless Self*—the first being the individual's *psychosocial* identity and the second being his *psychospiritual* identity, which are linked to each other by a life-giving tie—*is* psychological health, said Jung (1969b, p. 6). Anything less than this leads to despair and illness.

These ideas constituted Jung's second challenge, this one a scandal to the other major school of psychology of his day—Freudian psychoanalysis.

As is well known, Freud's model of psyche rested on 19th-century-materialist, natural-sciences assumptions in its image of psyche as an overheated engine driven by the steam of desire, the heat arrow always bordering on the red zone. Jung, who before his break with Freud around 1912 or 1913, was considered the "heir apparent" and "crown prince" in Freud's burgeoning psychoanalytic dynasty, saw the value in Freud's model of sexuality—as far as it went. The problem was that, although it went much farther than the Behaviorist model did in its recognizing of the primacy of the inner life, it did not go far enough.

For as some of the more interesting biographical work on Jung over the last decade or so has shown, Jung never fully embraced Freud's dogmatic assertion that it was *sexuality* that was at the core of psyche and that the power of the sexual instinct explained everything about psychodynamics (Shamdasani, 2003). Even during his heyday with Freud as a young physician in his 30s, Jung privately guarded his conviction that the merely sexual model was, although useful, fatally limited if pushed to the extreme.

As unquestionably the most brilliant "disciple" in Freud's inner circle, Jung finally expressed this idea publically, with the appearance in 1912 of a work that would come to be known as *Symbols of Transformation*—an elaborate, rambling, but unmistakable statement of Jung's belief in the primacy of the spiritual impulse in the psyche, not the sexual one. It made the break with Freud inevitable (Shamdasani, 2003). This schism caused Jung enormous professional injury and personal pain, throwing him into an anguished but also fruitful period of several years (Ellenberger, 1970).

But from that point on, Jung, emerging whole from that storm-and-stress as a still relatively young physician of about 40, never wavered from his courageous pronouncement—radical and off-putting for the psychiatric community of his day and still, to a considerable extent, in ours—that it was the longing for communion with the Transcendent, not the urge for sexual union with another, which finally powered psychic functioning.

As for Behaviorism, by the way, Jung scarcely deigned to comment on that trivial reduction of the psychic and ethical complexity of human experience to the voracious behavior of rats scurrying around in a maze, frantically in search of chocolate pellets.

In sum, by Jung's account, we come already equipped with psycho-*spiritual* urges—the archetypes. They are ancient, perhaps even timeless. They are inscribed in us as human beings. They exist and operate in the individual before and beyond the circumstantial construction of his subconscious and the scholastic cultivation of his rationality. In fact, they make up the dynamic field out of which both the subconscious and conscious minds emerge. And they reside, Jung claimed, not in a personal subconscious—which occults merely personal material that had been repressed because it was too painful to be aware of—but in the *collective unconscious*.

WHAT IS THE COLLECTIVE UNCONSCIOUS?

The Collective Unconscious as the Container of the Archetypes

This collective unconscious is the matrix (again, speaking in metaphorical terms!) that "holds" the archetypes. It might also be pictured in poetic terms as a force field. In it are the archetypes as concentrated areas of the field where various types of "meaning" have crystallized into psychological and ethical "formations of energy." It is *collective* because it is innate and universal in human beings. It is *unconscious*[2] because it exists in a much more ancient and much less accessible realm of psyche than either the person's experientially formed *sub*-conscious or secondarily schooled cognitive processes (Jung, 1969a, p. 95, p. 145f).

Jung intimated something of the frankly mystical nature of this collective unconscious at the core of all psychological functioning in writing that "the unconscious is not this thing or that; it is the Unknown as it immediately affects us" (Jung, 1969b, p. 68). In this statement, arguably the most important one in the twenty volumes of his *Collected Works,* the collective unconscious is tellingly portrayed as not only a psychological mystery. It is presented as *the* mystery of our *existence*. As such, *the collective unconscious not only lives in us* as psychological beings, but *we also live in it* as ontological beings.

This was a claim that was simply too much for the academic sciences of the late 19th and early 20th-century, laying Jung open to attacks from many quarters throughout his long career that he was just a fuzzy-headed mystic.

There is no question that he had pronounced mystical tendencies. His family on his mother's side was highly gifted in this way, and Jung had his own impressive otherworldly experiences throughout his paranormally saturated life (Jung, 1965; Bair, 2003). But fuzzy-headed he was not, for it is beyond question that Jung was one of the most influential thinkers of the 20th century (Ellenberger, 1970; Homans, 1995).

According to Jung, the archetypes—that are "in" or that "make up" the collective unconscious—are "the *spiritual correlates* of those physical instincts that determine our biological functions" (1969c, p. 138, emphasis added), "the inherited possibility of human imagination" (1967, p. 65) and "typical modes of apprehension" (1969c, p. 137). Looked at in broader historical terms, archetypes are "the functional disposition [of people throughout different times, places, and cultures] to produce the same, or very similar, ideas" (1956, p. 102). They are "the stock of inherited *possibilities of representation* that are born anew in every individual" (1969a, p. 156).

Later Jungians have pictured archetypes as "preconscious categories which [channel] thought and action into definite shapes" (Frey-Rohn, 1974, p. 92); "a kind of mold for the accumulation and discharge of psychic energy" (Odajnyk, 1976, p. 25); and "the structural nature of the psyche itself," "irreducible and primary" (Palmer 1995, pp. 8, 114).

Synchronicity: The Archetypal Orchestration of Psyche and Matter

Jung occasionally hinted that the archetypes may be pre-existent *ontological* realities as well as pre-existent psychological ones. In that case, the archetypal domain would govern, from an invisible but sovereign archetypal "command center," not only the emergence and structure and dynamics of the psyche but also the emergence and structure and dynamics of the physical world.

The archetypal realm would thus be what Jung, echoing Christian alchemists four centuries before him, called the *Unus Mundus,* the "One World," primal and transcendental (Jung, 1968a, 1969b). From it, the psychological and physical domains originally emanated and to it they must ultimately return—back into its mysterious embrace, its transcendent sea, where all dualities, such as that of the physical and psychological, are resolved and dissolved into a Divine One. This is an idea that is central in Buddhist psychology and metaphysics and an important one in reading Jung, who was deeply interested in Eastern philosophy and religion and wrote a good deal about it (1970b).

At any rate, a shared archetypal foundation for both psyche and matter would certainly help explain the phenomenon of "synchronicity," a term which Jung coined (Jung, 1969c, p. 419ff).[3] This is when a psychological and a physical event correspond in a way that is undeniably meaningful, even to the point of being overwhelming, to the person experiencing it. However, it is astronomically improbable to the point of being simply impossible that this "parallelism" of psyche and matter could have been caused by any known physical laws. A synchronicity is a rending of the fabric of ordinary space-time, a "rupture" of conventional science's cosmological symbols and narratives. This accords with Jung's view of Western science as finally being contingent, archetypally symbolic, and not absolute—although undoubtedly important in countless ways in our empirical lives (Main, 2004).

One explanation of synchronicity is that a synchronicity may take place when an archetype in its physical manifestation and the same archetype in its psychological realization come together in a way that has been orchestrated by the particular type of "meaning" that that archetype represents—which is, as we have already seen, precisely what archetypes do in our lives. They generate meaning.

A synchronicity underscores some particular meaning by bringing the physical and psychical worlds together in a singularly impressive manner under the power of an archetype and in the service of the individual's psychospiritual advancement. In that case, a synchronicity becomes a "clue" that has been sent by the archetypal realm to the individual, which he must then decode in order to further his life narrative.

Jung thus said that synchronicity is a *meaning-full* (that is, archetypally structured) *co-incidence* (of the physical and psychological-ethical world).

More on the Nature of the Archetype, Its Manifestation in Archetypal Symbols, and the Difference between the Two

It is important to stress again that although archetypes are "the functional disposition to produce the same, or very similar, ideas" in people everywhere, they are *not* those historically recurring ideas *themselves*. Although this is a fine distinction and a difficult idea, as Jung was always the first to admit, it is crucial in nearly every form of Jungian and post-Jungian psychology (Alister and Hauke, 1998).

An archetype *cannot* be the object of thought because it is the source from which our ability to think comes in the first place.[4] Just as a radio emits sound waves but is not the sound waves—which could never "double back" on themselves to "hear" the radio, which, in a sense, exists "before" the sound waves and is therefore "superior" to them—so thoughts cannot double back on themselves to "think" the archetypes.

But wanting to stay away from speculating about what might be ontologically or metaphysically "real" and therefore beyond the reach of psychology, Jung simply asserted that archetypes, as the epistemological "lenses" *through* which we see, cannot, therefore, be *what* we see through them—any more than a set of contact lenses is the tree we see when we are looking at it through the lenses.[5] We will examine this difficult but rewarding idea in greater depth in chapter 2.

Yet, although it is impossible to experience archetypes directly, it *is* possible to experience and work with them *indirectly*—and in a highly compelling and creative manner.

This is because archetypes manifest themselves in and to consciousness as *archetypal symbols, characters, and narrative structures*, which we not only *can* know directly but which indeed we constantly produce—especially in our dreams, artistic creations, life narratives, founding cultural narratives, and religions. These archetypal symbols, characters, and stories are enormously resonant within us.

They can be categorized to some degree so that we can study and work with them, but in the last analysis, they only point back, and also point forward, to the primordial mystery and transcendent longings of the human being.

In a previous study (2007), I offered one possible grouping of archetypes, which I give below. But such an exercise in classification must always be taken as incomplete and with a grain of salt as at most a legitimate convenience. Such a grouping of archetypal symbols is far from the primal-transcendental reality of the archetypal realm itself, since any "taxonomy" of archetypes is simply an attempt to categorize a mystery so that we can talk about and work with it.

Archetypal events include: birth, baptism, battle, initiation, education, vocation, friendship, courtship, matrimony, repentance, atonement, ritual sacrifice, death, and final judgment.

Some of the most prominent *archetypal landscapes and edifices* are the wilderness, city, home, place of instruction, edifice of worship, battlefield, heaven, and hell.

Certain *geometrical shapes* are also prominent: circles (often as mandalas), squares (especially crosses), and triangles (sometimes in three-person godheads).

Some *numbers* also seem to have particularly profound psychological and spiritual significance and are therefore probably of archetypal import: (1) signifying unity; (2) duality; (3) the reconciliation of tension in a new (i.e., third) perspective which unites but transcends the opposing polarities; (4) the creation of a new foundation upon which the new perspective can become established; and (5) the quintessence of it all. The prime numbers also have psychospiritual significance.[6] We will examine some of these archetypes for their educational significance in the following chapters.

Two conclusions follow from Jung's idea of the collective unconscious, its archetypes, and the fact that we can only experience them as archetypal symbols, figures, and narratives.

First, symbolic imagery is a better way to explore the depths of our being than "propositional language"—that is, the theoretical constructs, specialized vocabularies, and reasoning procedures of a particular area of intellectual inquiry, whether it is physics or anthropology, history, or biology. For, it is symbolic imagery that best captures the emotional and experiential complexity of "man's search for meaning," and ultimately this existential quest neither originates nor culminates in reason (Frankl, 1976). "The intellect is undeniably useful in its own field," wrote Jung, "but is a great cheat and illusionist outside of it whenever it tries to manipulate values" (1969b, p. 32).

Thus, it is not the one-to-one, syllogistic *signs* of strict cognition but the open-ended, mythopoetic *symbols* that emanate from our unconscious that matter most in making sense of our lives. In chapter 4, I lay out the difference, which Jung found crucial for psychology, between the sign and the symbol. This has many educational implications and applications, which is the purpose of this book to explore.

Second, when an individual experiences archetypal imagery in dreams, art, religion, and so on in profoundly intuitive encounter with the ground of his being—which Jung, in terms reminiscent of Hindu philosophy, called the Self (1969b)—the result is a *numinous*, or spiritual, feeling. This psychospiritual vibrancy is the natural consequence of the individual contacting what it perceives—and even better, *apperceives*—as the *mysterium tremendum et fascinans*.

And again, Jung stressed that, whether or not one's awe at this "tremendous and fascinating mystery" is *really* about something Divine or finally boils down to just the expression of the individual's *wish* to contact the Divine, is impossible to determine. God may or may not exist. We cannot know for certain.

But this much is clear. The need to live in the light of one's personal sense of Ultimacy (Tillich, 1956) is the most powerful of all of human motivations, the true center of all psychic functioning, and we search in vain for health and peace until we each access it in our various ways—and then live in dynamic relationship with it. For some, this will be the Christ or Buddha within, the Hindu Self, one's Higher Power, or what have you. But whatever it is, without it, as Abraham Maslow (1968, p. iv) concluded near the end of his career, "we get sick, violent, and nihilistic, or else hopeless and apathetic."

With the heavy emphasis in Jungian psychology on symbols, it is not surprising that the mystery of the archetype can best be approached by imagery. We have already looked at the image of archetypes as lenses. Let us entertain a few more tropes in our approach to the mystery of psyche before marshaling Jung's perspectives on and terms about psyche to enrich our understanding of and engagement with various educational issues.

Further Images of the Archetypal—and the Archetype's "Light" and "Dark" Sides

Imagine wind creating patterns in the sand. We cannot see the wind (the primordial/transcendent archetype) that is carving various figures in the sand. However, we do see the figures that the wind creates (personally and culturally variable archetypal images and narratives). By analyzing the wind's invisible operations in its visible traces in the sand, we can infer various things about the structure and dynamics of that universally shaping breeze.

Consider, for instance, a particularly potent archetype: the slain-then-resurrected *savior archetype*. This archetype has been embodied in various *archetypal characters* and *archetypal narratives* in history—such as those of Osiris, Bacchus, Tammuz, and Jesus. We do not know where this (or any) archetype comes from nor will we ever fully be able to take in its ultimate significance. We only know that it is one of the general ways in which many people have made sense of their existence for three millennia. However, in the group of symbolic figures that this particular archetype has left as both avatars and witnesses of its presence, we gain just that much more insight into "the archetype of the savior."

Now, *all archetypes have a light and dark side, a conventionally "good" and conventionally "bad" side*—although what seems to be "good" is not always or only good, and what seems "bad" is not always or only bad. This is a crucial point in Jungian psychology and psychotherapy (Mayes, in press, 2016).

We see this psychospiritual dualism very clearly in the archetype of the king, one that has had not only spiritual but also political significance throughout history. Let us look at one of U.S. culture's more recent instances of the operation of the dark and light sides of the king archetype.

In 20th-century U.S. politics, President Kennedy captured the popular imagination as an *archetypal image* of the light side of the *archetype* of the king who felicitously presided over his Camelot. President Nixon, on the other hand, embodied the archetype's dark side—his Evil Empire unveiled and unraveled in the calamity of Watergate. In fact, Kennedy was, as we know, certainly no saint, and Nixon was undoubtedly not without his virtues.

But Kennedy and Nixon were not so much individuals in their world-historical archetypal roles as they were the focus of the collective *projection*[7]—a term minted by Jung to explain the externalization onto another of what is actually an inner issue—of the light and dark sides of the archetype of the king by a people onto two magnetic personalities. One of them was attracting projections from the positive side of the archetype and the other negative projections from its tenebrous flipside.

At least as much as who Kennedy and Nixon "really" were, eliciting the terrific intensity of the collective national responses to these two individuals, their falls equally resulted from the supercharged archetypal energy that citizens projected onto them—the light and dark side of the archetype of the king. "The king" is thus one of the inborn categories, one of the archetypes, of how human beings see, set up, and go about their existences. The two presidents were *archetypal figures*, indeed *archetypal symbols*, who drew forth from a nation what was ultimately its own world-historical light—and its own world-historical darkness.

More on Science as Symbol

Since the sciences are taken today to be the ultimate standard of what is *"truly true,"* the litmus test of what is *"really* real," it cannot be stressed too much that according to Jung, even the hard sciences are, in the final analysis, conscious sign systems, just one among many, that simply embody symbolically an aspect of the archetypal realm within which we all necessarily live, move, and have our being.

Mathematics, the core of the hard sciences, would seem to be quite impervious to a prerational/postrational archetypal analysis. But it is not, at least according to such luminaries of math as Gödel and Poincaré—and as even the distinguished philosophers of mathematical logic, the early Ludwig Wittgenstein and Bertrand Russell were finally compelled to admit.

Gödel argued that numbers are basically just another system—quite useful in that little bandwidth of "reality" that we call "empirical"—but not ontologically privileged in what William James called our "pluralistic universe." Like every merely conceptual system, said Gödel, mathematics is self-enclosed, self-legitimating and, were thus finally found, after rigorous disciplinary-self-reflective analysis, to hang upon certain unprovable assumptions.

The Nobel-Prize-winning physicist Wolfgang Pauli thus asserted (Pauli and Jung, 2001) that before numbers became the tools of a particular sign system known as mathematics, they were and remain instances of "an archetype of order which has become conscious" (Jung, in Von Franz, 1991, p. 268). The *sign system* of mathematics at the secondary level of cognition grows out of *the archetype of order* at the primary level of the unconscious. This has implications regarding math and science education, which we will explore in chapter 2.

Even a glance at a few different cultures shows that there are many ways of embodying and putting into practice the inborn archetype of order (Von Franz, 1974). For instance, the four quadrants of a sacred circle painted in the sand by a Hopi Medicine Man in order to heal a patient symbolize a cosmic process that the number 4 does not in any normative sense or usage of it have to a mathematician in the equation "$4x=20$." Both the medicine man and the mathematician use that particular concretizing of "the archetype of order" known as "four," but its meaning is radically different for the two people. Each way comes with very different assumptions and purposes, and they are both valid.

To take another example of the archetype of order becoming embodied in yet another way, we can also look at alchemy—a topic of enormous interest to Jung (1968a, 1969b; 1970a. In renaissance alchemy, we see a different mustering of numbers, one which ultimately was about psychological processes, according to Jung, much more than transformations of matter, making alchemy the precursor not so much of chemistry as of psychology (Jung, 1970a; see also Edinger, 1985).

In alchemy, the number "1" is the primal unity out of which all things emerge; "2" is the dialectical tension that powers all physical and psychic processes; "3" is the resolution of the tension in a higher synthesis, like the apex of a triangle; "4" is the grounding of the higher solution in a new system, pictured as a square foundation; and "5"symbolizes the completion, or ethical essence, of the process—from which we derive the word *quint*-essence (Von Franz, 1974).

The curriculum of the Rudolf Steiner's *Waldorf* system of holistic education reflects this understanding of the archetype of order in its treatment of numbers, where children learn, play with, and create artistic products from the deeper archetypal significance of the numbers (Trostli, 1991). Here, children are taught the mathematical uses of numbers only after they have internalized the archetypal "feel" of each number from 1 to 10. This is accomplished through studying myths that use numbers symbolically.

Armed with this basic knowledge of some of the major terms that Jung used to approach the mystery of psyche, let us now begin to apply it in our own approach to the mystery of education.

THE ARCHETYPAL CLASSROOM
(AND THE POLITICS OF THE SPIRIT)

As we will see in some detail in chapter 1, the depth psychology approaches to education, ranging from classical Freudian and classical Jungian to post-Freudian and post-Jungian, all start with the assumption that our conscious processes—our practical and disciplinary "cognitions"—are outgrowths of and thus secondary to the fundamental and transcendental operations of our psychodynamic and psychospiritual processes.

As we have seen, Freud located this primary ground of all mentation and symbol-making in the *personal* subconscious. But Jung imagined it much more expansively as existing ultimately in a *transpersonal* repository of universal symbols—the collective unconscious and its archetypes. I will continue to elaborate on this point in the following chapters, but the focus will be on the educational implications and applications that flow from all of this.

For now, it is enough to say that the theoretical establishing of a realm of primary processes, and then the deepening and widening of what "primary processes" means—from the Freudian personal subconscious to the Jungian transpersonal collective unconscious—abounds with significant implications for education, which is the purpose of this study to appreciate and harvest.

As I have argued in previous studies (2005a, 2007, 2009b), one of the great potentials of a Jungian-oriented vision of education is political. Jungian pedagogy can serve as a powerful tool in resisting the hegemonic corporate approach to education, which determines a good deal of schooling today. For, although devotedly focused on the teacher's and student's individual psycho-spiritual dynamics, Jungian pedagogy also deploys a wide array of psycho-dynamic and psychospiritual perspectives and terms to critically interrogate the political dynamics of educational policies, processes, and settings in contemporary U.S. schools.

The major focus of that critique in this book is on the toxicity of the business-based approach to education which—through the mechanisms of standardized instruction, state-defined/state-enforced curricula, and high-stakes standardized tests—sees and handles students (or rather, monitors and controls them) as "human capital." It does this so as to mold them to the fiscal purposes of a corporate state that is always restlessly in search of ever-greater efficiency and profitability in the new global marketplace.

The Dean of U.S. Educational Historians, Lawrence Cremin (1988), prophesied three almost three decades ago in his magisterial work, *American Education: The Metropolitan Experience*, that the most ominous threat to American democracy in the 21st century would be the cancerous growth of the military-industrial complex into what he called "the military-industrial-*educational* complex." Cremin's prophecy has come to pass.

The result of this dystopian, corporate form of education—which is less and less "education" and more and more just "training"—is a psychologi-cal, intellectual, and ethical diminishment, even violation, of the student. Class after class, term after term, year after year, the standardized mode of (mis)education finally turns the student into a socially engineered object, a functionary of a particular political economy, not a free agent in individual psychospiritual growth.

In a disruptive contrast to this view of what education is and should be about, a Jungian pedagogy insists upon the primacy of both the personal sub-conscious and—even more powerfully and fundamentally—the transpersonal, cosmically situated processes of the collective unconscious (Mayes, 1999, 2001, 2002) in envisaging and bringing to pass in the classroom what it means to teach and learn profoundly.

Archetypal pedagogical theory insists that because primary psychody-namic processes and, even more deeply, primary psychospiritual ones are the matrix out of which cognitive processes emerge, it then follows that the teacher and curriculum should be closely attuned and richly responsive to this fact in what the teacher teaches, how she teaches it, her relationships with her students, theirs with each other, and how all of this can enrich her and her student's larger existential and even spiritual commitments in the formation and nurturance of their ever-expanding life narratives.

If this does not happen, the development of secondary but still vital cognitive capacities in the classroom—the importance of which no one would deny—will be compromised. For, it is a basic law of depth psychology that the primary processes, if unattended to, reactively turn toxic, strike back, and undermine what is going on at the secondary level. The archetypal approach to educational theory and practice offers a way of integrating primary and secondary processes in an educational synergy, which I aim to illustrate in this book.

This book expands upon what I have laid out along these lines in my previous work while also suggesting new trails to explore in Jungian educational theory and practice: the idea of a "shadow curriculum," some multicultural implications in the classroom of what I call the post-Jungian "collective *cultural* conscious," the use of Jung's interpretation of Kant as an epistemological framework for curriculum and instruction, and the distinction between what I call "Training in the Service of the Sign" as a miseducative instrument of psychosocial oppression and "Education in the Spirit of the Symbol" as an educative means of psychospiritual liberation.

To begin with in chapter 1, however, I deal not with archetypal psychology in education but look first at Freudian and post-Freudian theory in education since 1922 till the present. My reason for this is two-fold.

First, since the depth-psychological approach to curriculum and instruction began in early 20th-century Freudian theory and extends into the present as post-Freudian "self-object theory," it is historically accurate and theoretically sensible to begin here (Mayes, 2009a).

Second, there is a great deal of value in this by-now almost century-long study of the psychoanalytic aspects of education, and all of this adds to a Jungian view of education, just as a Jungian view of education adds to it.

After this, I continue to explore ideas about archetypal pedagogy and curriculum theory and practice in education from my previous books. I also suggest a variety of new ones in the mythopoetic terms that Jung's view of psyche so abundantly provides us as educational scholars and practitioners.

Before I do, however, I would like to thank the students in my summer 2015 doctoral seminar in curriculum theory in the Brigham Young University's Department of Educational Leadership and Foundations for their generous and insightful help in providing written comments and critiques on several drafts of this Introduction. Equally important to me were their comments, questions, and critiques in class discussion.

Any book that aims at some sort of significance is to some degree a joint effort with another or others. This is even truer of the present book, for the reader will note that at the end of each chapter is a commentary on that chapter by one of these students, along a brief description of his or her educational career. Each one is a member of a cohort that is finishing its doctoral coursework in educational leadership and is on the cusp of researching the dissertation. They have all been teachers and administrators in the public schools. I believe the reader will find their commentaries as theoretically rich and eminently practical as I do—that happy blend of theory and practice that characterizes each one of these students, who have also been my teachers.

NOTES

1. I use the adjective "psychic" in this book as simply another form of "psychological," not to suggest the parapsychological, although the parapsychological is a concern of Jungian psychology.

2. "Supra-conscious," as Rudolf Steiner put it, is possibly a better characterization (Wehr, 2002).

3. The idea of an archetypal "ground" of existence from which both empirical reality and our symbol systems then emerge has recently found some theoretical support, although still marginalized by current normative science—as, for example, in the work of David Bohm (2003) in physics, Rupert Sheldrake (2009) in biochemistry, and Michael Conforti (1999) in biology. Bohm has hypothesized an "implicate order" from which the various systems that govern the physical universe emerge. Similarly, Sheldrake speaks of "morphic fields" from which particular species and individuals come and to which they resonate ("morphic resonance"). Conforti puts forth a similar suggestion in biology. These theories point to the possibility of an underlying archetypal structure to things, which we cannot know directly or express in any conventional symbol systems since they are the *a priori* matrix from which our expressions and symbolic systems emerge. Furthermore, the idea that there is an archetypal substructure to both psyche and the physical world would explain the occurrence of "synchronicity"—a term Jung invented. This is when something that is going on with an individual psychologically corresponds to, and even seems to be confirmed by, a completely unexpected and unpredictable happening in the empirical world. This happens in a way that, although undeniably significant to the individual in the message it contains, is so improbable that it could not be a matter of the usual operation of physical law or mere chance. For instance, one dreams that a friend whom one has not seen, heard of, or even really thought of for 30 years dies. The next day, posted on Facebook, is a notice from a mutual friend that that friend suddenly passed away of a stroke. Here, psyche and the empirical world seem joined in a way that could not be explained by mere chance but might have something to do with a common structural foundation for both psyche and matter (von Franz, 1984).

4. As such, archetypes are preanalytical and may bear some similarity to Heidegger's idea of the *Urgrund*—or "primal ground" of existence (Heidegger, 1964; Nagy, 1991).

5. Jung did, however, cross the line into metaphysics and ontology at various points in his work despite his protestations to the contrary, rendering his claim to neutrality regarding metaphysics and ontology more than a little questionable (Charet, 1993; Noll, 1994; Palmer, 1995).

6. For more on the archetypal significance of numbers, especially numbers one through four, see Jung, 1969c; see also see Von Franz, 1984, for a discussion of the relationship between numerical archetypes and different conceptions of time.

7. Jung coined the term "projection," which has found its way into popular usage, as well as the popular notions of introvert and extrovert.

Chapter 1

The Psychodynamics
of Educational Processes

Since the advent of depth psychology clinically and academically over roughly the last 130 years, many psychoanalytic theorists have been keenly interested in and vocal about the relevance, indeed the indispensability, of psychoanalysis to education.

These psychoanalysts have asserted that to be emotionally vibrant and existentially valid, educational theory and practice must honor the fact that teachers and students are first of all supremely complex emotional beings whose conscious thought processes are *secondary* ones that grow out of the deeper soil of the *primary* processes of the subconscious.

In this chapter, we will review some major Freudian and post-Freudian contributions to educational theory made by psychoanalysts. We then move on in the following chapters to an exploration of some of the even deeper psycho-*spiritual* aspects of education that Jungian psychology has made it possible for us to develop. In its mythopoetic approach to the enduring enigma and transcendent trajectory of psyche, Jungian psychology offers us new horizons in educational theory and practice.

DOMINANT THEMES IN THE PSYCHOANALYTIC VIEW OF EDUCATION OVER THE LAST ONE HUNDRED YEARS

Primary and Secondary Psychological Processes

From about 1920 on, psychoanalysts who have engaged in educational theorizing have unanimously agreed on one point above all—one that insists upon a radical revisioning of all educational processes.

What the psychoanalytic educationists have argued is that the traditional concern of curriculum and instruction—*cognition*—is, although
of course crucial to education, finally dependent upon primary processes
(Mayes, 2009b). The secondary processes of cognition necessarily emerge
from the fertile soil of the precognitive ground of the subconscious. And this
will be the case no matter how "objective" a concept may seem.

Indeed, it may be all the more true the more daunting a concept may
appear as, after having *actually* undergone many mysterious transformations
in the subconscious realm, it now strides onto the brightly lit, public stage
of consciousness and consensual reality, wrapped in the institutional robes
of a normative discourse, and proudly declares itself to be sovereign. This
is a psychodynamically dangerous move.

After all, it is never wise to deny one's origins, one's heart and soul, one's
very infrastructure. It results in self-alienation, and alienation from, as well
as some form of psychological, physical, or political violence against, the
"Other" (Levinas, 1996), the *thou* of humane interaction, unethically turning
him into a mere *it,* an object (Buber, 1965).

This is a point that should interest educational scholarship greatly, but it
has not. Two other approaches dominate research in curriculum and instruction, excluding a depth-psychological perspective.

The first is the statistical measuring and managing of facts and concepts—
decontextualized thoughts learned in isolation from richer discussions that
explore and might even critique them. The purpose is to memorize these cognitive "items" for a standardized test, which are then forgotten as soon as the
test is over. This treats a concept as if it were an empirical entity, a cognitive
commodity. Such things began with the famous assertion of Edward Thorndike, the father of "educational psychology," and the IQ test over a century
ago, that "whatever exists, exists in some amount and can be measured."[1]

The second approach is the coopting of cognition as an ideological instrument in the service of some political program or other. The political Right
and Left are equally culpable here in their attempts to commandeer curricula
in order to prove their points and advance their causes. None of this is new.

Since the opening decades of the 20th century, the psychoanalysts who
have most energetically called for psychodynamically sensitive approaches
to teaching and learning have also been the ones who have most lamented its
absence in formal education.[2]

The overarching point made over almost the last one hundred years by
psychoanalysts writing about education has been that, whether in the formal
pedagogical setting of a classroom or in our many everyday interactions,
there are countless complexities at every level of one's being in what it
means to "have" or "convey" a thought—just as there are in receiving and
metabolizing the thoughts of another (Mayes, 2009a).

Teaching and learning are not so much something that we *do*—and *only* do with certain credentials in official spaces set aside for delivering a state-determined and increasingly state-monitored curriculum. Educational processes are something that we *are*. Optimally, each individual *is* an ever-evolving act of teaching and learning in emotionally responsible, ethically subtle, and ever-emergent *I-Thou* encounters with other similarly engaged individuals, not *I-It* master/slave non-relationships, in which a person is dominating another—from sexual domination to political domination.

"Mental Hygiene in the Schools": The Early Years of Psychoanalysis in Education

It is on classroom dynamics, mostly in public school settings with young children and adolescents, that the early psychoanalysts trained their focus. Their crusade was to promote "mental hygiene in the schools" (Redl and Wattenberg, 1951).[3] As that phrase suggests, the earliest psychoanalytic statements about education were essentially *clinical*, out to solve students' academic "problems" from within the system, and mostly geared toward promoting the student's "adjustment" to that system. This is not surprising for two reasons.

First, the earliest psychoanalyst-educational theorists were physicians for whom the medical metaphor "mental hygiene" would come naturally. This was all the more the case since they were still more or less struggling, as Freud himself had done, for acceptance into a medical establishment that had looked askance (and, as it turned out, would always look somewhat askance) at their "soft science"—its immersion in passion, contradiction, anxiety, guilt, dreams, and the indeterminacy of symbolism (Ellenberger, 1970; Jansz and van Drunen 2004).

Eager to demonstrate their practical usefulness in the schools, the psychoanalytic pedagogues relied heavily on Freud's 19th-century, biologically determined, mechanical model of the psyche as a battleground between the hyper-moral *superego* and the rapacious *id*. Between these warring forces stood the ego, struggling always to find a compromise between them by employing "the reality principle," a middle point that that would allow the individual "to love and to work," as Freud famously defined the goal of analysis, and to receive some measure of gratification in socially functional ways.

What these psychoanalytic observers saw in the schools was a prime site for furthering this psychosocial objective through the student's healthy engagement with the teacher, his fellow students, and a "developmentally appropriate" curriculum—Freud's model of development being the touchstone, of course, for what was "appropriate" in human development.

Second, not a few of these psychoanalysts in education would eventually experience Nazism. Many of them were Jews. Some of them, like Bruno Bettelheim, who had been in Buchenwald concentration camp, finally found refuge in the United States. They had seen what moral monsters the *Hitler-schule* ("Hitler Schools") had spawned. This was something that *any* school system was capable of if it existed solely in the service of the state and a program of total control of the individual for some "greater" socioeconomic or world-historical purpose.

Fervently dedicated to democracy, therefore, the psychoanalysts involved in education warned that a school system that did not intelligently attend to each child's psychodynamic uniqueness and complexity would cause children to become repressed, confused, and conformist—mere creatures of the state, primed to fall into lockstep according to either the seductions or punishments proffered by the next Rightist or Leftist demagogue to appear on the scene.

One of the best safeguards against this, and in general against the "herd-mentality" that Freud had early and often warned against, was to handle educational processes with psychodynamic care and skill (Freud, 1930). But of course, these psychoanalytic theorists *were,* after all, promoting a "system" of schooling.

However, they felt it was an enlightened system that valued the rights of the individual, for whom they were advocating. Clinical in its orientation, institutionally geared in its aims, early psychoanalysis hoped that its efforts would bear fruit in the schools by fostering the growth of emotionally balanced, intellectually honed, and politically critical individuals in an essentially just state.

The Psychodynamic Origins of Academic Problems

One of the psychoanalysts' most frequent points was that teachers must always consider the possibility that a student's educational problems may primarily be psychodynamic ones, and this was true for all students, not just those labeled as "emotionally disturbed."

A girl whose father sexually abused her mother every night might find it too painful, too literally close to home, to study about the maltreatment of female slaves on plantations by their masters. A boy whose mother had turned him into her oedipally enmeshed captive, her "little man," to compensate for her sense of abandonment and sexual frustration because of her unfeeling, adulterous husband, might be symbolically resisting his mother's demands on him (which he was powerless to do at home) by refusing to perform well for a demanding female teacher in a classroom.

Equally problematic were certain students who did *well* in school, but not out of a passion for learning. Rather, it was to gain affection, however conditional and inauthentic, from parents and teachers whose affirmations depended on the child's stellar academic performance. Such "learning for love" by the desperate child would eventually deaden the child's "love of learning." It would make of him a kind of scholastic circus monkey, doing well in school in order to get scraps of affection from an only provisionally loving audience—one that could turn hostile if the child's performance was not up to its expectations (Ekstein and Motto, 1969).

In such psychodynamically twisted forms of (mis)education, the child learned an emotional lesson that ran far deeper than any curricular content could ever do, and it was one he would carry with him the rest of his now-neuroticized life—namely, that he was a slavish mental *object* of other's expectations, undoubtedly stemming from *their* own unmet because unexamined needs, not a robust *subject* whose mental growth was of a piece (and at peace) with his own emotional depths. This point is at least as important today as when it was first made by the psychoanalysts many decades ago.

Also of continuing relevance is the early psychoanalytic message to teachers that there are many compelling and defensible reasons that a student may resist what a teacher has to say. These reasons may not be wrong, bad, or requiring "remediation," as it used to be called," or "intervention" (as it is now called).

A teacher could, for instance, be ill-informed, flat-out mistaken, or generally limited in her scope about something. Or she might be dictatorial and demeaning in her presentation of the "correct" concept to the now thoroughly dispirited, disempowered student. In short, she may be ideologically or psychodynamically violating a student by forcing something down his throat that runs counter to his deepest intuitions or contradicts his most energetic convictions—not to mention those of his family and culture.

This was not to say that a student must be pampered in petulant whims or toxic prejudices. It *was* to say that the teacher should not only take a psychologically informed view of why a student isn't "learning" something but might sometimes do well to also reflect on how he, the teacher, is teaching it in the way he is—and why. So adamant have the psychoanalytic pedagogues been about the need for the teacher to reflect on the emotional bases of his own ways of knowing something and teaching it that in the literature during the 1920s through the 1950s there were calls for the teacher to undergo analysis during her student-teacher year, just as an analyst-in-training must do.

The Transference and Counter-transference between Student and Teacher

Key to psychodynamic and ethical sanity in the classroom, felt the psychoanalysts, was that the teachers understand and be able to work with *the transference.*

A phrase drawn from psychotherapy, "the transference" refers to the patient's propensity—her compulsion, in fact—to subconsciously project, or "transfer," her issues onto the analyst. These issues often stem from her earliest (mal)formative relations with her mother and/or father, which she now proceeds to replay with the therapist. The patient's unwitting projection of her issues onto the psychotherapist provides him, if he is perceptive enough, with buried information about the deeper problems that have brought the patient to therapy and that underlie her present pain.

But misused by the therapist, the transference can become a problem. For through the window of the transference, the unscrupulous psychotherapist may salaciously peer into his patient's weaknesses and may sometimes even go so far as to exploit them for his own gratification—emotional, sexual, or both.

In addition to the inherently craven nature of such an act, it creates a cruel power imbalance between the therapist and the patient, and is thus a contradiction of the therapeutic goal of helping the patient regain her power, or maybe even simply experience it for the first time. The patient now finds herself more colonized and crippled than ever before, and, in a colossal betrayal of her trust, all of this has happened at the hands of the very person who had promised to aid in her liberation.

As already noted, the relational issues that underlie the transference are rooted in early distortions in the patient's relationships with primary caregivers, typically the mother or father. Now in adult life, they persist with a dire inexorability to blight the individual's relationships with others, especially intimate others—from one's lovers, children, and friends, to one's boss, doctor, therapist, and teacher. For this reason, Freud called the transference "a new edition of an old problem."

Some theorists believe that at the heart of this "repetition compulsion" is the person's subconscious desire to recreate again and again in relationships the initial relational misshaping with the parent(s) in the hope of finally finding a way to resolve it (Esman, 1990; Greenson, 1990). But since the individual has heretofore done this in an alienated, un-self-reflective way, the net result has been one relational train wreck after another in the patient's life. To reflect on all of this with a wise and compassionate other in order to work through and grow beyond this repetition compulsion is arguably the paramount purpose of therapy.

But the matter is even more complex than this. For the therapist to help the patient work through her projections requires not only psychodynamic delicacy and ethical probity on the therapist's part it also entails that he has already largely worked through such relational issues in himself.

Otherwise, what the patient is projecting onto him may all too easily simply cause him to counter-project his own relational issues back onto the patient, so that now not one but two new editions of old problems are taking place in a perversely complementary fashion in the consulting room. This *folie a deux* is what is clinically labeled the "counter-transference" (Jung, 1963). It was to provide some sort of defense against it that Freud finally required every psychoanalyst-in-training to undergo his own analysis by a senior psychoanalyst.

The relevance of the transference to education and educational processes is multifaceted and significant, as I have discussed at length elsewhere (Mayes, 2002). The transference is not limited to the analyst-patient relationship in the confines of the consulting room. It probably operates to some degree *whenever* people are in a relationship of any consequence to them. And the more intense the relationship—especially if that relationship involves a power differential between the participants—the more insistent the surges and more subtle the sway of the transference.

Thus, authority figures such as bosses, politicians, physicians, policemen, clergypersons, and teachers are especially prone to being objects of someone's "transference neurosis" since their positions of authority make them representatives of the parent in the individual's subconscious. This then trains the individual's entire range of fantasies and fears, loves and hates, aggressions and submission about the parent onto the authority figure. And what the psychoanalysts have stressed from the beginning of their involvement in education is that few relationships are as emotionally charged, existentially impactful, or as shot through with all sorts of power differentials as that between the teacher and the student.

Some of the best statements regarding the transference in the classroom are still to be found in the earliest psychoanalysts, who offered cautions that teachers still do well to heed.

Aichhorn (1925) wrote to teachers that when a student's response is puzzlingly inappropriate, it may be that the student is transferring a parental issue onto the teacher. "In such cases, what you see being enacted before your eyes are really only repetitions and new editions of very old conflicts of which you are the target but not the cause" (p. 88). This is so, noted Anna Freud, because "there is in the individual a compulsion to repeat in later life the pattern of his earlier love and hate, rebellion and submission, disloyalty and loyalty" (1930, p. 109)—a compulsion that the student aims at the teacher.

This need not be a bad thing, said Blos (1940, p. 494), one of the great psychoanalytic educational theorists of the World War II years, if the teacher is psychoanalytically sensitive. For, the teacher, who in some senses is a "safer" person than a parent, "may be in a better position than the parent to help the adolescent deal with new emotions, and may receive the transferred feelings of the student as a parental figure."

This makes sense in light of the fact that, next to the parent, the teacher is the single most likely object of the student's projections regarding his earliest caregivers, as two later luminaries in the field, Redl and Wattenberg (1951, p. 235), would claim to explain why knowledge of the transference was a pedagogical "must" for the teacher.

"The Emotional Experience of Teaching and Learning"

But whether to help the teacher deal with inappropriate projections from the student, to resist the impulse toward counter-projection within himself, or simply to channel and enhance in a general way the flow of emotions in a classroom, the teacher must understand and handle the transference.

For, depending on how they are navigated by the teacher at the helm, the quick and shifting currents of the transference can either carry the students on the ship of the classroom into open vistas of relatedness and liberation or those currents can dash all aboard the classroom liner against outcropping rocks from the subconscious: misunderstanding, greed, aggression, submission, and finally a sense of rejection and disempowerment for everyone involved.

Thus, it is that a psychodynamically wise pedagogy affirms that deep educational processes must grip and transform both the teacher and student in their depths if their interchanges in intelligence are also to be transactions in transformative love, grounded in a deep mutuality that forms around the occasion of a living curriculum. Then, and only then, do we rise above the level of mere "training" in a classroom—the bland transmission of information, boring imposition of a theory, or demeaning inculcation into a dogma—and move into the admittedly riskier (but when did growth ever come without risk?) yet existentially more abundant realms of truly educational processes.

No pedagogy that blithely ignores or cautiously tries to end-run what Salzberger-Wittenberg (1989) calls "the emotional experience of learning and teaching" can hope to create or nurture teachers or learners who connect deeply with each other, with what is being studied, and ultimately therefore with themselves. Where so much is at play, such processes will be either rich or rife with transferential possibilities, depending on the psychoanalytic knowledge and skillfulness of the teacher.

In none of this did the psychoanalytic educationists mean to imply that the teacher should try to play the therapist with his students. That would be professionally and ethically wrong. However, just as psychotherapy is in many respects an educational process, in which not only the patient but also the therapist learn a great deal about themselves in interaction with each other, so educational processes—if they involve and shape the student and teacher in their depths—will have profound emotional consequences for both of them.

The goal for the teacher, therefore, is not to do therapy but to create a *therapeutic classroom environment* for students in which they not only expand cognitively but deepen psychodynamically. In the therapeutic classroom, thought and feeling are wedded. This makes cognition emotionally relevant and sturdy. Conversely, it makes emotions wise and efficacious through thinking clearly and courageously about them.

As much as classical behaviorism (with its reinforcement schedules), the brain sciences (with their ultimately arbitrary and frankly unexciting metaphor of the brain as a computer), or a strict cognitive science (with its conceptual maps) might wish to deny or minimize passion in teaching and learning, passion persists. Our thoughts are compelling to us and moving to others to the very degree that they are charged with authentic desire that stems from the thinker's existential core and reaches out to his dialogical partner's core.

Where this is not the case, concepts become sterile tokens, and education becomes mere training. To be sure, there are fewer emotional and existential challenges for the teacher who is simply going through the motions of merely training his students, but there are also fewer things of ultimate import to be given or gained.

Training has its instrumental roles and goals. These are by definition secondary, however, necessarily limited, and operating only in the day-to-day realm of what Heidegger (1964) called the *ontic*. But let us never confuse the *ontic* instrumentality of mere training with those radically transformative *ontological* encounters at emotionally and existentially fundamental, primary levels with self, world and Other which—involved with our most vital emotional processes—alone fully merit the name of *education*.

POST-FREUDIAN CONTRIBUTIONS
TO EDUCATIONAL THEORY AND PRACTICE
IN THE SECOND HALF OF THE 20TH CENTURY

Object-Relations Theory

Around the early 1950s, the term "self-object" became prominent in psychoanalytic theory and it has had ever-widening consequences for psychoanalysis and psychoanalytic pedagogy since.

In "Self-object" psychology, also called "Object-relations" psychology, a "self-object" is the image that one has in one's own psyche of someone who has been pivotal in the formation of one's own sense of self. This idea is central to Object-relations psychology, where *it is the need for relationship that is psyche's driving force*. The infant's earliest relationships with others, who become internalized as the infant's self-objects, are the foci around which one's egoic self-identity forms, in either positive or disastrous ways depending upon the nature of one's original self-objects.

With this extreme privileging of the lived, subjective world of the individual, Object-relations psychology is quick to point out that a figure whom the individual has internalized and then constructed his inner world around is not exactly the same as the "real" person.

Rather, the self-object is the person's assemblage of impressions, images, and impulses *about* that person. This assemblage comprises his internal rendering of, and determines his way of relating to, that person. Internalized persons are referred to as self-*objects* because in a sense they are psychic *things*, emotion-laden building-blocks, that the individual employs—*must* employ—in defining who he is.

Object-relations psychology departs from classical psychoanalytic theory in crucial respects. However, it draws heavily from classical Freudian psychology in its topological models of the "terrain" of the psyche and how psychic energy either flows over that terrain or is diverted, even dammed, on it.

Thus, Object-relations psychologists have retained the idea of the super-ego, ego, and libido and its mechanisms such as repression, sublimation, reaction-formation, and transference. However, the self-object theorists move the psychoanalytic enterprise away from Freud's insistence that the sexual drive monolithically controls psychodynamics from a single throne in the center of the psyche. They direct psychoanalytic theory toward a much broader, potentially freer, and less biologically determined set of assumptions than the sexual hypothesis does.

For as such influential self-object theorists as Kohut (1950/1978), Winnicott (1969/1992), and Fairbairn (1940/1992) insisted, the powering nuclear core of psyche is the individual's need to grow as an integral ego whose evolution is constantly being nourished by ever more satisfying kinds and degrees of meaningful relationship with others.

As a form of intense communication, sex is one type of such generative relatedness. It is not to be minimized. But neither is it to be exaggerated. For it is the need for relatedness to others that is the core psychic imperative, let that need be filled in whatever of the many ways it can and must be. Sex is but one the varying types and degrees of intimacy across the spectrum of human interconnectedness.

To be able to *see* the Other and to *be seen* by him in tempered compassion, risky openness, and creative curiosity, to be a whole and developing self in deepening types and topics of communication with other such selves—this is what powers the psyche. To live in such relatedness to others is health. To lack it, or to look for it in ways that compromise the integrity and creativity of the ego, is illness.

It is interesting to note in passing the similarities of Object-relations psychology to the Existentialist thought of the mid-20thcentury, in which they both arose (Kaufmann, 1975).

For instance, one discerns parallels with Existentialist theology, such as that found in Martin Buber (1965) in the Jewish tradition, with his assertion that goodness resides in rich *I-Thou* encounter in dialogue with another. Evil, says Buber, is the opposite of this—namely, the abasing program of turning that person into a mere object of one's own self-absorbed, colonizing will. There are also echoes of Paul Tillich (1956) in the Protestant tradition and his credo that the individual's quest for relationship with the Divine and the ongoing actualization of her most authentic self are existentially "ultimate" and made visible in relationship (Tillich, 1956).

The correspondences between Object-relations psychology and the ideas of Jean Paul Sartre (1956) in the agnostic and atheist tradition are also impressive, with his idea that living "in good faith" means boldly discovering what makes life possible and endurable for oneself as a "being-for-itself"—an *etre-pour-soi*—and then moving forward to make this actual with others in the world.

Perhaps the most impressive correspondence between Object-relations psychology and Existentialism is with Martin Heidegger (1964), whose central idea is that the human being is not truly *human* and not really *being* as an authentic individual—what Heidegger called a *Dasein*—if he is not ontologically grounded in himself and in rich communication with other such *Daseins* in a process he called *Mit-Dasein, Being-with-Others.*

The first and most important self-object according to Object-relations psychology is typically the mother, then the father, then moving on to all sorts of influences from especially significant others. When one's self-objects are mostly beneficent and generally affirming of one's existence and its potentials, the individual has an excellent chance of living in health and creativity. One's ego has been established, from its very first feelings, in being at home in life, of being worthy of being with others, and of being safe in *being itself*—and therefore of being safe in Being, itself.

When the opposite is the case, when one's self-objects are cruel and condemning, or even simply contradictory or dismissive, one's life becomes a relational wasteland. One feels oneself perpetually blurring out of existence in solitude, while remaining sharply focused, fixed, and trapped in condemnation. The result is a shamed alienation from self and others manifesting as guilt, anger, fear, and either servility or arrogance in the face of the Other.

OBJECT-RELATIONS PSYCHOLOGY IN EDUCATIONAL SETTINGS AND EDUCATIVE PROCESSES

Given self-object psychology's focus on relationship, not sex, as psychodynamically primary, on one hand, and the symbolically maternal role of the teacher in pedagogies of deep emotional care, on the other hand (Noddings, 1985, 1995), it is not at all surprising that Object-relations psychology has had such a signal effect on psychodynamic *pedagogies of care*. This has been especially true over the last several decades in psychodynamic pedagogy's emphasis of the maternal self-object role of the teacher.[4]

In formal educational settings, the person who is generally most key in the student's formation of her view of herself as a learner is the teacher. Thus, in Object-relations terms, it is not too much to say that it is the teacher who is one of a student's primary *pedagogical self-objects*. The student's relationship to this self-object is of the greatest significance in the formation of his "learning ego." The term "learning ego" (Anthony, 1989, p. 108) refers to one's sense of who she is in life in general as someone who is capable of engaging life's challenges, learning from them, and thereby emerging from them in the form of a wiser, ethically enhanced person.

A teacher's respectful, emotionally clear, and compassionate interactions with a student can go a long way in fostering this capacity in the student. The teacher does this by being what may be called a *positive pedagogical self-object*.

In relationship with the teacher, the student can know and "grow" herself internally as a multifaceted learner throughout her life. Conversely, a teacher who is a power monger, withering, curt, or self-aggrandizing can instill a voice in the student's psyche that will reverberate throughout the student's life. This voice will bring her down in internally disturbed waves of sadness or cynicism whenever she attempts to engage in any deeply educative process or creative project. The teacher as a good pedagogical self-object is liberating, as a bad pedagogical self-object, enslaving.

In short, the effects of a good or bad teacher can be system-wide, stretching far beyond the classroom and into the student's entire life. We are all teachers and learners in many of the most important ways and settings throughout our lives—not just within the confines of a classroom. Moreover, we cannot know ourselves as good and efficacious beings apart from how we see ourselves as learners. Life *is* learning. How I either prize or disprize myself as a learner will tell me in great measure how I see myself as a being who is either powerfully navigating the world or who is simply an object being tossed hither and yon by life's squalls.

The integrity of one's learning ego is part and parcel of one's ego-structure in general, and the teacher is uniquely significant in the formation of that learning ego. It is no surprise, therefore, that teachers loom early and large as self-objects in many students' lives and will continue to do so throughout the lifespan. An individual's relationship with these pedagogical self-objects has a terra-forming effect in determining how she traverses the many landscapes of all of life's educational processes.

As powerful shapers or misshapers of the student's learning ego, teachers are almost invariably a force in contributing to the student's sense of her own existence as either an ongoing adventure in existential expansion or a rigged game of diminishment. With a history of teachers as positive self-objects in her life, the student has a better chance of coming to live in meaningful relation *to* her world and *for* her world through educational interactions with others.

Some of those educational interactions in her life will occur in a classroom. Most of them will not. But whether or not in a formal educational setting, they will all optimally be interactions in which the individual—drawing upon her internal store of good pedagogical self-objects—will know how to teach generously and to learn courageously. She will be able to be *both* a good teacher and a good learner in those countless venues of educative exchange between authentic beings that are the staple of a nourished and nourishing existence.

OTHER EDUCATIONALLY USEFUL TERMS FROM SELF-OBJECT PSYCHOLOGY

Self-object psychology offers other useful terms that have become standard fare in the literature on psychoanalytic pedagogy.

There is, for instance, what Kohut (1950/1978) calls "the mirroring transference." In how the mother responds to the infant, the infant comes to know who it is. If in looking into her eyes, the infant sees acceptance and security, it learns that it is welcome into a world that is fundamentally safe. If the infant sees rejection and anxiety, it learns that it is unlovable and that the world is to be feared. For good or ill, what the child sees in its mother's attitude toward him is his existential mirror. This mirroring transference is the child's first and most basic relationship—the primal paradigm of all future relationships.

The mirroring transference is very important in the classroom. In a teacher's responsive or nonresponsive attitude to a student, in her encouraging or discouraging eyes, in her realistic faith in him or her convenient dismissal of him, the teacher, as a good or bad pedagogical self-object, mirrors to him a soon-to-be-internalized assessment of who he is, or might become, as a learner.

This does not mean that the teacher should exaggeratedly praise a student's work beyond its merit. A good self-object speaks truth in love. Besides, unrealistic praise would ultimately do the student no good but would dangerously inflate his ego for a while until unforgiving realities later set in and mercilessly burst his bubble.

However, being a good pedagogical self-object does require that the teacher sees all that she can see in a student, build on his strengths, be cautious in identifying a student's "limitations" and patient with them, celebrate his victories not only in his strong areas but also (and sometimes especially) in his weaker ones, and help him be all that he can be in a given domain. In this way, the teacher tends to the student's *holistic* growth in many aspects of his being and provides the student with multifaceted lessons in efficacy across the spectrum of his experiences.

In a related transferential dynamic that Kohut termed "the idealizing transference," the infant sees what it might become in the paradisiacal goal of its mother's face. She is the focus of his gaze; she, his *summum bonum.* She is not merely what is desirable and good in existence. She *is* existence.

In a lesser but still influential way, the teacher, in her response to a student's work, indeed in her response to his very *being*, becomes for the student both the symbol and the embodiment of what he might become as not only a lifelong learner in this or that field but as a being whose very existence is constituted in learning.

The fact that this is a heavy responsibility for the teacher to bear does not make it any less necessary for her to do so. It is inherent in the archetypal dynamic that comes into being whenever there is a teacher and a student (Mayes, 2005). This is why it is necessary for the teacher to understand the psychodynamic threads that are profusely, organically interwoven in the living tapestry of her work.

It merits repeating that none of this should be taken to imply that the teacher is a therapist or should try to play that role. However, in her relationship to her students, she will inevitably create a classroom environment that is either encouraging or discouraging in the growth of their learning egos. Although not a therapist, she, in her potent role as a teacher, creates a space that is either a *therapeutic classroom*—or its opposite, a *nontherapeutic classroom*, where students, across the range of abilities in her curricular domain, will be less likely to become the best they can be in that context.

The classroom that serves the mirroring and idealizing needs of the child provides the child with what the great Object-relation theorist and child psychiatrist D.W. Winnicott calls a good "holding environment" that a mother offers the child. The classroom is a good holding environment whenever the teacher creates *a safe space for the student to grow in*, just as the mother creates safe spaces, physically and symbolically, for the child to develop in (Elson, 1989).

Providing a good holding environment may actually involve the physical act of the mother lovingly holding the infant. Yet, even when it does not, it does entail the mother providing the child with a physical and emotional environment that is appropriate to its needs and beneficial to its evolution—an environment, in short, that *holds* the child.

Similarly, the teacher creates what might be named a *good educational holding environment* for her students by letting them know in a variety of explicit and implicit ways that they are secure in her classroom.

She takes seriously the ethical and emotional imperative that in her class-room no student will be mocked or ignored that each student will be seen and valued in his unique reality to the degree that he wishes to disclose himself and that it does not violate the teacher's *own* healthy emotional boundaries to respond to. She also calls for her students to support each other in the many conversations and activities of their classroom community, however much their inclinations, opinions, and aptitudes may differ.

In a good pedagogical holding environment, one and all feel safe to join in the existential adventure of the discovery and creation of emotionally, intel-lectually, and ethically resonant knowledge.

With the emotional and existential stakes so high, it is understandable that a teacher might feel overwhelmed in her work. This is probably a major reason that so many teachers burn out, and it is a common problem not only in teaching but in all the helping professions, which tend to draw people who feel a higher sense of *calling*, a *vocation* almost in the religious sense of the term. These are people whose caring natures may too easily lead them into excessive emotional involvement with those whom they serve, vicarious suffering for them, and an exhausting sense of responsibility toward them.

One approach to understanding and preventing burnout in not only teach-ing but all the helping professions is to turn to Winnicott's (1992) notion of "the good-enough mother."

It is not the perfect mother (whatever *that* might be) but the *good-enough mother* who is best able to create a realistic and therefore viable holding environment for the child. Winnicott's phrase "good-enough mothering" is meant to distinguish it from the toxic ideal of *perfect* mothering. In "perfect mothering" the mother would always and unerringly be available to the infant, meeting its every desire almost before it arises, with no boundaries on mother's part to resist the voracious creature's constant clamoring.

Paradoxically, such an impossibly "perfect" mother would not really be perfect all. This is so because attaining this "ideal" would require of the mother that she entirely foregoes her own identity, her healthy needs, and boundaries. Thus compromised, she could not ultimately really be relating in health to her infant.

What is more, such a mother would not be allowing the infant to experience the opposition that it is necessary for it to confront, in healthy and monitored doses, of course, so that it can begin to realistically mature in processes that will compel it to grow. In this fashion, the child evolves in health, feeding positively upon the mother's *actual* humanity, not negatively osmosing her *neurotic* perfectionism.

Likewise, the "good-enough teacher" creates a classroom that is a holding environment for her students. In it, the student experiments with various funds of knowledge, modes of relationship, and ultimately therefore various kinds of self-creation. Such existentially rewarding forays into the unknown bring with them some degree of risk. This is a given. But it is risk that is salutary and exists in the service of the constant expansion of the self in responsible freedom.

Necessarily, the student and the teacher will sometimes stumble, fall short, or even land on their faces in this consequential existential journey. But in a classroom that is a good pedagogical holding environment such things are interpreted as growthful events—educative in revealing what does not work and in helping the students cultivate a certain steadiness of vision and the enduring will to carry on even when the stars seemed aligned against him. "True love never did run smooth," said Shakespeare. Neither did true creativity.

In short, where there is the impulse to create, there must also be the room to fail. Failure is not the opposite of creativity; it is its precondition. There is nothing that can be standardized or psychometrically assessed about the creative process—nothing that can make it a predictable and risk-free journey down a much traveled road of dull signposts that direct everyone to the same dismal, impersonal terminal of consensual reality.

Rather, creativity is filled with emerging anxieties, mixed motivations, and sometimes killing doubt. It is replete with false starts, bogus leads, and simply lonely wandering in a wilderness. The road to creativity is messy, poignant, paved with our mortal limitations, humming with primary processes, and littered with crumpled up and discarded pages from a sketchbook or manuscript.

The good-enough teacher therefore finds both rest and energy in the gentle use of humor. A frank but still good-natured and even tender recognition of all of our inescapable mortal limitations is a defining feature of the good holding-environment classroom, where teacher and students are wrestling with questions that typically defy simple explanations, and may indeed defy *any* single explanation—no matter how clever.

For there is no explanation or theory of anything of real cognitive or ethical moment that is so complete and "correct" that it will not leave at least some residues of uncertainty, some traces of the inexplicable, and often plenty of room for alternative perspectives and explanations. Humor reminds us of all this. Humor allows us to forgive ourselves and others for all our imperfections. (In chapter 6, we will look at humor in the classroom in more depth.) The ease and forgiveness of self and Other that must characterize a good-enough classroom are powerful antidotes to burnout in teachers and discouragement in students.

Another idea from Object-relations with pedagogical significance comes from W.R.D. Fairbairn (1940/1992), who spoke of over-intellectualization as a schizoid position. This occurs when the individual constructs elaborate intellectual structures around himself as a fortress against authentic engagement with others.

Fairbairn's work calls attention to the fact that "overvaluation of mental contents" is ultimately a desperate attempt "to heap up values in the inner world" to the exclusion of external reality and therefore is symptomatic of an unhealthy "libidinizing" of thoughts and theories, typically concluding in some form of "fanaticism" (1940/1992, pp. 15–20).

With the emphasis in current educational practices upon factual information and disconnected cognitive items to be reproduced on standardized tests, Fairbairn's warning about schizogenic education casts a worrisome light on what is happening in the schools, where students are "heaping up" more and more chunks of disconnected, personally irrelevant "knowledge" and "information" for tests. This precludes their *being in* a living curriculum and *being with* each other. Too much of this can lead to a "schizoid position" in the student.

Fairbairn's cautions about how hyper-intellectualization are especially relevant to scholars in the university, where "'intensive inquiry' may in fact be pathological, and may lead us to consider carefully the degree of psychopathology incorporated in all research or intellectual work" (Hall, 2002, p. 39). When things reach this pass, the life of the mind has so far distanced itself from emotion and relationship that cognition now does not merely ignore the existence of passion and relatedness but has declared war against genuine existential desire.

THE PSYCHOANALYTIC CONTRIBUTION TO EDUCATIONAL THEORY AND PRACTICE

Drawing on the fullness of psychoanalytic theory from its classical formulation by Freud to its development almost a century later by post-Freudians, various notable psychoanalytic theorists have used depth psychology as a way of approaching the mystery of what it means to teach and learn. What they have claimed—mostly to the deaf ears of colleges of education (Mayes, 2009)—is that teaching and learning are thick with emotional dynamics at every turn.

From the simplest to the most abstract, concepts are laden with instincts, personal and cultural commitments, memory, ingrained patterns of relationship, despair and hope, and, in brief, all of those constricting nightmares and great dreams that not only invest our lives but *are* our lives. Any concept is necessarily a site of psychodynamic complexity. We are therefore severely limited in our view of what it means to teach and learn if we see it in strictly cognitive terms. For cognition—despite its enormous importance—is a secondary process.

What comes first are the forever enigmatic processes in psyche's depths. It is in the womb of psyche that all mental motions first quicken and then gestate, and it is from this womb that they finally emerge. It is in that matrix of our precognitive desire, and then striving toward the higher ground of our trans-cognitive goals, that cognition is best understood and employed as the premier mental instrumentality it is—but not as a sterile thing in itself. Sterility is the fate of any concept when it is isolated from its deep origins and stripped of its transcendent purposes in psyche.

Additionally, the delicate transactions between individuals in teaching and learning reflect the first and most psychodynamically formative relationships in an individual's life as those relationships live on in him and shape his way of being with others.

Where educative processes are good, in and out of school, the person can build on what she already has in her rich inner world of Object-relations— a world that was founded upon her very first interactions in teaching and learning and that now extend productively into all educational situations and events. In the therapeutic classroom, good educative processes also allow one to repair damage in one's inner world previously wrought by distorted mirroring transferences and faulty holding environments.

It is in psyche that we live, move, and have our being. Educational settings and processes in which this fact is honored are most likely to yield the richest cognitive fruit.

COMMENTARY BY BLAINE EDMAN

Blaine Edman is the director of Technology Services for a large suburban district in Utah. He previously has served as a high school principal, junior high principal, assistant principal and middle school teacher.

Throughout my career as a teacher, assistant principal, principal, and now district technology director, I have attempted to identify and define the conditions in which, in my experience, learning occurs best. This quest began as a young public school teacher when I found myself reflecting on what might be the key ingredients to what I called "foundational learning." By that I meant, and mean, as Mayes also means, learning that is for the whole student as an existential being, someone in constant development.

I saw that type of learning occurring when, for instance, I helped a student understand a concept that she was not *memorizing* to duplicate on a test but one that she was *learning*. I knew this process would change the way she *understood* in general and so would think more deeply about her world.

As a middle school math teacher, I would see foundational learning take place the moment a student grasped exponential growth or when he learned to render a word problem into a formula or a graphical representation. Something *happened*. The student's life was changed.

I would also think back to times before my career as a teacher when I was taught important concepts that impacted my way of being.

I began to put together a three-component model of foundational learning. First was a worthwhile concept to be learned, second was a motivated student, and third a skilled teacher who could help make the connection to that deeper level. The attractiveness of the text, the hardware in the classroom, the architecture of the school—these were ancillary. It was the connection of the teacher, learner, and the relevance to the student of a concept that made the difference.

My theory was challenged when I realized that some of these truths and understandings in my own life came from reading a book or from listening to a lecture. These were occasions when I had no personal relationship with the author or teacher. Yet, even then, I realized that I really did have that connection. Even in these impersonal settings, those authors or speakers had somehow been able to build a connection with me—the reader or listener.

I now recognize that psychodynamic components were at play. For even here, the emotional connection of the teacher with his reader or listener is a necessary component. This is a connection that, as Mayes makes clear in this chapter, is formed in the primary processes of the subconscious and not just in the secondary cognition of the conscious mind.

This realization has important ramifications in the area of educational technology, in which I now work. The extent of the modern access to information could scarcely have been imagined a few decades ago. In this chapter, Mayes asserts that what psychoanalysts have claimed is that teaching and learning are thick with emotional dynamics at every turn. Although it might at first seem strange, the nature of learning in the Information Age reinforces Mayes' idea.

If teaching and learning existed purely in the secondary, conscious world of gathering facts and making cognitive associations, conditions would be ripe for an explosion of self-educated individuals no longer in need of teachers. Yet this is not the case. The emotional dynamics of education still require a connection between learner and teacher, even if that connection exists over a YouTube channel, posts on a blog, or pages in a book.

For all of the power of technology to dispense information, its greatest power in education is to facilitate connections between teachers and learners. Past boundaries of time and space, and beyond one's level of credentialing (which are no longer nearly as important as they once were) technology provides the means to connect teachers and learners in all sorts of novel ways— ways that bring their own emotional dynamics into play and in a form that is quite new to most of us.

The need for research into this issue in order to help teachers understand the psychodynamic implications of learning in this new digital age is now greater than ever.

NOTES

1. Although this entire quote is generally ascribed to Thorndike, it was one of his students who added the phrase "and can be measured."

2. See, for example, Aichorn, 1925/1951; Bettelheim, 1976; Blos, 1940; Castoriadis, 1991; Fenichel, 1945; A. Freud, 1930; Hall, 1904; Klein, 1975/1932; Pfister, 1922; Redl & Wattenberg, 1951; Zachry, 1929.

3. See also Aichhorn, 1925/1951; Isaacs, 1932; Pfister, 1922; Zachry, 1940).

4. For extensive treatments of these ideas, see Barford, 2002; Britzman, 2003; Ekstein and Motto, 1969; Field, Cohler, and Wool, 1989; Salzberger-Wittenberg, 1983.

Chapter 2

Jung's Archetypal Epistemology

Jung's insistence on the need to attend to the student's psychological depths was at least as spirited as any of the depth psychologists who were concerned with education. And it was more philosophically grounded than most of theirs were. This is because Jung's position was not solely a psychodynamic one but rested on epistemological foundations—a theory of knowledge—that Jung had been developing since his college days and that frequently appeared in their mature forms in his writings (Bair, 2003).

To this topic, we will turn after a brief presentation of some of Jung general statements about education and its purposes. After the discussion of Jung's epistemology, we will then apply what we found to a wide variety of topics in pedagogy and curriculum.

JUNG'S INTEREST IN EDUCATION

Jung's interest in education appears only occasionally throughout his writings although he did write some essays on the topic in one of the volumes of his *Collected Works* (1954). However, when Jung's concern with educational issues did emerge, his passion about the subject was pointed. Jung declared that "it cannot be the aim of education to turn out rationalists, materialists, specialists, technicians and others of the kind who, unconscious of their origins, are precipitated abruptly into the present and contribute to the disorientation and fragmentation of society" (in Frey-Rohn, 1974, p . 174, p . 182).

In what is perhaps his greatest work, *Aion: Researches Into the Phenomenology of the Self*, Jung declared in words that are even more relevant today than when he wrote them over 60 years ago: "A predominately scientific and technological education, such as is the usual thing nowadays, can ... bringing

a spiritual regression and a considerable increase of psychic dissociation"
(1969b, p. 181).

Jung believed that when a culture's educational systems ignore the
dynamic depths of the individual, the negative consequences of this neglect
must multiply across individuals until the whole body politic is infected with
"psychic dissociation."

And unlike many depth psychologists of his day, Jung stressed not only
the adverse psychological and political harm caused by such state-enforced,
miseducative practices. He gave equal weight to the *spiritual* damage they
worked—nothing less than a "spiritual regression" of the individual and collective psyche, a reversal of the perennial human impulse toward the transcendent, a devolution in the direction of something spiritually and ethically lesser.

When this happened, some form of totalitarianism (Right or Left, what did
it matter?) lay on the horizon. The result of such miseducation, Jung goes on
to emphasize in the same passage, is inevitably to "neuroticize the masses and
prepare them for collective hysteria" (1969a, p. 181).

Not only a master analyst of how the individual and collective psyche
shape each other but also a military physician who had witnessed the two
global conflagrations that had wasted the first half of his century, Jung was
not overstating the point in warning of "collective hysteria." He had seen firsthand how precarious sanity and civilization are. Like Freud, he lived in the
anxious awareness of how we are always teetering on the brink of collective
madness and mass slaughter in the grip of some political ideology or other.

Like the psychoanalysts whom we examined in the previous chapter,
Jung believed that a culture's educational systems could be either a bulwark
against this "psychic dissociation," "collective hysteria," and "spiritual
regression"—or it could be a catalyst of it.

Jung voiced the warning of depth psychologists everywhere that an
overemphasis in education on the secondary processes of cognition, technical
expertise, and political programming to the exclusion of the student's
emotional and symbolic depths would finally cripple, even paralyze, that individual psychodynamically and ethically in what he identified as "the rational-
ist and political psychosis that is the affliction of our day" (in Frey-Rohn,
1974, p. 61).

And in damaging the individual, the distortion must inevitably extend
into the entire civic realm. For, as Jung often pointed out, a culture is, after
all, a collection of individuals. If those individuals had—class after class,
term after term—been emotionally starved and thus intellectually distorted
throughout their formative educational years, what could they finally produce
but an unhealthy society? Jung thus cautioned that "where rationalistic
materialism holds sway, states tend to develop less into prisons than lunatic
asylums" (1969b, p. 181).

The post-Jungian analyst and scholar Andrew Samuels (2001, p. 139) is on the mark, then, when he declares that education which is "confined to precise techniques learned and applied at the workplace" are "psychologically demeaning" to students, teachers, and also principals, whose unhappy task it is to enforce such things at their schools. As Jung put it, corporate education "blots out" the individual—and it does so across the span of the person's formal education: it "begins in school [and] continues at the university" (1967a, p. 153).

This is unwise and unethical, said Jung, for several reasons. It creates the "mass man" of technocratic society and thus robs the individual of his uniqueness. It accomplishes this totalitarian goal by doing violence to teachers', students', and administrators' psychosocial needs. And last but not least, it grossly impinges upon the delicacy and sanctity of the archetypal relationship between teacher and student. All of this contributes to psychological, social, and ethical disarray (Jung, 1970b).

It is no wonder that the arts, humanities, and theology have so often turned to Jung as the psychologist whose work offers insights into the processes involved in their own work in a way that no psychologist before or after him has done half as well.[1]

This degenerative asymbolism in Western culture has not happened overnight. Jung anticipated the postmodern critique of the 18th century's commitment to "the scientific method" and its stark empiricism that, for all its undoubted technological benefits, also launched us toward the terminus of our current psychosocial desolation (Becker, 1966; Foucault, 1980).

Jung identified the Enlightenment as the intellectual epoch when Western culture began to disprize symbolic reality, bit by bit stripping symbols of their status and power in individual and social life and granting ontological reality only to what could be reasoned and then assessed by some sort of tool—physical or conceptual.

In education, the view of intelligence—damaging in its epistemological naivety and psychosocial effects—as a sort of "thing" that can be statistically measured and programmatically managed is symptomatic of this reductionism. As already mentioned, this "scientistic" approach to education was stated in Edward Thorndike's famous proclamation in the opening years of the 20th century that "whatever exists, exists in some amount, and can be measured."

Jung's view of psyche and its educational implications are dialectically opposite to Thorndike's. This is important because Thorndike's reductionist, positivist view of what intelligence "is" and what education "should be" currently dominates a great deal of educational theory and practice. The hegemony of Thorndike's shockingly simplistic and emotionally withering view of intelligence, even a century after he promulgated it—indeed, *more so* now than ever—now hangs over colleges of education like a dark spirit (Popkewitz, 1987).

Jung's unique vision of the psychospiritual depths of psyche offers a broadly principled and singularly powerful psychospiritual base to resist this quantification of the spirit and bring us to a higher and brighter view of education.

In this chapter, we will look at some of the epistemological aspects of Jung's vision to better understand his radical difference from what dominates current educational discourse and why Jung's work is so important in resisting that hegemony. In chapter 4, we will look at a specific epistemological issue—the difference between a "sign" and a "symbol"—to even further refine our sense of the power of Jungian psychology to clarify educational issues and offer psychospiritually robust alternatives to the present poverty in much pedagogical and curricular theory and practice.

JUNG'S EPISTEMOLOGICAL ROOTS: KANT AND ROMANTICISM

Jung and Kant

Although Jung appears to have had a list of favorite philosophers—Schopenhauer, Spinoza, and Nietzsche ranking high among them—it was Immanuel Kant, especially *The Critique of Pure Reason* (1781/1997), that occupied the highest place and most influenced him (Pauson, 1988; Nagy, 1991).

What intrigued Jung in the *Critique* was Kant's radically subjectivist argument that we can never know absolute reality, which Kant called *Das Ding-an-sich,* the thing-in-itself. Things as they *really* are—ontological certainty about a thing-in-itself—must forever lie beyond our inherently limited reach. This is the case because "absolute reality"—whatever *that* might be, and even assuming that such a thing or state of affairs even exists—can be registered by us only through the two innate filters that make up our consciousness. Outside of these two filters, we can see nothing.

It is from the vantage points and in the terms that these dual filters allow that we must register in our own foreshortened way a forever impenetrable existence, whose nature may or may not bear some resemblance to what our filters are showing us. These two filters, our dual modes of apprehending existence, are what Kant called our "mathetic" and "poetic" faculties.

"Mathetic faculties"—"mathetic" referring to mathematical-like reasoning—refers to our various kinds of analytical capacities, our "systematicities."

These feature our ability to engage in deductive and inductive reasoning; our construction of disciplinary fields each with its own specialized, internally consistent rules of interpretation and expression; and our hardwired perception of things as existing in three-dimensional space-time. In mathetic reasoning, controlled replicability, precise formulations, and economy of explanation are key. This is why the principle of Occam's Razor is the first commandment in the mathetic domain—the simplest explanation of something is always the best. In some current brain science, these things are seen as left-brain functions (Jaynes, 2000).

"Poetic faculties," on the other hand, refers to such right-brain functions as intuition, feeling, impulse, art, and mysticism.

The poetic impulse aims at transcending established paradigms, problematizing consensual reality. This threatens the procedures and boundaries that the mathetic faculty has labored so painstakingly to establish, and it is why the poetic faculty tends toward the radical and even the revolutionary. The poetic faculty is holistic, feeds off hunches, spontaneously combusts in symbolism, and is often opaque and indirect so as to point us in the general direction of something indeterminate but compelling, even absolute in its own way—something that the precision of the mathetic prevents us from seeing because of the delimitations that exactness requires.

In brief—and using a typology of personality that Jung was instrumental in devising—the mathetic faculty relies on thinking and sensation, the poetic faculty on feeling and intuition (Jung, 1971). That being said, however, and as theoretically useful as this division of consciousness into two faculties is, it is also artificial.

After all, few scientists have chosen their work without drawing upon deep feelings rooted in their values, sometimes rooted even in spiritual commitments, about what they are doing when they do science, why they are doing it, whom they are doing it for, and whom it might be used against.

Many of the great scientists have confessed, even happily announced, that it was intuition that led them to their most important discoveries—discoveries which may scandalize consensual reality and strafe bomb previous paradigms. This has been the case in the most revolutionary epochs in the history of science, according to the physicist and historian of science Thomas Kuhn (1970) in *The Structure of Scientific Revolutions*.

On the poetic side, the artist labors to give form to what is clamoring to emerge from him lest it simply degenerate into a mess of disconnected impressions and self-indulgent emotions. These may be cathartic, but they are not art. To communicate something to others, the artistic product must enter the world as an embodied pattern of some sort (Cassirer, 1965).

This is a pattern that will be either loved or hated by the critic and general audience, but it *is* a pattern, however fringe or even shocking. And it must, in any case, be seen in the context of the history of other such artistic patterns that preceded it, even if the present artistic product represents a rejection of that history and an attempt to start a new one.

In how we *know* and how we *create*, we are mobile, always shuttling back and forth on the continuum between the hypothetical poles of the purely mathetic and purely poetic.

Jung preferred the Latin to express his Kantian view of things, claiming that we can never know the absolute *esse-in-re* (*Das-Ding-an-Sich*, a being/

thing-in-itself). We can only know the *esse-in-re* after it has passed through our epistemological filters.

There, it appears as either the *esse-in-intellectu*—the-being-in-intellect, our mathetic faculty, our cognition and perceptions—or the *esse-in-anima*—the-being-in-our-soul, our poetic faculty, our feelings and intuitions. And of the two, it is clear that, although Kant gave these faculties equal weight, Jung, along with depth psychology in general, privileges the poetic faculty (Kirschner, 1996; Rowland, 2005).

This is evident throughout Jung's writings but nowhere more so that when he wrote that "between *intellectus and res* [that is, between the mathetic intellect and an ontologically absolute 'thing,' whether concrete or abstract], there is [the poetic] *esse-in-anima*, [which] makes the whole ontological argument superfluous" (Jung, 1971, p. 44f).

The "ontological argument"—the question of whether or not the *intellectus* can adequately capture the *res*, whether intellect can discover "really real reality"—becomes unnecessary in light of the inescapable fact that all we can know of reality, indeed all we *need* to know, is its significance *to us* in our ongoing life project of becoming more whole, clear, powerful, and sensitive within ourselves and in our relationships with others.

And since Jung considered questions of value and feeling as lying in the poetic domain, he saw it as the most important of the two epistemological domains. Although "the intellect is undeniably useful in its own field," he declared, "[it] is a great cheat and illusionist outside of it whenever it tries to manipulate values" (1969c, p. 32).

Jung's elaboration of the idea of the *esse-in-anima* emerges as one of his most valuable contributions to the philosophy of psychology.[2]

This brief presentation of Jung's interpretation of Kant reveals the philosophical foundations of both his and depth psychology's privileging of deep psychodynamic processes (*esse-in-anima*) over cognitive ones (*esse-in-intellectu*). It is useful in explaining why both Jungian Analytic Psychology and Freudian Psychoanalysis consider emotional processes to be primary and cognitive ones to be secondary. On the spectrum between mathetic and poetic ways of knowing, it is obvious that Jung's veers strongly in the direction of the poetic (Rowland, 2005).

Depth Psychology and the Romantic Movement

In depth psychology's emphasis on the poetic and emotion laden, its indebtedness to 19th-century Romanticism is also evident (Kirschner, 1996). Depth psychology's basic assumptions and even some of its practices date from early in the 19th century. In a sense, psychoanalysis was "gestating" during that century before emerging in the form of the medical model of "psychoanalysis" that Freud presented at the end of that century (Ellenberger, 1970; Kirschner, 1996).

John Keats' idea of "soul-making" illustrates the connection between core Romantic tenets and psychodynamic theory (Woodman, 2005). By soul-making, Keats meant the individual's creation of himself in this "*vale* of soul making," as he called our earthly life—not a vale of tears, an idea Keats rejected. Each person, said Keats in Kabbalistic tones and terms reminiscent of Jewish mysticism, is a spark of the Divine evolving into its proper, god-like identity through the dialectical tensions that this life allows, indeed that this life *requires* the soul to pass through so that it can evolve into an eternal being.

This life was the stage in which the spark's transformation into a transcendent, god-like soul could begin to occur—"through the medium of the heart, and in a world of circumstances." And it would happen—so the Romantics variously asserted and exemplified in their poetry—through the mining of experience for its hidden, even cosmic kernels of understanding that lay far beneath, and also above, what merely empirical observation or "objective" reasoning could disclose.

We see this Romantic ideal exemplified in one of the most important documents of the Romantic period, Wordsworth's autobiographical poem *The Prelude,* first appearing shortly after his death in 1850, a mere 25 years before Jung's birth.

There, Wordsworth engages in the creative use of memory to reimagine his past through the lens of the poetic faculty in the present. This poetic retrospection would unveil new types of significance *in that past* from the vantage point *of the poetic present.* But this retrospective process immediately doubles back on itself in a wonderful way.

For that revisioned past now invests the present with new emotional richness and ethical significance since, after all, the present is the organic outgrowth of the past. This new present is richer, however, because it is now the product of a reimagined, existentially fuller past. Grounded in this now-enriched present, one can now go on to envisage previously unimagined possibilities, even transcendental ones, *in the future.* This possibility of "transcendence," whatever that term might mean to a given individual, is a key difference between Jung and Freud. In Jung, one finds a much greater hope of it than in Freud.

And as the Romantics demonstrated in their work, soul-making required attending to and working with *symbols* as they welled up in dreams, presented themselves in art, and even, as in the Romantic theorist Coleridge's case, were called into being in drug-induced states of altered awareness to announce messages that beggared the tiny scope of ordinary, ego-based consciousness.

Through the emotionally supple uses of memory, introspection, and symbols, the individual would thus, in attending first and foremost to his depths, fashion himself into a powerful soul. This "soul-making" was our fundamental mortal mission, according to Keats—one which might, he suggests, extends beyond this life—but which in any case needed to be started now.

One need not strain to see the connection here between Romanticism, on one hand, and depth psychotherapy, on the other. Soul-making, like deep psychotherapy, mines the power of symbols to understand the past, revision the present, and forge past and present together in generating a life narrative of hope in a more creative future (White and Epston, 1990). Psychoanalysis is in this sense the clinical embodiment of Romantic self-creation (Kirschner, 1996; Woodman, 2005).

Drawing on Romantic theory and on Kant, Jung—and in large measure psychoanalysis generally—sees the poetic faculty as more emotionally and existentially fundamental than the mathetic.

The poetic and mathetic both mediate consciousness. But the poetic is more magnetically drawn toward the depths of psychodynamic functioning, while the mathetic is more magnetically drawn to the surface level of cognition. Therefore, from the psychodynamic point of view, the poetic is of greater existential moment than mathetic, more attracted to and expressive of our depths, where meaning lies. There can be no doubt that the whole psychoanalytic enterprise privileges the poetic domain, although the *analytic* nature of the mathetic domain is also vital: Psyche comes first, analysis of psyche comes second, and it is therefore called *psychoanalysis.*

Naturally, this epistemological position will have many educational implications, some of which we have already examined from a psychoanalytic perspective. But Jung's epistemology goes one step more deeply than even this, pushing beyond the subconscious into the realm of the archetypes and the collective unconscious, where all of our thoughts and feelings are structured at the most fundamental, primal, and also transcendent levels. Let us look at the idea of the archetype, which was discussed in the Introduction chapter, in a bit more depth here.

THE ARCHETYPES AND THE COLLECTIVE UNCONSCIOUS[3]

As we have already seen, Jung felt that there was more to our psychodynamic depths than just the awful clumps of agonizing consciousness that had to be hidden behind the soiled black curtain of the subconscious, as Freud claimed. And whatever it was that did lie beneath the conscious and subconscious mind was, Jung felt, not just a reaction to trauma.

It was—he increasingly observed in his clinical practice and discovered within himself—nothing less than the origin and goal of all psychic energy and its infinite transformations. Freud was right that the subconscious preceded consciousness, but Jung believed that something even deeper preceded the subconscious and that this "something" structured all mental activity, conscious or subconscious, mathetic or poetic.

The Idea of the Collective Unconscious

This "something" was, as we have seen, the collective unconscious. It did not so much lie *beneath* conscious awareness and subconscious dynamics, although it could be pictured in that way, as it *surrounded* both the conscious and subconscious mind. For, it was at once deeper than the subconscious mind as well as higher and broader than conscious awareness.

To suggest its unfathomable depths and ultimate unknowability, Jung called it the *unconscious*. And to indicate that it was something that lives in each of us, something that we are all born with, he called it *collective*. In talking about the archetypes and the collective unconscious, we are frankly in the midst of an enigma that, like most mysteries, communicates with us in paradoxes, since linear, dichotomistic thinking can never fully capture the *trans*-rational (but not irrational) contours of mystery.

There are Jungians who, as I do, interpret Jung's intentions in his writings as being essentially "spiritual," however an individual might uniquely understand that term. Yet, it should be noted that Jungians are pretty equally divided about whether Jung's intentions could ultimately be characterized in this way. The other camp sees him in more strictly Existentialist (1991) terms. Nevertheless, it is a more spiritual orientation to Jung that is taken in this book.[4]

But what is meant by that highly charged word spiritual in this context?

For those who do take a more spiritually inclined view of Jung, the unconscious is often imagined as that Cloud of Unknowing in medieval mysticism—nowhere fully graspable but everywhere fully grasping us—which the great mystics have always born witness to (Underhill, 1961). It is the "fullness" that transcends all of our language and conceptualizations that the Dominican Meister Eckhart wrote and preached about.

It is also the emptiness, the *Nada* of the 16th-century Catholic mystic St. John of the Cross, negating any form or picture of ultimate reality that we could conceive or imagine but from which all of our conceptions and imaginings arise and back to which they point. It is the Great Void of Buddhism, *Sunyata*, from which all things proceed and to which they return (Suzuki, 1964).

The collective unconscious is thus another of the many names for the great Unknown that encompasses our lives and is also at their core. In the Gnostic tradition, which interested Jung greatly, this is the God-beyond-God (1969c, 1968b, 1970a; see also Hoeller, 1982). We inhabit the collective unconscious because we are *ontological* beings, but the collective unconscious inhabits us because we are *psychospiritual* beings.

By accessing the collective unconscious, the individual might gain direct experiential knowledge—*Gnosis*—of a Divine Mind beyond any religious dogma or ecclesiastical tradition (Hoeller, 1982). It is this Gnostic God-beyond-God of which Jung was probably speaking when he was asked during a BBC interview if he believed in God, and he replied: "I do not need to believe. I *know!*" (1959, p. 428).

The Idea of the Archetypes

The collective unconscious is "made up" of archetypes. In a sense, they are its "elements." They can be pictured metaphorically as those places of "congealing" or nodes of energy where the whirling, all-encompassing Cloud of the Unknown, the collective unconscious, has "crystallized" into varied "structures." These structures, the archetypes, are embedded in us as the inborn ways human beings engage their existence and also connect with the timeless as beings who live *sub specie eternitatis*—as self-aware creatures of eternity.

To experience the pull of the archetypes is to step into a zone that Jung called the *temenos*, a *sacred zone*. It is a psychospiritual field that is so existentially compelling, so experientially extraordinary, so simultaneously primal and transcendent in our experience of ourselves and the universe, and so often accompanied by "synchronicities" (a term coined by Jung), that it inspires in one a sense of the *numinous,* the spiritual, and may easily take on the aspect of a "religious" experience.

However, we must be careful not to call archetypes "spiritual" in any simply pious sense, for they have a dark side as well as a light side, which would make them the source of our sense of good *and* evil. If the archetypes *can* be called spiritual, it is in a Gnostic sense that we must do so, as containing all dualities and emanating from the Ground of Being, which is nondual. This Ground, as the source and resolution of all dualities, is the *Unus Mundus*, the transcendent "One World," which is a phrase that Jung appropriated from the medieval Christian alchemists and their Gnostic arts (1968).

The Paradox of the Archetypes as the Unknowable Source of Knowing

We have already seen how Jung's presentation of what an archetype "is" creates an epistemological paradox, of which he was well aware and often wrote. *Because archetypes are the ultimate sources of our ways of knowing, we can never know an archetype in and of itself.* The archetypes that *enable* thought are *unable* to be known by the thoughts they produce.

In other words, the archetype, being existentially and qualitatively *prior to*—and in that sense even "superior" to—the dependent, conditioned knowing it generates, is ungraspable by that knowing. The archetypes, and the collective unconscious that "contains" them, are forever inaccessible to the thought they produce, especially merely conceptual thought or cognition. Poetic modes of apperceiving come closer to the realm of the archetype, but they still do not totally capture the archetype itself. For, the archetypal matrix is of a different order of reality, a transcendent order, just as, in the metaphor used earlier in this book, a radio is of a different order of reality than the sounds it produces.

As Jung frequently pointed out, such conundrums as this one—what enables us to know also prevents us from knowing what enables us to know—always pop up to exasperate us whenever mind studies itself. We can never jump behind our minds in order to ultimately know our minds. For, what would we then be knowing with?[5]

We see Jung's indebtedness to Kant here as well as his reworking of Kant. Like Kant, Jung believed in *a priori* epistemological structures that both enable and limit our apprehension of reality.

However, it is the archetypes and the collective unconscious that are the ultimate categories and basis of mind for Jung, not the mathetic and poetic faculties as in Kant. Indeed, like every other mental capacity, the mathetic and poetic capacities also arise out of the archetypal matrix in a Jungian view, although the poetic faculty is "closer" to that archetypal matrix than the mathetic faculty, the poetic being the "favored child" of the two.

Jung readily admitted that the collective unconscious and its archetypes "is a controversial idea and more than a little perplexing." He knew that these ideas could easily be dismissed as a sort of exotic irrelevancy. Except for one thing: The idea of the archetypes and the collective unconscious that in some sense "contains" them explains a great deal that is otherwise hard to explain.

After admitting the difficulty of the idea of the archetypal realm, Jung was quick to add that "I have always wondered what sort of ideas my critics would have used to characterize the empirical material in question" (1967, p. 77, n. 15).

The Explanatory Power of the Theory of Archetypes

"The empirical material in question" is the recurrence of similar symbols, narrative patterns and themes, and the types of characters which exist in the myths and legends of vastly scattered places and times throughout history and that persist even now in the ways we interact every day, the movies we watch in the evening, and the dreams we have at night—among other things that typify human existence. The universal recurrence of such patterns, themes, figures, and symbols across time and cultures is precisely what one would expect to stem from an archetypal realm.

And even taking into account the geographical transmission of some myths and legends, it is difficult to totally explain the persistence of such parallels over time and across the spectrum of the human experience except by positing an archetypal layer of consciousness that spans all human epochs and cultures, that is inborn and that never ceases expressing itself in individuals and their societies in culturally variable but still essentially similar forms.

The hero's cycle is a good example of this universality and one that will be used throughout this book (Campbell, 1949). A young man[6] hears a call to adventure, leaves his small village, and ventures into a perilous wilderness where he meets both menacing beasts, evil enemies, and wise helpers who know how to make restorative potions and useful amulets. Along the way, he sometimes comes across a damsel in distress whom he saves and who in turn inspires him to carry on his journey toward a defining battle with a particularly loathsome embodiment of evil. He triumphs and is then rewarded with a boon that symbolizes the wisdom and strength he now possesses to return to his people as a culture hero with a renewing vision for them.

This story, in one culturally and/or individually specific variation or another, is as old as humanity's most ancient foundational narratives and myths but also as current as tonight's crime drama on television and as insistent as a dream that one cannot shake the next day.

Indeed, archetypes in narrative and imagistic form are common in our dreams, where, when ego consciousness recedes, the archetypes emerge every night to put on their strangely mystical and mythical dances for us in the darkened theater of sleep in the form of archetypal characters, symbols, and story lines (Vedfelt, 2001).[7] They also reveal themselves under extreme psychic duress, which may create pressure fissures in ego consciousness that become so great that they finally split the psyche wide open, even beyond the realm of the subconscious, revealing archetypal landscapes filled with archetypal characters who, along with the archetypally possessed individual, are now living out archetypal dramas.

When such powerful psychological phenomena overtake and then obliterate ego consciousness and its reality principle, the individual becomes possessed by the archetypal realm—literally goes "out of his mind"—its personal conscious and subconscious dimensions. He loses himself in the collective unconscious. He becomes psychotic.

Often completely identifying with an archetypal character in a catastrophic erasure of his actual personality, the archetypally possessed individual ardently believes everything that he does and that happens to him is certain evidence of a totally extraordinary, even supernatural chain of events, sometimes taking the form of a plot against him by others who "just do not understand" the plane of being on which he, now either a favored or damned soul, is living (Samuels, 1991).

This psychosis illustrates a basic Jungian tenet that *psychological health lies not in a total immersion in archetypal energy but rather in a constructive flow of energy between a strongly intact ego in line with the reality principle, on one hand, and the archetypal realm of mythic imagination, on the other.* This "axis" between the egoic and archetypal realms invests the ego with a sense of universal meaning while grounding the psyche's archetypal impulse in daily reality (Edinger, 1973).

An archetype varies in how it gets embodied and "dressed up" according to the culturally distinct times, places, and circumstances in which it is appearing and then getting expressed. These are the historical conditions in time and space in which the individual must experience, interpret and express—in his own and his culture's terms—the reality of the transtemporal, transspatial, transpersonal archetype as it is operating on him in the *here-and-now.*

When a person or culture gives viable voice and impressive image to their experience of an archetypal reality, then the archetype takes on a form that is at once universal and specific. It can become art. It can become a religious experience. Indeed, if it is powerful and generally appealing enough, it can be the foundational moment and myth that even *begins* a new religion.

As noted in an earlier chapter, the form the archetype takes on is either that of an *archetypal narrative*, archetypal *symbol*, or an archetypal *figure*. Thus, the hero's cycle is an archetypal *narrative*. The boon he receives is an archetypal *symbol*. The hero himself is an archetypal *figure*. The hero's cycle, as an archetype, appears in stories as distinct as ancient narratives from now extinct cultures to soap operas on daytime television. A dream you had just last night might also fit a particular archetypal configuration. In fact, at least one of your dreams last night probably does.[8]

These archetypal narratives, symbols, and figures can be categorized and then worked with in various ways and fields—from cultural anthropology to psychotherapy, from literary criticism to historiography.[9]

Let us explore them in educational terms.

Commentary by Tom Sherwood

Tom Sherwood, M.Ed., has been the principal of Jordan High School in Sandy, Utah, for 7 years. Prior to his principalship, he worked as an assistant principal and science teacher.

I am going into my 12th year as a high school administrator (eight of those years as a principal) and my 19th year in education. I have an M.Ed.

in educational leadership and policy, am currently finishing my coursework for an Ed.D. in educational leadership and foundations from Brigham Young University, and am beginning to research my dissertation.

I mention my experience and education to emphasize the following point: I struggle every day as a leader of a large educational institution in defining the purpose of education—which *must* be concerned with education as *meaning.*

When I entered education, it was with the hope of enlightening minds and changing lives for the better. I wanted nothing more than to be a mentor to youth who needed someone to believe in them and thus be able to teach them something enduring—and in this manner to truly have served them along their way. As I entered educational administration on the heels of the *No Child Left Behind* legislation, I had these dreams as an educational leader.

However, the educational system of which I had hoped to be an integral part was rapidly changing. The new accountability models and focus on quick, measurable outcomes rapidly changed the focus of education from concentrating on the individual to constantly worrying about aggregate statistics. Schools, teachers, and students were beginning to be measured by such rubrics as "adequate yearly progress" or "student growth percentile." In the name of the god of "21st-Century Skills," we may have sold our soul as an educational system to "accountability."

In the opening of chapter 2, Mayes quotes Jung: "It cannot be the aim of education to turn out rationalists, materialists, specialists, technicians and others of the kind who, unconscious of their origins, are precipitated abruptly into the present and contribute to the disorientation and fragmentation of society." As I look at the current state of education in America, it is very disheartening to see what we are doing to children of all ages by subjecting them to our current "scientistic" approach to classroom instruction, which harms what Mayes characterizes in this book as the archetypal relationship between the teacher and student.

The best description that I have heard, one that accurately but sadly portrays our current approach to education, is a phrase that Mayes quotes from Donald Schön: "technical rationality." Inasmuch as we are trying to solve the problem of education by recklessly using "technical rationality" pulled from other areas such as business or government without taking into account the unique setting and circumstances of education, we are guilty of creating what Jung described as a technocratic society, which robs individuals of their uniqueness.

Along with Jung, I firmly believe that each individual is imbued with a unique and precious soul. It must be handled with a certain amount of care and a tremendous amount of reverence. As educators, we have been given a sacred responsibility, which the current system is ignoring. Instead of allowing each individual to develop their talents and seek after their passions, we are trying to mold them all into worker-bees ready to fill their niche in the economic juggernaut. Is that really my purpose as an educational leader?

It is shocking to me to see how far we have strayed in education from any connection to things spiritual. The idea of a collective unconscious as described by Jung is fascinating to me and is supported by the work of various philosophers. Most relevant, of course, is Plato's theory of learning as remembering. It holds that we once knew of the universe and its mysteries and, in our current state, are simply trying to relearn what we once knew. This supports Jung's idea of archetypes and an underlying collective knowledge that may become accessible if the relationship between the teacher and student is archetypally alive.

The spiritual has been abandoned in education for fear of it becoming "religious" and thus breaching Jefferson's famous wall of separation between church and state. This is an understandable, necessary concern in a pluralistic democracy, but it can leaving schooling spiritually empty.

Mayes suggests a response in his presentation of Jung's Gnostic epistemology. In educational settings, this would translate in the simple but powerful idea of each student pursuing his or her own highest vision in a way that is relevant to the curriculum, is nondogmatic, and thus allows conversations that are legally permissible in the classroom, according to various Supreme Court rulings. This is an excellent and workable way of introducing spirituality into the public school classroom. It may be our last chance of saving the spirit in U.S. education.

NOTES

1. See Barnaby and D'Acierno, 1990; Dourley, 1984; Handy and Westbrook, 1974; Kelsey, 1984; Snider, 1990; Ulanov, 1999.

2. Brooke, 1991; Kelsey, 1984; Nagy, 1991; Pauson, 1988.

3. For a more in depth discussion of the collective unconscious and the archetypes, see my *An Introduction to the Collected Works of C.G. Jung: Psyche as Spirit* (in press, 2016, Rowman & Littlefield).

4. Admittedly, Jung, for various reasons which go beyond the scope of this study, seems to have jumped around quite a bit, and may even played cat-and-mouse from time to time, in his writings about whether or not the collective unconscious and the archetypes were "just" psychological—mere "products of our imagination"—or whether they were "spiritual" in a way that had some sort of ontological status. The question, in other words, is whether or not the collective unconscious and archetypes have, or at least provide access to, a *reality* that both precedes our psyche and may be calling it on toward the Timeless.

Jung's statement later in life seems to tip the balance in the direction of spirituality, when he unequivocally stated, "just once and as an exception," that the collective unconscious and its archetypes are the "place" where the Divine mind and the human mind overlap, and that the Divine mind had built the archetypes into the human being so as to form a sort of "communication-link" between God and humanity (1977, p. 667).

5. Buddhist meditative techniques can be viewed from a Jungian point of view, as does Mocanin (1986), as techniques of so stilling one's primary and secondary consciousness that one actually *does* come into contact with the primal structures of thought behind thought.

6. The hero's cycle revolves around a young man. As yet, there has not been enough work done in what the outlines of an archetypal heroine's journey might be, as feminist Jungian scholars have noted (Lauter and Rupprecht, 1985; Rowland, 2005).

7. See also, Feinstein and Krippner, 1998; Houston, 1996; Samuels, 1991.

8. The force of the archetype can also be discerned at the personal level as when, for example, in therapy, one member of the couple sees the other as his or her savior. The tremendous archetypal force of this projection—sometimes going beyond anything that can be identified in the patient's personal, family-of-origin issues—can go a long way in explaining the religious intensity of the person's initial attraction to the mate as well as the sense of cosmic betrayal when the mate cannot live up to the archetype. Then, the light side of archetypal savior projection onto the mate disappears and the mate is suddenly invested by the patient with the dark side of the savior archetype, now seeing her former marital savior as the opposite of a savior, indeed as the very devil himself.

9. See Gray, 1996; Kalsched, 1997; Schwartz-Salant, 1995; Tarnas, 2006; Wheelwright, 1974.

Chapter 3

The Archetypes
of Teaching, the Politics of
the Classroom, and the Case
for Archetypal Reflectivity

THE ARCHETYPES OF TEACHING AND LEARNING

Few human interactions are as universal or meaningful as those between a teacher and a student.

The Buddha's final sermons to his disciples still inspire the most scrupulous study and disciplined practice among students from Bangkok to Boston. When Mary Magdalene sees the resurrected Jesus at the entrance to the tomb at the end of John's Gospel, she addresses him with a single word, "Rabbi"—Teacher. Moses and Mohammed abide for many as prophetic pedagogues who delivered lessons that must be studied from generation to generation for the inexhaustible meaning in their messages. And Lord Krishna's counsel to Arjuna on the field of battle in the *Bhagavad Gita* still vouchsafes lessons in moral courage for us all to contemplate.

At the base of cultures are just such foundational narratives as these (Berger and Luckmann, 1967). Their primary purpose is personal *in*-struction in the service of cultural *con*-struction.

The hero at the center of the story is also a cornerstone of his culture, and his role is primarily that of a teacher. His words establish and his deeds evidence the society's "fiduciary commitments," their unspoken but everywhere operative "articles of faith," upon which the culture rests. These are those axiomatic and treasured beliefs and worldviews that are bodied forth in a culture's rules, rituals, and other modes of exchange and interaction, all of which may even come to be codified at a higher level of abstraction in that culture's legal system (Bruner, 1996). And all of this begins with the culture hero as teacher.

The scope of teaching and learning is very wide. Not only are teaching and learning key to the founding and maintenance of cultures; they are present as well in the smallest settings.

In what D.W. Winnicott (1992) has gracefully named "the romance of the nursing couple," the mother and child, in hushed isolation, learn together the protocols of adequate feeding, letting each other know what works and what does not work in this first classroom for the infant. In this sense, "The full breast is the first curriculum the baby must empty and digest in order to meet the goal and requirement of satiation" (Ekstein, 1969a, p. 49).

Perhaps this is why we so often use eating imagery in talking about educational processes. One devours a book, consumes information, chews on new ideas that a lecturer pours forth or dishes up, tries to get the flavor of an argument that somebody has brewed or cooked up, takes time to digest facts or concepts, and sometimes is even required to regurgitate knowledge on tests, which may leave a bitter taste in one's mouth or stick in one's craw so much that one is simply fed up and could just spit!

There is a fundamental connection, it seems, between *taking in* knowledge and ingesting nutrients. In the tiny confines of the nursing room no less than in the great halls of history, teaching and learning are the heart of the matter.

Between these two extremes take place the engagements and exchanges of the rest of life. They vary greatly in social scope, degrees of closeness, and possibilities of sharing, of course—from the tough talk in the boardroom to the mellow after dinner conversation in the living room, from the joke in the lunch line to the chants on the protest line, from life-changing conversations over days on road trips to brief, excited discussions about a movie on the short trip back home. Despite their differences, all of these exchanges are alike in being potential sites and sorts of educational processes.

Indeed, these encounters are existentially substantial to exactly the extent that the conveying and receiving of personally important points of view is going on. Otherwise, all that is happening is just "idle talk." Except in the most formulaic and therefore trivial situations, our communications generally aim at much more than the mere transmission of information. That is what computers do, and that is all they do, which is why they must always be limited in education to the role of tools that may *facilitate* but must never be allowed to *dominate* educational processes between the teacher and student.

In our daily discourses, from the thousand-and-one "micro-semiotic" encounters of life partners in the course of a week—from chitchat to the addresses of leaders to assembled political bodies and even nations, the intention of the exchanges is to convey an emotionally tinged view about something to someone else. This may well involve an attempt to shape that other's view, and, if one has entered the conversation in good faith, to be shaped in turn by the other's views. We can hardly *be with* each other without *being in* an educational process with each other, and in that process we will usually alternate between our roles as teachers and learners.

Such a core fact about human life is archetypal by definition. The roles of teacher and student are engraved in our existential DNA.

We are teachers and students from cradle to grave. Whenever teaching and learning are going on, an archetype is therefore activated, or "constellated" as Jungian psychology has it. This means that an archetype's "energies"—again, a term to be understood in a symbolic, not necessarily literal, sense, as noted in the previous chapter—have been evoked and embodied in the actors and their acts in a present situation. It is safe to say that, given this centrality of teaching and learning in human experience, the archetypes of "teacher" and "student" are never far from us and are always on point of constellating.

Ironically, the numinosity of the archetype of the teacher and student relationship—the psychospiritual core of it—in deeply educational processes is a potential and a problem in current formal school settings. Why is this?

To answer that question in the American context requires a brief overview of the history of U.S. public education in the last 150 years.

The Teacher's "Vocation" versus Corporate Education

Schools are the official spaces that a culture sets aside and dedicates as its formal educational sites. Their purpose is to validate and pass on the culture's worldviews and practices to its children regarding everything from the nature of the cosmos to how to cook an egg. Teachers and students come together in these spaces in historically embedded, socially constructed, and personally experienced ways and roles that obviously vary greatly across cultures (Pai and Adler, 2001).

In Western industrial and postindustrial societies, schooling has increasingly operated in the service of the great nation states that arose at the end of the 18th- and throughout the first half of the 19th century and have been evolving ever since (Schumpeter, 1975; Hobsbawn, 1999).

The rise of public schools in the United States is part of this world-historical nation-state movement, especially in the last 140 years as public education has operated more and more in the context and for the purposes of industrial, and now postindustrial, society (Tyack, 1974; Cremin, 1988). Schools deliver an "official curriculum" (Eisner and Valance, 1974) the process and goals of which are more or less determined, monitored, and enforced by the state (Foucault, 1980).

Behind the rhetoric of providing equal opportunity for all in a meritocratic democracy, public schooling in the United States, despite its undoubted successes, has equally functioned to deliver varying levels and types of skills, information, and knowledge *differentially* to children depending upon their social positioning, their *habitus* (Bourdieu, 1977)—which has traditionally meant their family's socioeconomic status and ethnicity.

This amply documented stratification of educational resources and opportunities available to a student in the U.S. public schools depending on the child's social positioning has tended perpetuate a given social order, conserving certain distributions and dynamics of power (Bowles and Gintis, 1976). It is a sad but true fact of U.S. educational sociology that nothing so predicts a student's score on college entrance exams as his or her parents' socioeconomic status (Morrow and Torres, 1995).

Furthermore, students learn a great deal about what their "proper role" in society will be through the constant flow of explicit and implicit messages that they receive in the school it is their lot to attend—from the attractiveness of the school architecturally, to the quality of the labs and playing field and library, to comments dropped by teachers in the classroom, to differential academic and vocational counseling, to how experienced and stable or inexperienced and transient the school's staff is (Kozol, 1991).

This, and more, leads to widely disparate educational experiences for students and thus to different possibilities and life paths for them after their schooling. In short, schooling becomes to a considerable extent a vast "sorting machine" in the service of presently constituted power(s) to train children into their roles as "worker-citizens" (Spring, 1976).

In the United States, as the corporate state tightens its grip on schools more with each passing year, public schooling has become one of its primary means of reproducing present power relations and in shaping children's consciousness to conform to that existing order—or rather, in instilling "false consciousness" in them as it is called when the worldview of one's oppressor is internalized because one has been taught to consider it good and true or in any case inevitable—"just the way things are."

Through scholastic means the corporate state thus legitimates and consolidates its hegemony. And this is largely accomplished through high-stakes standardized testing, with its rewards for compliance and high performance and punishments for low performance or resistance—in addition to other forms of both concrete and symbolic surveillance and control of virtually everything that now goes on at a school site (McLaren, 1998).

So complete had the strangle hold of corporate interests on public school already become by the end of the 20th century that the Dean of American Historians of Education, Lawrence Cremin, warned in 1988 in his masterpiece, *American Education: The Metropolitan Experience*, that the paramount threat to American democracy was no longer simply the military-industrial complex, which President Eisenhower warned of in a farewell talk to the nation, but the growth of the military-industrial-*educational* complex. Cremin proved prophetic. This complex now bestrides American education like a colossus.

American public education over the last century has increasingly come to reflect the assumptions and requirements of the corporate system in which—and for which—it works. The teacher in corporate America, increasingly seen by both "neo-liberal" and "neo-conservative" reformers in managerial, technocratic terms, is now compelled to deliver an official curriculum devised by "experts" in pursuit of higher international test scores and greater geopolitical competitiveness in the transnational corporate capitalist economy.

Ironically, of course, such modes of miseducation defeat their very purpose by stifling individuality and creativity, the twin engines of economic greatness. And in the balance, this corporate model of education alienates the teacher from her work, especially those teachers whose sense of calling and practice spring from the archetype of the teacher in all of its historical, cultural, and psychospiritual richness.

No doubt there will always be some degree of tension in the 21st-century classroom between the state's demand, legitimate up to a point, that schools promote a profitable and efficient society, on one hand, and the delicate archetypal dynamics of teaching and learning, on the other hand. These two goals need not be antithetical. After all, the healthier and more intellectually engaged the children in our schools, the more balanced and constructive the adults they will become, and the more productive and just the society they will make.

However, U.S. education is now being reduced by the state, with a historically unprecedented speed and thoroughness, to the mere transmission of disconnected bodies of official "knowledge" and masses of utilitarian "facts"—none of which is to be critically questioned but merely reproduced on high-stakes standardized tests. Schooling exists now, more than ever, in the stranglehold of a commodity-obsessed fixation on technology and in the service of the "the bottom line." In such an archetypally unfriendly, even hostile, environment, the heart, soul, *and* mind are being driven out of education.

Teachers and students are decreasingly allowed to be living *subjects* in psychospiritually exciting engagement with each other through the medium of a cognitively rich and ethically relevant curriculum. Instead, teachers and students are being tragically transformed by the withering corporate touch of the state into *objects*.

As Jung (1969a) predicted, such a dystopian educational scenario, in which "technical rationality" (Schön, 1987) is the card that trumps all others, must conclude in "psychic dissociation," "collective hysteria," and "spiritual regression" in a people—the decline and fall of democracy. This is something which the psychoanalytic pedagogues have always warned about, Jung inveighed against, and John Dewey (1916) argued against in *Democracy and Education*.

To resist the now almost complete intrusion of the state in the schools and to do so in the service of their students' and their own growth in an intelligence grounded in psychospiritual well-being—this is the heroic struggle of the teacher who chose her work under the inspirational pull of the archetypes of teaching and learning.

To stay true to that psychospiritual, civic, and ethical sense of calling, she must everyday renew her efforts to erect a firewall between her students and the encroachment of the state—its program of merely "training" children into a kind of robotic obedience, or diagnosing them as medical problems if they consciously resist or for whatever reason cannot conform, and are then medicated into submission until they *do* conform by the very corporate system that created the problem in the first place.

It is imperative that the teacher be her students' champion on their shared mythic journey, their archetypal Wise Elder and also Magician with her existentially restorative potions and protective amulets—symbolic of the *I-Thou* relationships she exemplifies and invites around a living curriculum. She must regularly rededicate herself to tapping into the archetypal wellsprings of her sense of calling through reflectivity on her practice.

In this manner, she is better armed—even with the current constraints she labors under—to transform her classroom into a *temenos*, a sacred space abounding in the archetypal graces of teaching and learning. She and her students thereby win not only a political victory but, even more significantly, they experience ever greater psychospiritual growth in the triumph of deeply educational processes.

ARCHETYPAL PEDAGOGICAL REFLECTIVITY

The Archetypal Dynamics of Conceptual Change

One way in which the teacher can find this professional self-renewal in the service of her and her students' psychospiritual maturation in critical intelligence is by engaging in what I have called "archetypal reflectivity" on her practice (Mayes, 1999, 2001, 2009b). This consists in introspection and journaling, dyadic work, and group processes in terms of archetypal symbols, narratives, and figures about one's sense of calling as a teacher, one's pedagogical practices, and how one's role as a teacher fits into the larger narrative of one's life.

For, the Jungian theorist Irene de Castillejo's (1973, p. 22) observations about physicians—that "in the great machine of modern medical practice" they have become "cogs," alienated from "the archetype of a healer"—are equally germane to teachers, who need to be able to draw on *the archetype of the teacher* to counter disaffection in their work. Bolstered by archetypal energy in their roles, they can view and renew their practice against a broader, more numinous, and even eternal backdrop of meaning. This can empower teachers, investing them with archetypal *mana*, revitalizing them in their political struggle, and feeding them in their and their students' holistic unfolding.

In examining the educational implications and applications of the archetypal realm in this and following chapters, I discuss archetypal symbols, figures, and motifs that have proven useful to me and the teachers with whom I have worked over the last two decades in reflecting on our practice. The teacher thus has psychospiritual material ready to hand that she can use in weaving her professional narrative into the broader archetypal patterns and symbols that comprise her larger life story (Houston, 1996).

Meditating in these terms on her sense of calling, her pedagogical practices and her existential purposes, the teacher finds psychospiritual renewal and development, enabling her to explore alternate ways of seeing and being in the classroom. At the same time, these practices help form a deeply principled basis for resisting the state's excessive presence in today's classroom.

In previous studies (2003, 2005b, 2009b), I have examined teachers in terms of such archetypal roles as Priest or Priestess, Zen monk, Shaman, Trickster, Wise Elder, and the archetypal Great Mother or Great Father. I have also looked at the student as a hero or heroine passing through the stages of the hero's cycle in his or her emotional and cognitive emergence. Additionally, I have made suggestions (2009b) regarding an archetypal approach to conceptual change theory.

Conceptual change theory deals with why and how a person clings to a presently held idea in favor of a new one, even in light of the fact that the new idea is backed by evidence that logically merits the change. The dynamics of conceptual change were originally formulated mostly in cognitive terms as "cold cognition"—so called because the ideal was to create a student in the image of a scientist changing his views under the weight of objective evidence (Posner et al., 1982; Chi, Feltovich, and Glaser, 1986).

However, in the more emotionally nuanced terms of "hot cognition," conceptual change theory began to consider the personal psychodynamics of why one may understandably, even justifiably, hold onto a concept in the face of strong countervailing evidence (Duschl and Gitomer, 1991; Pintrich, Marx, and Boyle, 1993).

The reluctance to change an idea despite compelling evidence can additionally be seen in the archetypal terms of the ancient narrative of the sacrificially slain but then resurrected god whose death ultimately brings new life to his people. In these terms, the refusal to change a concept in light of compelling new evidence can be understood as the archetypal hero "stalling" on the road to resurrected vision and enhanced ethical maturity, because he will not let his old idea, and ultimately himself, be sacrificially slain in the service of his and his people's revival in a new conception. He will not die to be reborn. But then again, who does submit to such processes easily?

Having a sense of the archetypal enormity that may underlie changing a concept grants us a deeper understanding of and compassion for the student who clings to a present idea against the facts. To learn something new may mean to die to something that one loves and that has been essential in one's identity, personally and/or culturally. At least, it may *feel* that way at first to the student. Even, and sometimes especially, scientists have been known to cling to a theory because of their personal and professional investment in it.

This must be honored in the student and care must be taken to assist her in her journey toward conceptual change. For changing an idea, when it is felt by the student to be calling her very existence into question—when, that is, she perceives it as a clear-and-present threat to her identity—activates in her depths the fear of the obliteration of that identity.

This is nothing less than the fear of death itself, oblivion. Here we are in the universal zone of the archetypal Hamlet's "to be or not to be." We are also approaching the core of all our psychodynamic processes according to Existential psychotherapy—the strengthening engagement with or neurotic avoidance of the question of one's mortality (May and Yalom, 1995).

Changing an idea may be felt by the student to implicate her very existence, stimulating what the Jungian Donald Kalsched (1996) calls "archetypal defenses of the personal spirit," as when the student falls into an almost autistic posture of primal helplessness before a hostile cosmos, and then projects archetypal demonic imagery onto the teacher who, in calling for conceptual change, becomes The devil himself in the student's eyes—an archetypal monster who turns out to be none other than the embodiment of the student's own archetypal shadow.

Other puzzles and paradoxes await us in the archetypal realm that helps us understand why educational processes can be so emotionally intense and refractory.

For instance, in resisting conceptual change, the student, in recoiling from the death of an old idea, is *refusing* to draw on the energy of the savior archetype in undergoing a transformation for the sake of his people.

On the other hand, in clinging to what may be a problematic idea rooted in his cultural commitments, he is also attempting *taking on* the savior archetype. Single-handedly, against all evidence, and under duress, he is nevertheless straining to defend his culture's norms against new ideas that, in fact, it might be wise to consider because doing so would help him enrich his community. In sum, the student is possessed by the savior archetype at the same time as he flees from it. Such contradictions are typical of the subconscious and unconscious and come to bear on educational processes in many influential ways.

We will examine other archetypal processes in the classroom in what follows exemplifying how *secondary* cognitive processes can either be blocked or enhanced by *primary* psychodynamic and archetypal processes at personal and transpersonal levels. First, however, an example of archetypal reflectivity.

A Personal Example of Archetypal Pedagogical Reflectivity

I would like to offer an example of my own reflectivity as a teacher of educational psychology. In doing so, I do not mean to privilege my reflectivity or to set it up as some sort of standard for other teachers to follow. Like Mark Twain, I would not speak of myself if I knew anyone else half as well. I simply hope that by offering this personal portrayal of *archetypal pedagogical reflectivity*, I might encourage others to do so in ways that are most rewarding to them in deepening their own practice.

I have chosen to frame my reflectivity in the rest of this chapter by drawing upon certain elements in the hero's cycle as presented by Joseph Campbell (1949) in his classic study *The Hero with a Thousand Faces*. I have employed the hero's cycle in a book-length study (2009b), where I used it as a lens for viewing a wide range of issues in contemporary American schooling. I will now draw upon only selected characters and motifs in the hero's cycle to reflect on my practices and experiences teaching an undergraduate class with intending elementary- and secondary-school teachers generally ranging from 18 to 25 at Brigham Young University in Provo, Utah, in the United States.

According to Campbell, the archetypal journey commences with a call to adventure. If the novitiate hero is to develop, he must respond to that call in the affirmative—and not, like Jonah, try to deny the beckoning voice of fate. Stopping one's ears to the call typically results in being swallowed by the Leviathan of depression. "The Jonah Complex" refers to any refusal to do the inner and outer work that is necessary to advance on the path of individuation—one's life task, never fully accomplished in this life, where there are always inner issues to wrestle with, but with one constantly approaching the goal in ever closer approximations, as if always pushing just a little farther the asymptotic limit in calculus.

The hero accepts the call by crossing a perilous threshold—usually one that leads to a spooky forest or monster-infested desert. This begins his quest for the grail, the holy cup that holds the blood of God, symbolizing individuation, the *personal* discovery of *the image of the god* within, the *imago Dei* at the core of psychospiritual dynamics (Heisig, 1979; Jung and von Franz, 1986).

The hero cannot embark on this quest without giving up his previous life. Along with St. Paul, the archetypal hero must die a certain death by "put[ting] away childish things" to become an adult (*1 Corinthians* 13:11). The person who will not respond to this challenge will always remain a psychological and ethical child regardless of chronological age—caught in the self-imposed constrictions of the archetypes of the *puer* or *puella,* Latin for "boy" and "girl," which shuts down the potential for psychospiritual expansion (von Franz, 1981)

Having chosen to go over the threshold, the hero soon meets a Wise Old Man or Woman who already completed their own archetypal quests long ago when they were young.

These Wise Elders tantalize their budding charges with riddles and oracles, thereby teasing the *puer* and *puella* out of the smug certainties of their previous worldviews, much as the *koan* posed by the *sensei* functions for his monks in Zen meditation. This requires the young hero to rise to Robert Frost's challenge "to seek a newer world" by searching out a higher wisdom—symbolized by a boon that the hero receives at the end of his quest. He may then return to his people as a culture hero renewing society.

In my teaching, these archetypal images, characters, and motifs cast light on my practice—its problems and possibilities.

Defamiliarizing the Student's World

I teach several sections of an undergraduate class entitled "The Foundations of Education." This class is taught by most of the faculty members in my department and is a requirement for students who are preparing to become public school teachers.

I first present a given issue in contemporary U.S. education in its standard historical, political, and philosophical contexts. We then take as long as we like, referring to the syllabus in only an approximate way according to the rhythm and range of our needs as a community of discourse, to explore an array of complex and controversial issues. The goal is for each student to deepen and refine his or her sense of calling as a teacher—and to explore what that narratival elaboration on oneself as a teacher means in the larger narrative of one's life.

My approach to The Foundations of Education is disruptive, dealing with problematic aspects of American education socioeconomically, ideologically, psychologically, and ethically. In doing this, I consign myself to the status of an outlier—*out-land-ish* in the politically conservative landscape of the religious culture in which I teach at the largest religious institution of higher education in the United States. To make matters "worse," I let students grade themselves, which they wind up doing probably even more strictly than I would.

For I want to practice what I preach in the very first class, when I announce that my teaching practice is informed by Paolo Freire's (2001) insistence that authentic educational processes must be liberatory and that I do not want for any of us to operate according to what Freire (1970) calls "the banking model" of education.

I of course read and comment on all of their work closely and do not retract from my responsibility as the archetypal Wise Elder, the guide on our intellectual trek over a semester, where we are bound to meet many curious conceptual beasts, some of them dangerous. What I will *not* be in our class is the head banker who controls the capital in a marketplace classroom. What I intend is for us to create a democratic community of discourse, a free zone of liberated learners.

The banking model dominates, I tell them, when teaching is the mechanical "transmission" of information *into* the student, not the meaningful "transformation" *of* the student (Kane, 1999). In banking education (which is not really education at all, but merely training), the teacher (who is not really a teacher at all, but simply a functionary) just pours "intellectual capital" into the "checking account" of his students' uncritical heads so that the students now possess a few deposits from the teacher's cognitive currency of institutionally approved/imposed "knowledge."

Such knowledge makes up the cultural "capital" that the students could now draw upon in the intellectually and ethically vacuous game of upward social mobility (Bourdieu, 1977). Such things have nothing to do with the creation of real knowledge, for the students have had no role in engaging and assessing ideas for themselves for their import to *them*. This lacks the holistic relevance to the student that Dewey (1916) insisted is key to true education, which demands of itself ever more education in an internally generated, life-long adventure in learning.

In the banking model, the students' work is no labor of love, which profoundly educational processes by definition must be. Rather, the students' grim duty in the banking model is simply to slavishly grind through then reproduce officially imposed bits and pieces of quasi-intellection for the teacher on a test that merely mirrors the teacher's opinions, guaranteeing *his* power and his students' disempowerment. This confirms the professor in a narcissism that comes all too easily with "Ph.D." after one's name. Even more destructively, it trains students into ideological conformity, foreclosing their creativity.

Thus, I make it clear from the get-go that the prime educational directive in our class is that students engage all the material—books, lectures, videos, discussions—in a way that will most deeply touch and change them as spiritually called, ethically powerful, and critically astute educators, not instructional "middle-men" for the state.

"The Old King must die!" is the archetypal subtext of my introduction to the class, which even this early on I endeavor to make implicitly ring with the mythical narrative from Jessie Weston's (1957) classic study *From Ritual to Romance* about the death of the Old King and his moribund reign and the installation of the New King and the redemption of the land in fertility and the people in freedom.

But now, the land is dry and cracked, wasted, and the people are distracted and distraught, fearful of the lowering clouds of a plague they see approaching from the horizon. Will my students join me in killing the Old King to usher in the age of that New King after a poetic Last Judgment, where the apocalypse consists, in William Blake's visionary terms, in "the destruction of all bad art and science"?

Will we build in our classroom Blake's visionary New Jerusalem of unchained minds and hearts in apocalyptic education? Will we set "art and science" free—at least within our four walls every Thursday from 4:00 to 7:00 p.m.—free from the political and cosmic dominions that would enchain them as students and reduce them to pedagogical servitude under the Old King?

Will we (so my unspoken archetypal challenge goes) merely continue under the Withered Autocrat, the archetypal *Senex*—the old, shrunken, bitter grandfather who bears us no love and who occupies the seat of power from which he orders links to be locked around our necks so that we must bow to his curricular will? For that *Senex* has sneaked into our learning spaces and is ravaging teachers' and students' souls. As the Wise Old Man, the light side of the archetype whose opposite *is* the *Senex*, I am issuing the archetypal call to my young hero/heroine students.

And although I do not say this in so many words, I am sure that they perceptively register the message in another mythic vocabulary that they and I share and that I *do* explicitly deploy. I recite to them St. Paul's words that, I point out, are especially relevant to us as educators who are our students' only hope in the death-dealing establishment of contemporary public education.

"*Ephesians* 6:12," I announce. Many take out their scriptures to follow along: "For our struggle is not against flesh and blood, but against the rulers, against the authorities, against the powers of this dark world and against the spiritual forces of evil in the heavenly realms." They close their scriptures. There is the inevitable meditative silence. "I believe," I say after they have had time to take the scripture in, "that what we are facing, as teachers in the service of our students, is nothing less than what Paul is describing here."

Shortly after this, I then leap from The New Testament to Sartre's *Being and Nothingness* to introduce one of the Existentialists' ideas that will loom large in our class. I call upon my students to carry on their pedagogical work in the spirit of Sartrian (1956) "good faith"—in a way, that is, that corresponds to their most authentic vision and ongoing creation of themselves as teachers in the service of their students' and their own freedom; for, where there is disempowerment, there also are depression and anxiety.

Their liberation must inevitably contribute to their ability to advance their own future students' holistic health.

I have assembled readings that do not line up with the usual curricular suspects: the obligatory "methods" sections based on the most current "instructional theory," the latest and glitziest in brain science research, the drudgery of funding issues, the sad history of the devolution of teachers' unions, the often overly celebratory narratives about public education in America, and all the other bland ingredients of a typical class in the Foundations of Education, which are in general famous for being hoops of fire that intending teachers must jump through and which, if they are sane, they will forget five minutes after the final exam.

Rather, my students read about education as a psychospiritual and ontological fact that is at the core of the human condition, and one that can serve politically, psychologically, and ethically liberatory purposes—or not. But this it *must* do, or become degraded into the status of mere "training," an instrument of oppression in the hands of political forces that would violate the sanctity of Martin Buber's (1985) *I-Thou* relationships between teachers and students.

When that happens, I tell my students, the classroom morphs, like a video game populated by zombies, into a wasteland of *I-It* nonrelationship between broken beings who—now distanced from each other in what should be their joint labor of love—finally become alienated from themselves. Psychological and social dissociation, intellectual deterioration, and ethical devastation lie right around the next corner down that dehumanizing road. And *that,* I suggest to my students, is exactly where we find ourselves today in a great deal of what passes for "education" in America.

"What will you do about this," I conclude by asking after our first session, "as the frontline educational advocate for your students, and in defense of your own integrity? This class is about just one thing, and that is your response to this question. The answers that you come up with will be your own and need not at all agree with mine. That is not a requirement—not even remotely.

"The only thing that matters is that you come up with approaches to your sacred work as teachers that resonate with your best vision of yourself and your students, and that you then put that into action, constantly revising and improving, theory informing practice and practice informing theory, throughout your career—in the most courageous and compassionate manner that you can under the difficult circumstances in which you will work.

"There! That is our syllabus. Read the first three chapters of the book I've assigned as our first reading. Come prepared next week—although I do not give tests and I never take roll. I trust that your interest in becoming a better teacher will move you to read and will draw you here each week. It matters greatly to me that each of you be part of our conversation and share what those chapters meant to you, positive, negative or both. And be prepared for the possibility of being changed by a conversation—one in which you should be aware of the daunting prospect that your views may change others, too. Be responsible, for we have a covenant with each other to do our best."

To further upset my students' now rocked ideological and institutional world, I relentlessly drive home the message every class that in the study of American education we are dealing with issues of such intractable complexity that there simply is no such thing as the "Truth" with a capital "T" about these questions. "Anyone who comes to you with the capital 'T' truth about schools is after your money, your vote, or both. All we can hope to attain are humane, lower-case-'t' 'truths'—many with their strengths, but, like my own views, limited, too, and producing their own sets of problems."

With this realization, it dawns on my students throughout the next few classes that I was actually serious during in this first class when I said that the goal of our time together would be for *each student* to wrestle—individually and authentically—with these problems in order to come to her *own* conclusions about them. And, issue by issue, class after class, my students learn the wisdom of Kenneth Burke's (1989) great pronouncement, "Every way of seeing is also a way of not seeing."

This is a tough piece of ideological meat for my students to chew on in the flagship educational institution of a church where they feel they have been given the ultimate truth, with the definitive capital "T," and that it is their duty to convey it to a planet slip-sliding into an imminent world-historical apocalypse in moral relativism. What do I mean by saying there is no capital "T"? Am I in the service of the relativistic Evil One who now roams the world more craftily than ever?

Naturally, my students are shocked the first day and for at least a following class or two to have wandered into this *anti*-class, so unlike anything that, according to their comments at the end of the year on student evaluations, they had ever experienced at my university, where so many see compliance to authority as a virtue, indeed as almost a self-evident theological imperative, and where resistance—not to mention disruptive theory and practice—inspires the fear that one is toying with the thin wedge that the devil wields to open a tightly shut door that has been safely bolted by doctrinal correctness against all sorts of ethical night terrors.

In dramaturgical terms—and teaching is inevitably either good or bad theater—I set out to accomplish what Bertolt Brecht, the German communist playwright, tried to do in his drama, and that is to create what he called a *Verfremdungseffekt*, an "alienation effect," from the first moment the audience sits down.

The *Verfremdungseffekt* refers to the overturning of someone's expectations in a conventional setting—a theater or a classroom, for instance—by dismissing standard situational protocols and all their niceties, as reassuring as they are wrong. Both onstage and in the audience in the "theater situation," this throws sudden doubt over the previous rules of dramatic engagement and interpretation, calls into question all of the participants' "roles" from the playwright and actors to the person sitting in the last seat in the last row, and brings to awareness how empty and even hypocritical the hierarchy of those roles often is.

The *Verfremdungseffekt* ultimately, therefore, forces each person in the theater space to radically reconsider what they are presently doing, why they are doing it, and how it fits, or more likely doesn't fit, into what preceded this event in their life as well as what will soon come after in its narrative flow— and now its narrative dislocation. In short, each member of the audience is being called to globally interrogate his very identity, which he had thought would simply be more or less comfortably confirmed this relaxing evening at the theater—or this routine afternoon in class.

An experienced teacher can read his students, and what I read during this first class is a wide spectrum of incredulities scrawled in not-very-subtle strokes all over their faces.

Some of the students are happy and amble to the front after class to tell me so, to have found a class that promises to help them gain new ways of seeing and being, precisely what they so rarely find in the current U.S. higher education environment of "the corporate university" (Giroux and Myrciades, 2001).

Other students are simply disoriented, their dazed stares announcing as they leave that they do not know what hit them or what to expect out of this sheer incongruity in their conservative academic experience to date. And one or two betray by smirks and furtive glances back at me as they exit that the whole thing is clearly a joke, and one that they will be able to milk for an easy "A" with minimum sweat. But I have reason to believe that even these students come around.

After the first class, however, their shock at what they have just experienced in the first class confirms for a few students the fear they have finally found that renegade professor whom their parents warned them about, that wolf in sheep's clothing, a false prophet who will undermine their beliefs. This is not at all my intention. My goal is to help my students' make of their faith and their thinking in general something that is more emotionally mature, ethically nuanced, and culturally tolerant.

My end-of-term evaluations are filled with comments that my students' visions of teaching changed, and for some it has been a sea change. I read that my students feel that the term created in them a more energetic set of hopes for even their most difficult future student's potential if that student can be seen from many psychological, cultural, cognitive, and ethical points of view, and as a vibrant existential *etre-pour-soi,* a being-for-itself, not an *etre-pour-autres,* a being-for-others (Sartre, 1965). And I am convinced that this is what they are more hopeful of for themselves, too.

The evaluations inform me that my students come away with a more healthily skeptical view of current educational policies. In addition to the positive things that happen every day in the schools and which certainly need to be honored, my students are now also more aware of the intellectual and psychospiritual damage being wrought by many current miseducative policies and practices. Above all, they now feel more empowered to try to resist such things, at least in their own classrooms.

Many write that our class has offered them a more expansive view of what education should be, a better perspective on how their teaching fits into their larger life narratives, and a magnified vision of those larger life narratives themselves. What is going on here is ontological transformation of both myself and my students in the archetypal *temenos,* the "sacred precinct," of the classroom.

To choose to engage students in such ways is a high-stakes existential project—one that is central to my life and therefore one that I have reflected on from many angles over my 35 years as a teacher. Each mode of reflectivity has offered much.

Pedagogical reflectivity has helped me view my practice through the lenses of a wide range of theories of teaching (Brophy, 1994). Biographical reflectivity has yielded insight into family-of-origin and other personal issues that psychodynamically influenced my decision to become a teacher, and has clarified and refined my ways of relating to my students in health and compassion (Huberman, Gronauer, and Marti, 1989). Critical reflectivity has served me in honing my classroom acts to be more politically aware and proactive in what I include in the curriculum and how I present it to my students (Bullough and Gitlin, 1995).

However, it is archetypal reflectivity that has brought me to the deepest as well as the highest vision of my role as an educator in the service of my students' and my own liberation in the psychospiritual trajectory toward individuation.

The Archetypes of the Puer, Puella, and the Wise Elder

In this brief picture of my teaching an undergraduate class, it is clear that I have issued in archetypal terms the "call to adventure" to my young students. Many of them are still *puers* or *puellas,* who are prone to an "in-group/out-group" binary of themselves and others into "us versus them," where "we" are the children of light, "they" the children of darkness.

But all archetypes have both a light and dark side. The maturation of the soul entails that each of us integrates both sides of the archetypes that circulate within us—which is yet another way of understanding the idea of individuation. Our psychospiritual goal is to augment the light while discovering, drawing upon, and channeling the power that lies hidden in the shadows of the psyche.

In my classes, I draw upon the brightness of the archetype of the Wise Old Man, an archetype that is common in the patriarchal culture in which I live and thus nothing that would take my students by surprise. But I blend it with the archetype of the Trickster to create a mix that catches my students just off guard enough to find themselves in the midst of something novel, something that it may require actual *engagement* to cope with.

For as Jung claimed, not all that we have banished to the shadow of consciousness is bad. Unlike Freud, Jung did not view the personal subconscious as entirely a dump yard of everything so hurtful in one's life that one could or would not remember it. Much of what lies in the "shadow"—a term Jung introduced into the psychological vocabulary—had been cast out of ego-consciousness simply because it *had* to be occulted in order for the developing ego "to go on being" under circumstances it was then not yet experienced, adept, or self-aware enough to otherwise handle (Winnicott, 1992).

But now, with waxing maturity, such exiled things not only *can* but *must* be retrieved and rehabilitated. In this way, one comes closer to the always beckoning, never fully achieved goal of individuation—to be skillful in handling those contradictions in life and in oneself that are at the heart of our existential situation, contradictions that we do not merely endure but *are*.

Not to work with one's shadow means that one will remain self-righteously stuck in superficial "virtues" that do not answer to the depths of life's actual ambiguities. For, each individual is called to wrestle with life's paradoxes, like Jacob with the angel, so as to mature and connect with higher truth, a more nuanced heaven, mystically symbolized in Jacob's ladder to superior levels of awareness. As Edgar says in *King Lear*, "The ripeness is all."

The questing soul's frank recognition of and confrontation with its shadow is the precondition of emotional, intellectual, and ethical evolution. Refusing to face one's own shadow—paralyzed in the *puer or puella* position—means that one cannot further the progress of one's pilgrim soul but must freeze in a developmental fixation.

One thereby becomes merely a semi-personality—cloyingly "sweet," formulaically "kind," but impotent at last, and all too prone to project one's own denied darkness onto others by demonizing them. Or the 30-something professional football player may continue playing despite his doctor's warning after the eleventh concussion that the next one may disable him for life.

This is the outcome of staying stuck in the *puer* and *puella* archetypes.

I am determined that it will not happen in my class as my students' teacher, their Wise Elder throughout the forest of the academic term. As the Existentialist theologian Reinhold Niebuhr (1944) said, each of us is *both* a child of light *and* a child of darkness. It is archetypal wisdom to brace up to this fact and to handle it.

Many of my *puer* and *puella* students have come to the unfamiliar— indeed the *"de-familiarizing"*—zone of my classroom from religiously orthodox homes, where virtue is a given and has so far been relatively untested in their tender years. Their undifferentiated consciousness is symbolized in the hero's cycle by the rustic village in which we first meet the hero, blessedly but all unconsciously bundled up in an innocent bower of felicity. This bucolic setting is as charming as it is unreal. In that village, virtue is easy—a facile, self-congratulatory adherence to a cultural norm that it pays to observe.

In terms of Kohlberg's (1987) hierarchy of three levels of moral reasoning, some of my students are still stuck in Level One moral reasoning—"Good Boy/Bad Boy, Good/Girl Bad Girl"—where what is "good" is simply what one's parents say is good.

Or they are in Level Two, "Good Citizen" moral reasoning, where the ethical standard is whether or not an attitude or act accords with the social norms. And although "social obedience" is where many people tend to land and stay in the development of moral reasoning according to Kohlberg, individuation requires more than just good citizenship, which too easily degenerates into what Freud and Jung both cautioned against: "the herd mentality" or blind obedience to a corrupt state. Individuation, the highest reach of moral reasoning, demands exploring one's own depths and opening up to the depths of the Other (Levinas, 1996).

I therefore blow the pedagogical clarion from which issues the call for my students to leave the picturesque cottage of their country villages and its laudable but limited virtues and to cross the threshold into the archetypal forest of psychospiritual and ideological adventure.

I am summoning my students to take seriously in their lives and professional practice St. Paul's own reflective observation "When I was a child, I talked like a child, I thought like a child, I reasoned like a child. When I became a man, I put the ways of childhood behind me" (*1 Corinthians* 13:11). For, it is a developmental breakdown of a particularly seductive sort to cling too much to any doctrine—let that doctrine, political or theological, be ever so good and reassuring—if one does not face and shape oneself as an existentially unique being.

Furthermore, as Fowler (1981) has shown in his seminal work *Stages of Faith*, growth in one's spiritual commitments reaches its apex in a certain universalism. The seasoned believer comes to view many paths as leading to the same mountain top—and not in spite of his beliefs but precisely because of the message of compassion and hope that is at their core.

"No one has a monopoly on the truth" quickly becomes a sort of background mantra in our classroom discussions. The innumerable paths to the universal summit are marked by mutual respect in free and open discourse, where each is edified by each and the only binding rule is service to others. Of such free individuals is a living democracy made.

To remain stuck in the *puer* or *puella* archetype, leading at last to what Jung called "doctrinarism," results in an unspiritual life, for it must conclude in the pious fraud of sanctimonious intolerance of others' paths. This disregards the basic moral obligation that life lays upon us all—to grow in seasoned and reasoned compassion.

It bears upon this exercise in reflectivity to mention that some of my students' political naivety has to do with their religious belief that the United States is a country of special favor in God's eyes and will be uniquely instrumental in carrying out God's millennial purposes. This conviction in many of my students leads some of them to an exaggeratedly favorable view of the United States in their reading of current events and an overly celebratory interpretation of U.S. history.

All of this may result in these students embracing ultraconservative politics that simply dismiss as not only unpatriotic but also theologically suspicious those contrary voices that speak of America's shortcomings, even its sins. I introduce my students to these voices and that evidence in such works as Howard Zinn's (1990) *A People's History of the United States*, which sees America's past and present not from the point of view of the groups that have won but those that have lost and now live shakily and in shame on the margins.

One does not wish to deny or even minimize the greatness of America, but it is necessary to view it in a realistic light, sensible of what such Jungian cultural theorists as Adams (1996), Gray (1996), and Gellert (2001) have identified as *a nation's shadow*. (This is a topic we will develop in chapter 5.)

The American shadow includes the legacy of its genocidal program against its Native inhabitants, its treatment of African Americans, its colonization of various parts of the world to get cheap goods and extorted services while engaging in the corporate dumping of symbolically and actually toxic products, and its fevered "commodity-fetishism," as Marx called it, which, in its obsession with objects, turns those who covet those objects into its ultimate objects.

I do not ask my students to give up in their political commitments. What I do require of them is that they guard against the category error of confusing their idea of the role of America in a millennial future with her past and current realities—her virtues and grandeur, to be sure, but also her corrupt admixtures, which, as I demonstrate in the course of the term, are there on open display for all to see in the history of class, race, and gender oppression in U.S. educational institutions.

I call upon the *puer* and *puella* to cast off their immature, self-serving nationalism in favor of a more mature love of one's country that takes the good with the bad, as all true lovers must eventually do with what they love.

All of this includes but goes beyond the realm of politics or the ins-and-outs of the latest, and often politically and economically motivated, "research" into "cognition" and "instructional science" that make up the standard Foundations of Education class. More universal pedagogical and psychospiritual patterns and purposes, invested with the intimations of something that exceeds the day-to-day world, are at play in our classroom. Archetypal reflectivity makes this clear to me as a teacher and offers me insights into how my students and I may move in this realm with ever greater measures of grace and goodness.

My students and I are the particular actors in this dramatic space known as "the classroom." It is a space that is more likely to become a *temenos* of authentic engagement if I, as their teacher, engage in archetypal reflectivity upon my practice, learn to draw upon the archetypal energy inherent in the deeply educational relationship, and deploy it in ways that serve us all as growing souls with an eye to the eternal in what we are doing in the here-and-now classroom.

The Teacher and the Trickster

A few students persist in projecting onto me the archetypal energy and imagery of the Trickster even late into the term. After all, who *is* this incendiary character standing in front of class—he who seems to be calling into doubt, at first even seeming bent on demolishing, so much of what the student once thought was certain, virtually sacrosanct "knowledge"? Why has he done this? Is it some kind of elaborate practical joke he is playing?

I must confess that the Trickster is an archetypal role that I take on quite naturally and always strategically in the service of my students. My grandmother was a vaudeville comedienne in the Yiddish theater in New York City in the early 1900s so that my mother, who grew up in the wings, was constantly "on stage" around the house. I was raised in a constant rain of tragicomic one-liners, hilarious slapstick, and gentle irony—all those echoes of that lost Jewish art still alive in my classroom.

The purpose of such humor, often intentionally at my own expense and, of course, never at my students', is both to soften the shock of my unorthodox pedagogy in a conservative setting and also to make myself vulnerable to my students, always within limits that preserve my own boundaries.

In this fashion, I bear comedic witness to them that I care about them, that I trust them, that I am not in love with my own institutional "position," and that, even though I may sometimes resemble that consummate archetype of the prankster Coyote in Native American mythology, I would never lure them astray with my shape-shifting displays. My aim is simple. It is their growth and empowerment as teachers, and through the humor of the Trickster, they come to know it—to *feel* it.

And finally, to draw again upon my Jewish origins, I want my students to believe (for it is true) that I see each of them as an eternal spark of the divine Kabbalistic flame, evolving into transcendent personhood. Mine is "archetypal comedy" akin to that of King Lear's Fool, for the benefit of my sometimes naïve but nevertheless regal students (Welsford, 1935). Archetypal reflectivity upon my role has made this humor possible *in* me, comprehensible *to* me and, I trust, beneficent in its use *by* me in the best ways that I am capable of.

Happily, almost all of the students fairly soon begin to resonate to my approach and we settle in for an exciting ride for the rest of the term. But occasionally at the end of the term, an unfavorable student evaluation will make it clear that my class wasted the author's precious time.

There will always be a few students in the course of a year who will refuse to resonate to the call, entrenching themselves even more deeply as *puers* and *puellas* throughout the term. Nothing will ever change them from seeing me, as is always the case with the one who has issued the call to adventure in the hero's cycle, as "a dangerous presence dwelling just beyond the protected zone of the village boundary. . . . The emotion that he instill[s] in human beings who by accident [venture] into his domain [is] 'panic' fear, a sudden groundless fright" (Campbell, 1949, p. 81).

Although only several students will wind up evaluating me in this way in the course of an academic year, it is nevertheless the case that even one such evaluation can sting. Like many teachers, I would wish every student to like me—and even one student's misunderstanding hurts. For, just as the patient's rejection of a therapist can wound the therapist since he is so deeply involved personally in his patient's therapeutic processes, so the student can wound the teacher, who is no less deeply involved in his students' educational processes (Kirsch, 1995). This is just one of the many parallels between therapeutic dynamics and deeply educative ones (Mayes, 2005a).

Here is a place where reflectivity can also be helpful—in (ad)dressing the wound of the teacher who has been rejected by a student.

For I have come to see that most of these reactions to me are not finally to *me* but to something originating in the student's own psyche. Naturally, one must examine oneself to make sure that one has not done anything personally to cause this rejection. However, when that has been ruled out with tolerable certainty, it becomes likely that the student's negativity is a transference of some sort. And as with all transferences, it is rooted in the student's specific issues psychodynamically as well as at the transpersonal level psychospiritually since every transference, even the most personal, probably has an archetypal nucleus.

What may lie at the base of such a student's unhappiness with me is that I embody an archetypal paradox that the student cannot resolve. I am a contradiction for him, and contradictions can spawn frustration and aggression.

My nurturing nature and obvious care for my students soon constellates within them the archetypes of the Wise Elder and even Great Father. But because I am posing vexing questions that may not only be simply challenging the student but disorienting him, I may simultaneously be constellating in him the image of the Dark Magician. This archetype is symbolized by the *sol niger*, the black sun, of the alchemists. The Dark Magician is one who confounds things through the weird conceptual chemistry of his dubious arts—the dark light of his strange science.

The black robes I wear at graduation may thus have a dual significance in the deepest reaches of this student's unconscious mind. For those robes are for him not only a symbol of my archetypal status as Wise Elder. They are also, in their blackness, darkly emblematic of the perceived threat of a wizardry that this student persists in believing I am practicing. Even our gowns of official distinction are woven with the psychic threads of archetypal tensions.

The Student as Prometheus: Old Gods and New

Another important archetypal figure in educational processes is Prometheus. The student must be able to access the archetypal energy of Prometheus, he who steals fire from the gods to offer the light of rejuvenating knowledge to his community, to bring his heroic journey in the classroom to its fitting conclusion. But it is no small matter to rob a god—a symbolic form of killing that god. Still, this is central to the archetypal processes of changing an idea, and even more so if what is involved is the restructuring of a worldview. Thus, it is that one must sacrifice the old god. One must immolate him and his system on the altar of the new idea from a new god.

But this new god turns out to be none other than the student himself—finding the *imago Dei,* the "image of God," as the god within (Heisig, 1979).

Conceptual change is a kind of deicide and, when the new idea/god runs counter to something one's family, culture or nation has always believed, perhaps even deified, this deicide at the secondary level of cognition can cause considerable guilt and anxiety at primary subconscious and unconscious levels. Because I understand that the student may be projecting this tension onto me, I can respond to him with greater calm, clarity, and compassion. As the fruit of my reflectivity, I may be of greater service to him throughout the term, not defensively reactive to him.

Archetypal reflectivity thus requires close analysis of oneself and one's students to harvest the archetypal energy inherent in the teacher-student relationship and use it well. This is all the more important because archetypal energy, if poorly handled, can be destructive of the teacher, who to some degree is inevitably invested with it. We see this in the Wise Elder's shadow.

The *Senex* is the pompous, dried up, snappy Old Man, always making some dreadful little moral point or other that alternately bores and browbeats all who are forced to listen to him. He is a tyrant who demands total obedience from his oppressed and repressed subjects. He is the crotchety fool who thinks he knows it all simply because he occupies a position of some authority and has a wall covered with diplomas to justify it but which really just evidence his narcissism mixed with profound insecurities.

The shadow side of an archetype takes possession of one's psyche when one becomes so invested *in* an archetype that one ultimately comes to be possessed *by* the archetype, which necessarily includes its shadow. As we saw in chapter 2, this complete identification with an archetype is called "inflation" in Jungian terms. A teacher who overly identifies with the Wise Elder archetype, forgetting his all-too-human limitations, is ripe for possession by its shadow, the *Senex*.

Under the force and farce of inflation, the individual is so overheated with archetypal energy that it fries his reality-principle circuits. He has fallen into the seductive grips of a transpersonal dynamic that is now not enriching the personality with numinosity and a wholesome charisma but is obliterating that personality in psychic waves from a cosmic sea of ultimately untold depth and strength. Without the sturdy boat of an intact ego, one simply sinks into the archetype and drowns in its tempestuous waters. This was Jung's gloss on the scriptural warning that "it is a terrible thing to fall into the hands of the living God."

As the noted Jungian scholar Edward Edinger (1973) said, the key to the individuation process and the criterion of psychospiritual health is the creation and maintenance of an "axis" between the ego and the archetypal realm. One of the great misconceptions about Jungian psychology is that it is luring us to get lost in an airy-fairy land of mythical images and self-aggrandizing narratives at the expense of ordinary consciousness and in defiance of the basic rules and roles of everyday life to which we all must attend.

But Jung, a conservative Swiss and occasionally a military physician who began his career treating psychotic patients in a psychiatric hospital, was a realist. He knew very well that the shattering of ego consciousness by an excessive influx of archetypal energy results in psychosis. Without the ego and its reality principle to contain the superpotent brew of archetypal energy, one grows psychospiritually drunk with one's archetypal role. Then, in a sort of psychospiritual DUI, one will at some point inevitably drive the speeding vehicle of one's now grotesquely inflated sense of himself into the brick wall of unforgiving reality.

Thus, although the teacher may draw upon the archetype of the Wise Elder, he must do so circumspectly, without becoming so enchanted with it, and with himself, that he loses a proper sense of his own limitations, and thereby comes to lord it over his students with exercises of his classroom power. Indeed, much undue use of power by teachers in the classroom stems from archetypal inflation (Mayes, 2003) in response to a primal narcissistic wound (Kohut, 1950/1978).

Drawing upon the archetype of the Wise Elder to orient and energize his practice with appropriate power and charisma, the archetypally reflective teacher—steering clear of inflation—knows that he, like his students, is after all just another hero in the making, yet another learner in the University of the Cosmos. That University's curriculum presents the universal undergraduate that each one of us is with one educational threshold after another to cross in curiosity and courage.

Even the teacher has not entirely given up all of the small and self-serving village notions that delimit his growth, nor has he been purged of all of the biases that may be blurring his vision. He too has many borders and boundaries yet to cross. And he never forgets—if he is truly a *wise* elder—that the ultimate threshold of death, that final call to adventure, awaits us all, and that we are all marching inevitably toward it and must cross it one day … alone— a fact that makes novices of us all.

No less than his students, then, although hopefully on a more developed plane, the teacher knows that he is also a pilgrim. He too is a student on a muddy, twisting road whose signposts are often unclear, written in an other-worldly language. Wise Elder to his students, he knows that he is just a more experienced *student* than they. He is aware that he must summon and then respond to a deeper source in order to renew himself as an authentic being, and also, therefore, as a teacher. For, being a teacher is a big and inseparable part of his total existential constitution. Thus, it is as both a guide *and* fellow traveler that the archetypally reflective teacher comes to see himself.

Or perhaps he is the captain of the classroom "ship of thought" (Barford, 2002). His vision of himself in the classroom having been expanded and made more subtle by archetypal reflectivity, such a teacher better understands both his potentials and limits in his role. Not a captain who sits aloof in his privileged cabin, he works in solidarity with his students as fellow sailors, First-Mates all, on the waves of an ever-emerging sea of discourse, with the entire crew headed toward the same port—growth in principled freedom, individuation. This is the destination to which the needle always points on the compass of archetypal pedagogical reflectivity.

Commentary by Aaron Wilson

Aaron Wilson, M.Ed., is currently the assistant principal at a Granite Park Junior High, a Title I school with over forty languages spoken by students who come from over sixty different countries.

As educational practitioners, we can all appreciate the process of reflection that allows us to improve our craft, and in turn, improve outcomes in student learning. Reading this chapter can assist each teacher and administrator reflect on the fundamentally unique roles they play in education, the deep impact they have on students' lives and on society in general.

In viewing education and the relationship we have with our students through the lens of archetypes, the importance of our roles and the deeper meaning of student behaviors will "click" like never before. The hero's csycle and the roles it encompasses, for example, may easily be applied to the classroom, where the student is appropriately cast as the hero questing through the stages of his hero cycle, for, in fact, each person in some way *does* cast himself or herself in this role.

Students will have experiences at school that are problematic and hurtful in their greater journey, whether it is bullying, peer pressure, experiencing school culture that is incongruous with their upbringing, or a myriad of other things. If we understand students in Mayes' archetypally pedagogical terms, we will have greater empathy. We realize that we are asking our students to change their very existences. They are straining, heroically, to defend their background, their understanding, and nothing less than *themselves* on that battleground where these incongruities are being suffered but hopefully are also being worked through: the classroom.

As educators, we have deep archetypal roots in our roles. Mayes highlights this fact. By understanding our mentoring role to students through their journey, more deeply appreciating the importance of our relationship with them, and utilizing the powerful effect we have, we can "renew our practice against a broader ... eternal backdrop of meaning." This understanding can both "revitalize" and "empower" us, even in facing the toughest situations in our profession.

One of the toughest situations we face, Mayes notes, is the pressure to conform, which is exerted upon us as educators and also on our students. Mayes outlines the detriment to students if *information* is merely transferred to them rather than allowing them to grapple with *knowledge* in creative ways. Mayes fortifies teachers with an archetypal perspective as they not only impart the curriculum (which Mayes talks about) but also as they must handle student misbehavior (an area that needs to be addressed by educational scholars in the archetypal light that Mayes writes about).

As we come to understand our relationship with our hero students, we learn the psychological underpinnings of why they may project their tensions onto us and also have renewed eyes that allow us to archetypally reflect and compassionately respond to this. Doing so, Mayes illustrates, will allow us to channel the archetypal energy we inherently possess as teachers, using our unique positions to assist the student in ways psychologically conducive to their growth.

And as in this chapter, where Mayes encourages teacher to issue "the archetypal call to his young hero-students," he issued it *to us,* in our doctoral seminar with him this summer. We experienced what issuing and hearing the call means in the specifics of a relationship-driven classroom.

Archetypal reflectivity, helping the teacher understand his role as a mentor more deeply, helps that teacher create a classroom space where the individual student's voice enriches without dominating airtime in classrooms, where instruction is more responsively differentiated, and where more just and productive power relations exist in the classroom. This fosters in students healthier perspectives about their roles in society, a love of learning, and an ability to express themselves creatively throughout their lives.

Chapter 4

Training in the Sign, Education in the Symbol

Jung accorded the highest significance to the symbolic dimension in both our individual and collective lives. Human experience and expression are at their most valid and forceful, indeed they reach their highpoint, in "the symbolic life" (Jung, 1977). This is especially obvious in our religious and cultural narratives, dreams and art, but it is a fact that permeates all the *secondary* processes of our *cognition*. Symbols emanate from the foundational realm of *primary* processes, the subconscious and unconscious minds, from which they inevitably come and to which they eloquently point with an existential finality.

As both a psychotherapist and cultural critic, Jung claimed that the *desymbolizing* of our lives is the root of our psychological, social, and ethical maladies. He felt that an individual or culture becomes emotionally and morally ill when they are *demythologized*—that is, when they lose touch with their archetypal source, when self and society are estranged from the symbols that alone are capable of manifesting and bestowing archetypal *meaning*. Asymbolism underlies the existential crisis of contemporary man.

"Now, we have no symbolic life," lamented Jung in a conversation with a group of British psychiatrists,

> and we are all badly in need of the symbolic life. Only the symbolic life can express the soul—the daily need of the soul, mind you! And because people have no such thing, they can never step out of this mill—this awful, grinding, banal life in which they are "nothing but."... There is no symbolic existence in which I am something else, in which I am fulfilling my role, my role as one of the actors in the divine drama of life.... That gives the only meaning to human life. That gives peace, when people feel that they are living the symbolic life, that they are actors in the divine drama.... Everything else is banal and you can dismiss it. (1977, p. 273ff)

It is no wonder that the arts, humanities, and theology have so often turned to Jung as the psychologist whose work offers insights into the dynamics of their own work in a way that no psychologist before or after him has done half as well.[1]

This degenerative asymbolism in Western culture has not happened overnight. Jung anticipated the postmodern critique of the 18th century's commitment to "the scientific method" and its stark empiricism that, for all its undoubted benefits, also launched us toward our current psychosocial disarray (Becker, 1966; Foucault, 1980).

As mentioned previously, Jung saw the Enlightenment as the time when Western culture began to minimize the reality of the symbolic realm and grant reality only to the empirically observable and measureable world. In education, the view of intelligence as a sort of "thing" to be quantified was established by Edward Thorndike. He set the tone for a great deal of educational research and practice ever since his famous proclamation in the opening years of the 20th century that "whatever exists, exists in some amount, and can be measured."[2]

So what is a symbol according to Jung? We will look at this in more depth in this chapter in order to mine Jung's writings for some of their subtler educational implications regarding the importance of the symbolic domain in deep educational processes.

THE SYMBOL VERSUS THE SIGN IN
JUNGIAN EPISTEMOLOGY

According to Jung, the first thing to note about a symbol is what it is not. It is *not* a sign. Between a symbol and a sign there is a tremendous difference.

A sign means one thing and one thing only. A stop sign means to bring your vehicle to a complete halt before proceeding, and it has nothing at all to do with anything else except driving when it is planted by the side of a road as a big red token to be obeyed. The sign for a curve ball that the catcher flashes to the pitcher demands a curveball, not a fastball high and inside, and the catcher is not trying to communicate anything else to the pitcher except this strategic message to retire the batter.

A mathematical sign means to perform a specific numerical operation, and it certainly has nothing to do with how the person doing it feels about the operation. A no-smoking sign means just that, especially where oxygen is being used, lest everything go up in flames. Signs serve many purposes, often crucial ones.

A sign bears a one-to-one correspondence with what it signifies. The sign and signified are *isomorphic* to each other. To the extent that a sign is at all ambiguous, it is a bad sign whose unclear signification is probably based in a factual error and may lead to a procedural misfortune. An effective sign leaves no room for interpretation by the person who is processing it. A sign claims objectivity and demands obedience.

Subjectivity is forbidden in the world of signs, for subjectivity is what signs are meant to keep in check, even eliminate. Indeed, in the world of signs, anything else *but* signs are in-*sign*-ificant. Signs are the official motto in the kingdom of Nothing-But, where everything is either A or not A, B or not B, C or not C. The problem, of course, is that life is rarely like that.

Although the sign has its regulatory and instrumental purposes that no one would deny and can be enormously beneficial, it is a harsh taskmaster if it abandons its secondary role and tries to take control. Indeed, when it becomes the *master* and not just the secondary *tool* that by definition it is, then a sign has overstepped its bounds and has a marked tendency to enslave thought and action. For, a sign will not stand for any interpretive wandering by the individual—whom it may then brand as "deviant" if he strays too far in those interpretations.

The world of the sign is absolutist—a black-and-white journalistic photograph. The world of the symbol is dramatic—a varicolored, emotionally fertile, abstract painting.

In the black-and-white world of signs, the only imperative is to *reproduce* something or some state of affairs—"reproduce" in the sense of reflecting, employing, and perpetuating its assumptions and ways of doing things—not to *examine* them.

The net result of this is to bolster the beliefs and confirm the conventions of a certain established reality—in spite of the fact that what counts as real may vary across cultures. And even within a culture, the individual who challenges the authority of a governing sign system, or at least its appropriateness to *him*, learns the hard way the truth of Emily Dickinson's wry observation that "straightaway you're dangerous, and handled with a chain."

The sign's "yes or no" view of things is prone to produce an "I or other" mentality, an "in-group or out-group" view culturally and politically, a simplistically "true or false" way of evaluating an idea, and a judgmentally "good or bad" way of assessing morally complex situations. There is no in between in the domain of the sign. There is no place where subjectivity may creatively roam in search of the fruit of the imagination in resolving dialectical tension by moving to a higher plane of thinking—Jung's "transcendent function."

This is not to say that signs and binaries are not useful. Their syllogistic languages underlie and make possible the whole range of helpful technologies. It would be hypocrisy and ingratitude not to acknowledge those many ways our lives are made better by the languages of signs and what they produce. However, it is also true that *signs are as use*-full *as they are value*-less.

An instrumentality is always *full* of practical *use*. That is what makes it an instrumentality. But an instrumentality is *empty* of ethical *value*. That is why it can be deployed in such a wide range of different, and even contradictory, situations and for opposite purposes. A gun can be used equally efficiently to either kill or defend the innocent. The gun itself is without moral value. It is just an instrument. It is killing that raises the question of value.

Hence, value can be neither discovered nor communicated through any sort of sign—not even in the impressive but ethically neutral binary-operations of the newest computer on the market. Nor is value to be found *ultimately* even in conceptualizing, for, as Jung wrote, in issues of feelings and value "the concept is only a word, a counter, and it has meaning and use only because it stands for a certain sum of experience" (1969b, p. 33).

Certainly not mere signs, then, and not even the reach of concepts finally answer to the supra-rational complexity and situationally specific ambiguity of experience, from which value emerges. Values are charged with all of our precognitive passions and point toward our supra-cognitive aspirations. They are embedded in who we are primally and what we may become ultimately.

Indeed, values involve *all* aspects of our being—from the biological to the cultural, from the sensory to the spiritual. Values are an outgrowth of all the swirling circumstances and connections in both our inner and outer lives, and it is only something as nuanced as a symbol that can even begin to approach and express this.

The unidimensional sign or even the layered syllogistic concept could never do this kind of subtle existential duty. This is why education that is sign obsessed or aims at the mere reproduction of disconnected concepts for a test fails miserably when education revolves, as it should, around what the individual values and how to act on those commitments. The world of values is inseparable from our subjectivity, and our subjectivity lives, moves, and has its being in the domain of the symbolic (Kierkegaard, 1969).

To live the symbolic life is a courageous act of risk and passion in the service of one's own freedom, which, so as not to be self-indulgent or danger-ous, must dedicate itself to the freedom of others as well.

Thus, whereas the sign is designed to conscript and channel an individual's thoughts and actions in a definite but anonymous direction that has already been determined by some other agency or system external to him, the symbol aims to liberate the individual into an ever more nuanced and open sense of his own transcendent identity.

To be ethically wise and not emotionally sloppy, the discovery of one's own transcendent identity—what subsequent Jungians have called "the Self" with a capital "S" to stress its internal, psychospiritual nature—must labor in the service of liberating others and therein find its own salvation, as all the great Wisdom traditions throughout history have declared (Huxley, 1945).

Archetypal symbols are manifestations of the ultimately unknowable archetypes. They are guesses about and glimpses into the core mysteries of life, which is another way of "defining" an archetype. For, as Jung stated, in what must count as one of his most significant observations, "The unconscious is not this thing or that; it is the Unknown as it immediately affects us" (1969b, p. 68). The collective unconscious is nothing other than the mystery of life itself as it impinges on human consciousness and as human consciousness reaches out to engage it. The archetypes are the "categories" of that engagement.

In a professional medical community that was enamored of clinical "objectivity," Jung was courageously bucking the tide in insisting that a symbol is the only way of approaching the Unknown, which we cannot ever fully grasp but which fully grasps *us* in those areas of central significance in our lives.

The symbol is "the best possible expression," as Jung put it, "for something that cannot be expressed otherwise than by a more or less close analogy" (1971, p. 63 fn. 44). Pointing to the experiential, perhaps even ontological, possibilities that go beyond mere ego-consciousness and propositional reasoning, Jung characterized a symbol as "the best possible expression for a complex fact not yet clearly apprehended by consciousness" (1969c, p. 75).

Jung suggests something of the tremendous scope of the symbol, its depth and height—which does not deny ego consciousness or its systems but, enfolding them, exceeds them, in a move that is not *irrational* but *transrational*—in observing that "the symbol is the primitive exponent of the unconscious, but at the same time an idea that corresponds to the highest intuition of the conscious mind" (1978b, p. 28).

In Kierkegaard's (1969) terms, the distinction between a sign and symbol resides in the difference between stumbling through life as a dazed member of a herd—or striding through life in singular purpose and spiritual crescendo as "that certain individual."

In Heidegger's (1964) terms, it is the difference between the secondary *ontic* realm of operationalizing a *predetermined* agenda, on one hand, and the primary *ontological* realm of authentic Being, where the fullness of one's subjectivity *is* the agenda, on the other hand.

In Buber's (1965) terms, it is the difference between the master-servant face-off of *I-It* and the vivifying encounter of *I-Thou.*

In psychodynamic terms, it is the difference between the surface phenomena of secondary conscious processes and the deep core of all mental movements in primary subconscious processes.

In Jungian terms, it is the difference between the necessarily limited world of the day-to-day ego, and the discovery of the transcendent Self in the limitless world of the archetypal domain.

And in the classroom, it is the difference between *training in the service of something external to oneself*, in which the curriculum is a mechanism of control, and *education in existential growth toward subjective freedom*, in which the curriculum is a means of liberation.

TRAINING IN THE SERVICE OF THE SIGN, EDUCATION IN THE SPIRIT OF THE SYMBOL

Educational theorists and practitioners must be careful—as many presently are not, or not enough—to distinguish between "training" and "education." A Jungian approach to the sign and symbol is very helpful in clarifying this distinction. In what follows, I deploy this idea to present a pedagogical distinction between what I will call "Training in the Service of the Sign" and "Education in the Spirit the Symbol."

Training in the Service of the Sign

In Training in the Service of the Sign, the teacher more or less mechanistically transmits an "official curriculum" (Eisner and Vallance, 1974) which, however much he may or may not agree with it, he has had little or no role in creating. The official curriculum is made up of things ranging from "facts" to isolated concepts to official theories—announced, codified, and enforced by the state—which increasingly in today's schools are simply presented as "true" and are not to be subjected to any real degree of critical analysis in the classroom, much less radical critique or subjective appropriation.

The official curriculum inevitably contains various assumptions about "how things are" and "how they should be." These comprise what is called "the hidden curriculum" (Eisner and Vallance, 1985), which, in the last analysis, reflects and reproduces the worldviews of favorably socially positioned groups, whose political power determines what the official curriculum will be (Apple, 1990).

Standardized tests, the major means of enforcing the official curriculum, reward students who can and will perform well on them. Such students thereby evidence proficiency in and compliance to the structures and discourses of power. At the same time, standardized tests punish and push to the margins students who, for a wide array of reasons, many of them valid and compelling, cannot or will not do well on those tests (Jones, Jones, and Hargrove, 2001).

Training in the Service of the Sign—which is increasingly the reality of U.S. education—is not so much *objective* as it is *objectifying*. Teacher and student are not called upon to choose or change in any personally meaningful ways under the ethical pull of a true existential gravity in the classroom. To the contrary, students are simply required to "get" or further "develop" certain types of "knowledge" and "skills." The goal is to render the student more suited to someday filling a hierarchical slot in the corporate state (Giddens, 1990).

And to make matters worse, the slot that a student will fill is closely tied in to his parents' social positioning, which is both reflected in and reproduced by the "quality" of schooling that he has access to—"quality" now being defined as how well the school prepares a student for high-stakes standardized tests and the prestige of the university he will enter, assuming he makes it that far (Morrow and Torres, 1995). As already noted, no single factor so closely predicts a student's score on college entrance exams as the student's parents' socioeconomic status (Jones, Jones, and Hargrove, 2003).

Day after day, week after week, term after term, year after year, training in the service of the sign methodically and mercilessly dispirits both the teacher and the student by making irrelevant, indeed erasing, the possibility of *meaning* in the classroom. For, meaning comes into being when what happens in the classroom is something that students and teachers make their own in a way that enriches their life narratives, their *subjectivity*. Otherwise, their narratives are violated and become mere manuals in conformity, not personal stories of a unique being's unfolding.

To the degree that an educational system erases the teacher's and student's subjectivity and "gives in" to the hegemony of the sign, to that very degree the classroom becomes a site of alienation from self and others. When this happens, then, as Buber wrote, "The continuing growing world of *It* overruns [a person] and robs him of the reality of his own *I*, till the incubus over him and the ghost within him whisper to one another the confession of their non-salvation" (1965, p. 46).

As a professor of education, I see every day and have written about the personal and professional carnage all of this is creating in veteran teachers who are preparing to become principals in the graduate department of educational leadership in which I teach (Mayes, Blackwell, and Williams, 2004).

Such experiences leave scars on the soul for teachers and students. Too many of these scars, especially early in a person's life, can, as the psychoanalytic pedagogues whom we examined in chapter 2 lamented with one voice, so disfigure a student's "learning ego" that he will give up on himself as a learner, on learning itself as being anything applicable to him, and moreover cause him to condemn himself as not only a scholastic failure but also generally deficient as a human being (Anthony, 1989). This is a cry that has been the constant theme of the psychoanalytic literature on education for almost the last one hundred years (Mayes, 2009b).

On the other hand, but equally injuriously, the student who receives the message that he is good and important because of all the rewards he gets for scoring well on such tests will soon learn to forfeit the pursuit of his real self in order to "be" and do whatever is necessary to get a high score on the next test.

This causes him to live in what can be a paralyzing anxiety that he may not do so well the next time, leading to what Winnicott called living as "a false self" and what Jung called being possessed by one's *persona*. It breeds in the child the painful, neurotic, and even slavish practice of "learning for love," not the buoyant, liberating pursuit of "the love of learning" (Ekstein and Motto, 1969; Winnicott, 1988/1992).

Education in the Spirit of the Symbol: The Subjective Curriculum

In truly educative processes, the teacher is key in deciding not only *what the curriculum will contain* but also, like Winnicott's (1988) "good-enough mother," *how the curriculum will contain* his students in the classroom as a nurturing "holding environment." In this sense, the curriculum has the potential to be a living thing because, like the symbol itself, it is an occasion for *I-Thou* relationships to form as individuals join to generate multidimensional knowledge, which each student may then appropriate in his own way in the furtherance of his unique life narrative.

For we are narratival creatures after all, and to eradicate, or even minimize, the growth of a person's narrative is to minimize or eradicate the person (Ricoeur, 1979). Training in the service of the sign, in its rigidity and anonymity, is antinarratival. Education in the spirit of the symbol, in its ability to see a topic from many perspectives, its subtle ability to change to fit shifting emotional needs and tones in the classroom, and its focus upon individual interpretation, promotes the creation of a rich narrative in the student. Like a symbol, such a curriculum spurs on those constant "evolutionary emergences" within and between individuals that symbols also catalyze.

Education in the spirit of the symbol places a premium on not only *what* the curriculum contains but *how* each student experiences it in the classroom and then uses those experiences to elaborate, in passion and compassion, her wider life story. As noted in chapter 2, this is called "the subjective curriculum" (Cohler, 1989). As do symbols in general, education in the spirit of the symbol contributes to the student's richer life narrative, and it accomplishes this through the medium of the subjective curriculum.

Again, recall Jung's insistence upon how crucial it is to the individual's well-being to feel that "I am fulfilling my role, my role as one of the actors in the divine drama of life" (1977, p. 275).

In an ethically significant narrative of one's life—a narrative that is arching in a creative trajectory toward existential fulfillment in the future, one that makes redemptive sense of the often painful past because it is precisely *that* past that led to *these* present possibilities—the present is transformed into a vibrant focal point of significance. For, the past now leads to and the future emerges from a "now" that has become abundant in meaning and potential. The student catches a vision of herself as "one of the actors in the divine drama of life." Training in the service of the sign is concerned only with the "potential" of turning the student into an instrument of an imposed program—usually a political one.

A narrative of robust subjectivity with hope in the future is what constitutes emotional health and moral vision. The absence of such vision in an overly determined, sterile, fixed present is disempowering, another word for neurosis (White and Epston, 1990). Promoting health and vision as its central purpose, education in the spirit of the symbol is therapeutic. Training in the service of the sign, in its objectifying tendency, is neuroticizing.

Education in the Spirit of the Symbol: Creativity across the Curriculum

It is important to emphasize that there is nothing about a particular subject matter that inherently marks it as sign dominated nor anything that immediately confers the status of the symbolic upon another subject matter. It is just as possible to teach math in the spirit of the symbol as it is to teach literature in the spiritlessness of the sign.

The trigonometry teacher whose passion for the dance of a sine wave makes the brain waves of his students also dance is teaching in the spirit of the ever-expanding symbol. Such a teacher gives his students a glimpse of a landscape strewn with the sinuous blossoming of numeric functions.

The English teacher who cynically deconstructs one of John Donne's Holy Sonnets and trashes its noble intent just to make a fashionable political point has sullied something of tremendous archetypal worth, turning the poem into a mere sign of an ideological agenda, one that is here today but will be gone tomorrow with the next literary critical fad.

Education in the spirit of the symbol is as relevant to science education as it is to arts education because, in both, creativity is key, and creativity is by definition a symbolic function. Why is creativity a symbolic function?

A sign can only exist within the strict confines of a certain way of seeing and being. Indeed, it is precisely the nature of a sign to both represent and vigilantly guard a certain plane of thinking. The sign patrols this plane to make sure that nothing that does not conform to its rules may enter it or, if something foreign does appear, to expel or even destroy it. The sign fears what is new, but creativity must be ever in search of it, in the same way that one is always seeing something new in a symbol, which allows endless possibilities of interpretation on various planes of thought.

Furthermore, creativity involves the reconciliation of a tension between opposites by going to a higher plane to view the tension from a wholly new perspective and, from there, be able to resolve it in a novel way. A creative approach to a tension makes this move because the opposites exist on the same plane of thinking as each other, and they therefore share the same fundamental assumptions. Each pole of the opposition is simply a different way of applying those assumptions. But it is precisely those limited assumptions that are limiting vision and therefore creating and confirming the problem!

Thus, Einstein observed, "The significant problems we face cannot be solved at the same level of thinking we were at when we created them" (as quoted in Komar and Hatzoglou, 2005). Moving to a higher plane of thinking to re-vision and interpret something from that higher perspective is the essence of the creative act and exactly the effect of a symbol on consciousness. To encourage students to think creatively *is* to teach them to think symbolically. This is true in *any* discipline, art history or microbiology, and it is the purpose of a pedagogy in the spirit of the symbol.

The tension of opposites on one plane leading to a creative transcendence and resolution of those opposites on a higher plane is what Jung called the transcendent function (Jung, 1967, pp. 67–91). Approaching an intellectual or psychospiritual dilemma as an occasion for a higher resolution of two equal but conflicting claims in a "third," higher answer, the transcendent function is the essence of the process of individuation in the classroom and in life in general, according to Jung (Miller, 2004). This third answer, as the synthesis of the two competing claims and then a transcendence of them on a higher plane, is a creative act in interpretive possibilities, which is the nature of symbolic thinking.

Like all creativity, this solution must be worked out and attained through considerable intellectual and often ethical effort that changes the individual in a new vision of not only the question under analysis but also a new vision of herself. Such difficult things are not just "given." Jung used the Latin expression *tertium non datur*, "the third is not given," to indicate that the transcendent function, as the dynamic of individuation, requires hard work and personal *transformation.*

Such transformation of the student in the classroom is the goal of education in the spirit of the symbol. On the other hand, training in the service of the sign, with its objectification of the student in its view of her as "human capital" as in current corporate agendas for the schools, does not seek to transform the student. On the contrary, it aims at freezing and objectifying her. This is antithetical to individuation, which *is* a process of unending transformation, perhaps even a process of eternal progression (Hartshorne, 1984).

Training in the Service of the Sign demands of teachers that they be operatives of a socially engineered program that objectifies the teacher, student, and curriculum.

A pedagogy of the symbol invites the teacher to be a visionary, who in turn invites her students to think creatively—which is to say, *symbolically*—in every domain of the curriculum, in ongoing intellectual and psychospiritual growth.

Commentary by Jared Wright

Jared Wright, M.Ed., currently serves as the principal of Dilworth Elementary School in Salt Lake City, Utah. Previously he was the assistant principal at Clayton Middle School and a teacher at West High School, also in Salt Lake City.

I am sure that even just a pedestrian survey of public school people in the current political environment would reveal the unrelenting pressure that both teachers and administrators feel is operating in schools in what Mayes calls "training in the service of the sign." Teachers are required to follow strict pacing guides that are oriented against benchmarks, with rigid learning objectives and lockstep schedules for formative and summative student assessments. A teacher's pay and even his/her very career hang in the balance of what some distant person or impersonal algorithm has determined to be "adequate student growth" as represented on the latest standardized test.

As a principal, I also too often hear frustrated teachers tell me how they see lost opportunities to spend time on a lesson or activity that would be meaningful and context rich for their students. One teacher lamented to me just such a lost opportunity to teach about crystals and the water cycle on the first snow storm of the season when students became excited about the weather.

Confused, I asked her why she couldn't take advantage of that moment. She replied, "I'm not supposed to teach the water cycle until the spring. The pacing guide is very specific on that point, and the interim assessments don't align with the water cycle being taught in December." This type of controlled, sign-based rigidity is an example of the opposing force to what most educators feel are the best ways of teaching and learning.

Each year schools are given a single letter grade (an absolute "sign") that is developed using a normed scale of comparative student-achievement data that is derived from standardized assessments. The letter grade is a *sign* to the public, declaring the effectiveness, or ineffectiveness, of the entire school, which then reflects directly on the school principal, whose job is then often at risk.

Worst of all, students are regularly objectified by standardized assessments and by teachers who focus their instruction on items of information instead of helping students place knowledge into the context of their own lives. Robbed of their individual and unique characteristics, students are classified solely in terms of performance on standardized tests and on how well they respond to "mathetic" instruction, as Mayes calls it, referring to Kant.

Small wonder that politicians so often complain of a public system of education that leaves so many of its students without a high school diploma. Their "solution," however, is actually a primary cause of epidemic high school dropout rates as students leave school, tired of being treated as nothing more than an object whose purpose is to reproduce the required facts, figures, and demonstrate some basic skills (which, by the way, they would have naturally picked up with richer forms of instruction).

The challenge for education policy makers, administrators, and teachers is to discover what Jung called the "transcendent function" in order to successfully negotiate the sign-based barriers that will otherwise frustrate what Mayes calls "education in the spirit of the symbol."

An example of the transcendent function begins with the first pole: a belief that education is about helping students create the meaning of the content they are taught, as that content is decided by referencing students' life narratives. On the other side of the dialectical tension is the second pole: a belief that schools must also prepare students to demonstrate, by whatever measure or standard is required of them, adequate academic achievement so as to satisfy the demand by policy makers and purse holders for measurable outcomes. Can this tension actually be resolved in a transcendent solution? The answer is "Yes."

This transcendent solution occurs when a teacher teaches his/her students and not just the subject matter. It happens when classroom assignments and activities are designed to help students develop their own thoughts, ideas, and understanding instead of just preparing for the next test. It happens when administrators and policy makers value the symbolic and meaningful type of teaching and learning that Mayes argues for in this chapter—above that of sign-based, measurable-outcome-driven instruction. Under these conditions, students both become more integral beings and more successful in learning the curricular content at hand.

NOTES

1. Barnaby and D'Acierno, 1990; Dourley, 1984; Handy and Westbrook, 1974; Ulanov, 1999.

2. Although this quote in its entirety is generally attributed to Thorndike, in fact it was one of his students who added the phrase "and can be measured."

Chapter 5

In the Light of the Shadow Curriculum

In the first part of this chapter, let us first further look into some of the territory we have covered by going more deeply into archetypal shadow dynamics in teaching and learning, for they often constellate upon the ongoing call to adventure throughout the lifecycle of the class. Although the shadow may appear in any classroom at any time, it is especially prominent when the student is being encouraged to examine sensitive commitments that he has brought to the class.

The second part of this chapter is a closer look at Jung's studies in alchemy as symbolic of the individuating psyche. This provides us with unique and uniquely powerful pedagogical symbols and terms.

Third follows a discussion of what I will call the "shadow curriculum." This involves Jung's idea of "the inferior function."

Finally, we consider the Jungian notion of a *collective cultural conscious* and its archetypal shadow, applying these ideas to current multicultural educational theory and practice.

We will see how much light can be gathered from the archetype of the shadow in the classroom.

PART ONE

More on the Hero's Journey and Its Educational Implications

"Education for individuation," another term for education in the spirit of the symbol, revolves around the holistic well-being of the student, including her cognitive growth, of course, but with a special emphasis on her psychospiritual development (Mayes, 2005a, 2007, 2009a). Education for individuation aims at something akin to what the great 20th-century Curriculum Theorist Duane Huebner characterized in theological language as "education for ultimacy" under the beckoning "lure of the transcendent" (1999).

In both education for individuation and education for "Ultimacy" (Tillich, 1956), the student is invited to appropriate and employ what happens in the classroom in order to enrich her ever more vibrant and creative subjectivity. The focus is thus on the student's existential project of forging satisfying and evolving life narratives as they move toward individuation against the backdrop of the eternal (Ricoeur, 1976).

A challenge in education for individuation, however, is that the student may register the call for profound transformation, in not only cognitive but also deep psychospiritual areas of his being, as a threat to who and what he is—a perceived danger to his existence as it is presently constituted by myriad influences and commitments. This may give rise to a wide range of emotions in the student. In some students, those emotions may be resistive and even aggressive.

This can cause the student's shadow to constellate, which he then projects onto the teacher in a classic case of negative transference. Such negative transferences are called "dystonic" in psychoanalytic parlance.

The archetype of the *puer* or *puella* may constellate dystonically as the student's way of hunkering down in an act of rejecting the teacher's call for him or her to relinquish a simplistic opinion. This is typically one cherished by his or her family and/or culture of origin. As we have seen throughout this book, a sound general rule in both educational theory and practice is that it is important to recognize that cognition is not "cold," a strictly conceptual affair, but is "hot," fired with energy and imagery from the personal subconscious and collective unconscious (Pintrich, Marx, and Boyle, 1993; see also Mayes, 2009a).

In challenging the student to consider an issue more maturely in all of its complexity, and perhaps even its ultimate insolubility, the teacher easily becomes the target of various projections of the *puer* and *puella,* who now feel outmaneuvered, engulfed, and imperiled by the teacher.

The student will then instinctively, and often enough with a primal ferocity, lash out by projecting shadow archetypes onto the teacher who is beckoning her across her traditional thresholds—summoning her to leave her daisy-bedecked country home with its comfortable but limited certainties in order to enter an ambiguous forest with all kinds of spooky foliage that symbolize the complexity of ideological adventure. This is the beginning of the hero's cycle.

The beginning of every profoundly educative process is in this sense an archetypal summons to adventure, a clarion call to leave familiar regions of previous conclusions and their attendant commitments in order to cross the threshold into an unknown land that will involve the student in various metamorphoses, from small to great. This occurs not only at the beginning of the term but throughout it, as, layer by layer, the student's previous ideas are peeled away and core commitments are revealed. How will the student respond to this call that is always constellating in the deeply educative classroom? And for that matter, how will the teacher?

Much depends on how convincingly the teacher is able to give voice to the summons—and how skillfully he continues to do so throughout the journey. The teacher must have faith in the process being called into existence, for it is one that is calling his students into a new existence. And not only that. It is calling him too. This may require the teacher to not just present but also question some of his *own* notions, perhaps dearly held ones, ones in which he may even be academically invested. Not only the student's but also the teacher's ego structure is always on the line to some extent.

In all of this, there is no substitute for experience. The more a teacher has traveled with students through forests of authentic educative engagement, the more adept he becomes as a wise guide during the pilgrimage and the more credibly he may wear the archetypal mantle of the Wise Elder. This is only one of various archetypal roles that the teacher will play and archetypal apparel that he will wear throughout the course of the educative relationship with his students, but it is perhaps the most important one.

Filling the role of the Wise Elder can be difficult. The teacher must take it on without, in Jungian terms, becoming "inflated" by the role—the psychospiritual error of over-identifying with an archetype, not simply drawing on it to vitalize one's practice and indeed one's life. A key to individuation—the goal of Jungian psychology—is the creation and maintenance of an "axis" between the egoic realm and the archetypal one (Edinger, 1973).

This living link between these two worlds invests the ego with the universality of archetypal energy and charges it with meaning. At the same time, it keeps the intense power of the archetype workably contained in the ego so that it does not shatter the ego and render it problematic, even perilous, for the teacher and his students. Boring teachers are deficient in such archetypal energy. Arrogant ones who abuse their power over students are possessed by it.

The teacher must wear the mantle of the Wise Elder—but he must do so lightly lest he be possessed by its shadow, which will then spread over the entire classroom, casting a pall of fear that is death to real learning and meaningful change in *I-Thou* relationship. It is thus crucial that the teacher don the mantle of the Wise Elder deftly, for on the archetypal hero's journey it is the Wise Elder who is often the first of the hero's allies to show up on his path and also the one who miraculously appears at various crucial junctures along the way to see the hero through his ordeals. The archetype of the Wise Elder, whenever it appears in myth, is a pedagogical one (Mayes, 2001, 2002).

It is necessary in preventing inflation that the teacher knows his own limitations, as he discovers them in both "psychodynamic reflectivity" and "archetypal reflectivity" on his practice at subconscious and archetypal levels. Such reflectivity in the teacher will constantly reveal and offer guidance in handling, and sometimes even healing, these limitations. That the teacher be able to live and work productively in this tension between his archetypal status as Wise Elder and his existential limitations as just a human being is central to his practice as a teacher.

The teacher as Wise Elder who is aware of his shadow, his all-too-human shortcomings, can be the "good enough teacher" who *contains* the classroom, making it a nurturing "holding-environment" for his students (Winnicott, 1992). Otherwise, the student's understandable anxiety at hearing the archetypal summons to leave the comfort and innocence of his rustic village and family behind in order to cross the threshold of adventure might cause students to simply shut down in the *puer* or *puella* position, passively aggressively foreclosing the whole process.

Jung captured the dialectical nature of emotional, intellectual, and ethical growth in his notion that every archetype has a dark and light side and that, in general, every leap into a higher ideological and psychospiritual position results from a bipolar tension that, rife with doubt, is also rich with potential in the transcendent function—the dynamic of the individuation process (Miller, 2004).

The transcendent function allows the relocation of thought and feeling onto a higher, radically new, and invigorating plane where the old problem is now not only resolved but honored as having been the stimulus for existential evolution, a stage in the student's now-enhanced life narrative to individuation, the North Star of the never-ending quest toward wholeness.

At the outset of the journey, and indeed throughout it, a student may occasionally feel varying levels of fear and sometimes even anger. How could he not? He is being called upon to die to the old and resurrect into the new. In the Christian narrative, Jesus himself asked the Father to take this bitter cup away from him on the night before his crucifixion (*Luke* 22:42).

To be sure, the classroom may be a New Jerusalem for the student, a site of his existential liberation, but it may also be his Golgotha, the dread hill of dead *skulls* symbolizing *conceptual* crucifixion. This horror the student will sometimes project onto the teacher, who can go in the course of a lecture, even in one controversial statement or a glance at the student, from being clothed in the white robes of the Redeemer archetype in the student's tender eyes to being draped in the next instant in the satanic vestments of the

Tempter, the Evil One, and the Father of All Lies in the same student's now apprehensive eyes.

Of such volatile stuff, in the swirling primary processes of the subconscious and unconscious minds is the transference, made, evidencing how in the classroom the secondary cognitive processes of the ego are everywhere being impinged on and shaped by primary psychodynamics.

To change an idea, even just to reconsider one, often implicates the student's whole system. We have already looked at the idea of "conceptual change"—an important area in instructional theory—in archetypal terms of the crucified and resurrected savior. Here, the student and his ideas need to be sacrificed on the archetypal cross of a new vision, which the hero student, now in ideologically resurrected form, may bring to his people to renew them.

The student may well deploy all of his defenses to resist this archetypal summons to die to the old in order to rise to the new. His primary defense is to cast the shadow onto the teacher who would start the process. This should come as no surprise considering Jung's observation that the first archetype that is constellated when the ego feels threatened is that of the shadow or another archetype that is mistaken for it (Jung, 1967a, p. 96).

This darkness is constellated because, when what is known is presently being cast into doubt, then what one sees stretching before oneself may be experienced as utter darkness—a "darkness visible," as Milton characterized hell itself in *Paradise Lost*. The teacher must be aware of the student's primal panic and the "archetypal defenses of the personal spirit" that are set into motion because of the student's fear that by winding up in this class he has fallen into this infernal darkness visible (Kalsched, 1997). The teacher may then, in a flash, undergo an archetypal transformation in the student, who no longer sees him as the Wise Elder but the Devil, Trickster, Seducer, and Fool.

Unaware of this process, the teacher, caught in the shifting waves of a student's dystonic responses to him, may easily feel overwhelmed—especially when he is engulfed in a classroom *overflowing* with various students' shadow projections onto him. The teacher may then drown in these dystonic transferences—emotional breakers of colossal height crashing down on him.

Teachers can be deeply wounded by students. This is something the teacher must be aware of, adept at guarding himself against for his own sake, and know how to handle for his students' sake so that he does not counter transfer his own fears, born of his own shadowy vulnerabilities, back onto his students by demonizing or simply "giving up" on them (Mayes, 2002).

Equally important is the teacher's recognition that in the student's shadow lies not only the detritus of the psyche, as Freud felt, but also its unconscious potential, as Jung insisted (Jung, 1961). Since the essence of education for individuation is self-realization of buried potential, the student's shadow is not only a relevant, but also an essential, pedagogical consideration (Mayes, 2005b, 2007, 2009a).

PART TWO

An Alchemical Primer for the Teacher

The art of transfiguring debris into gold, of coaxing something of transfigured and transfiguring merit out of what has been rejected, was the alchemist's art, as Jung demonstrated in his crowning works on alchemy (Jung, 1969a, 1969b, 1970).

Jung saw the stages of the alchemical processes—to which the religious medieval and renaissance alchemists gave names such as *nigredo, calcinatio, albedo, rubedo:* the blackened matter, the calcified matter, the whitened matter, the reddened matter—as evolving symbols of deepening psychospiritual growth in each alchemical refining of the gross initial material, the *prima materia*, the primary matter. The original dark substance was moving through these stages to the final product of the spiritual gold, and goal, that the alchemist was striving to attain.

And because this evolution occurred through inner change of the alchemist *himself* as a spiritual practitioner, as well as outer change of the *material*—to such an extent indeed that the inner and outer processes were inseparable—Jung asserted that "the world of alchemical symbols definitely does not belong to the rubbish heap of the past, but stands in a very real and living relationship to our most recent discoveries concerning the psychology of the unconscious" (1970a, p. xiii).

Psychologically interpreted, alchemy is "a treasury of analogies that corporify or embody the objective psyche and the process it undergoes in development" (Edinger, 1985, p. 100). The "development" of the "objective psyche" and "the processes it undergoes" in that development being the teacher's stock in trade no less than the therapist's, alchemy thus emerges as relevant to the educative process as much as it is to therapeutic one.

In this sense, the teacher, working in the furtherance of his students' psychospiritual as well as cognitive growth, must, like the therapist, also be something of an alchemist. This is why the archetype of the Wise Elder often magically materializes to the hero in his journey in the aspect of a beneficent wizard, who of course is none other than the alchemist—he who brews up magic potions and crafts miraculous tokens and amulets for the hero to guard him against evil as he travels through the forest of transformative travail, his *educational* quest toward wholeness.

The classroom is the "retort"—the alchemist's test tube. In it, the student is immersed. The student's shadow—all of its negativity and all of its unrecognized potential—is the *massa confusa*, "the confused mass," the substance which the alchemist puts in the retort to begin the transformative process.

The alchemist initially found the components of the *massa confusa*, the confused (that is, undifferentiated) matter, by venturing into the most out-of-the-way midnight places, gathering up in his bag (embroidered, no doubt, with arcane symbols) discarded and even disgusting things that littered a lonely, often dangerous slum landscape. He ground these things up, and they became the *massa confusa* that served as the starting material of the *opus*—the spiritual alchemist's "work."

The medieval and renaissance religious alchemist saw his work as sacred and salvific, endowing him with the power and responsibility of a *salvator microcosmi* (a microcosmic savior) working under the sponsorship of the *salvator macrocosmi,* the macrocosmic Savior of the Universe, Christ himself. The *salvator microcosmi's* calling was to redeem isolated bits of degenerate matter just as they believed Christ would redeem the entire fallen universe.

In this, we see just how crucial it is that the teacher understands both the archetypal scope and the personal limitations of his unique calling.

When he does not understand his own limitations, the teacher, in a psycho-spiritually catastrophic move, identifies with the Macrocosmic Savior archetype to such an extent that it leads him into folly, exhaustion, and sometimes even serious mischief. In Jungian psychology, this is called "an inappropriate identification with the Christ-archetype."

Now inflated with his archetypal role, he no longer sees himself as merely a fallible *salvator* in the *microcosm* of his particular scholastic environment, a humble laborer for the Eternal in the small laboratory of his classroom. Rather, he now inappropriately identifies with the *salvator microcosmi* archetype, The Savior himself, and becomes possessed by that archetype, to his own and his student's psychological, ethical, and intellectual harm. This damage to the student assumes two forms.

The first results from the student wisely rejecting the teacher in his exaggerated sense of himself as a sort of pedagogical Redeemer, the font of all wisdom, he who has all the answers, the classroom "God" who knows all things. This teacher will brook no opposition. His delivers his lectures as if they were revelations which his students must accept as gospel truth and reproduce back to him, word for word, in the Last Judgment of the final exam.

This inflated *salvator microcosmi* who now believes himself to be the *salvator macrocosmi,* the one true ideological God of the classroom and beyond, will, Jehovah-like, punish a student for her "disobedience" in disagreeing with him by letting loose the full Old Testament force of his "righteous vengeance" on her. This can range from absurdly harsh grading of her work, to demeaning comments about her as a student or even a person in front of the entire class, and even to sexual predatoriness against her in either symbolic or actual ways.

But an opposite and equal harm to the student lurks in the shadows of the misguided and misguiding alchemist-teacher's classroom. This harm is inflicted when the student is seduced or otherwise falls prey to the teacher in his inflated role.

The student grows possessed by the shadowy archetypal energy of the Ardent Disciple. She becomes what Eric Hoffer (1990) ironically identified as "the true believer" in pursuit of what Christopher Lasch, with equal irony, named "the true and only heaven" (1991). She will then, like the teacher, discard the sanity of her ego and the healthy skepticism of its "reality function" to devotedly follow the quasi-God of the teacher into any and every kind of intellectual excess, even moral mischief, and call it good, even God's plan for her.

The horror of what happened at Jonestown and Heaven's Gate, where a mad "messianic" teacher-leader alternately coaxed and browbeat his student-disciples to follow him into death itself through their suicides, are the most extreme examples of what are finally not just moral but also pedagogical catastrophes when an inflated *salvator microcosmi* is possessed by the archetypal energy of his role and leads his student into intellectual suicide. Such a false Savior, drunk with the archetypal energy in him, dupes the student with the bogus promises of an unsustainable ideological salvation.

The hoodwinked student then becomes a rabid, even obnoxious advocate of her teacher's ideological *evangel* wherever she goes, an irritant to everyone she meets outside the classroom, where she never stops preaching the missionary message of her teacher-savior's arrogant ideologies as the answer to every problem. His alchemy has gone awry, and he has turned his student into fool's gold, not spiritual gold, because he has misappropriated archetypal energy. It has not made the student free but chained her by the neck to his pedagogical and ethical folly.

The spiritual alchemists of the medieval and renaissance periods were, as Jung discovered in assiduously studying their manuscripts over years, as careful to monitor and circumspectly shape their *own* inner transformations as they were the changes in the material in their test tubes. They knew that it was only through constant introspection on their own weaknesses that they would remain humble in the process of transmuting the initially undifferentiated material into the ultimately ethical gold.

So must the alchemical teacher reflect without fail or excuses upon his own classroom practices as he works upon the *prima materia* of his students so that he may wear his archetypal vestments in probity, health, and humanizing humor. Through archetypal reflectivity, he keeps his focus constantly trained upon his students' psychospiritual growth in freedom, not their enslavement to his potentially perilous intellectual art(fulness).

Otherwise he gets too puffed up in his scholastic power symbolized by the degrees that line his wall. To the psychoanalytically astute eye, these degrees finally evidence his attempt to escape from real life, in what Fairbairn (1992) has called a theory-encrusted "schizoid position," that is a defense against authentic engagement with others. But this is contrary to the purpose of education for individuation, which is the joint development of the student's and teacher's life narrative toward freedom, not the coopting of the student's narrative by the teacher's bizarre and archetypally "off" miswriting and dictatorial imposition of his own.

When all goes well in the alchemical classroom, it is precisely the "shadow-stuff" of the students' *massa confusa* that will finally emerge—through the alchemy of the academic term in the alchemist-teacher's laboratory class-room—as the precious spiritual metal known as the Philosopher's Stone, the *lapis philosophorum.* It is the student's most uninformed notions that have been the material out of which higher vision has been crafted. The climax of the alchemist's meditations and labor, this is also called The Spiritual Gold. It is the "gold" that the spiritual alchemists were aiming to make, not the crass medium of marketplace exchange.

For the alchemist-teacher who is faithful to his calling as a true *salvator microcosmi* in the service of his students, the Philosopher's Stone is the student herself, who, now empowered with new intellectual acuity and ethical force at a higher stage of differentiation, is a step closer to the goal of individuation. The student emerges from the classroom retort with a more complex, complete, and compassionate intelligence. Along with the spiritual alchemists anciently, then, the teacher, at the end of a successful term of transformation, might proclaim, *Aurum nostrum non est aurum vulgi:* "Our gold is not vulgar gold"—not the gold of the world but the gold of the spirit.

It takes a teacher in healthy communion with the Wise Elder archetype to know how to contain this process, in a delicate dance with his student's shadows and at their service, but never at their mercy, and certainly not projecting the shadow of his own personal wounds, intellectual limitations, or professional pride back onto them. If the teacher can accomplish this, then what was rejected in the student is now that much closer to being (re)solved—melted and shaped into yet another educative form of archetypal gold in the student's larger life narrative toward individuation.

Like alchemical processes, educative processes entail both peril and promise. But this is always the case with creativity, which requires a mature confrontation with the shadow, especially one's own—the darkness in the light, the light in the darkness—as in the opening lines of St. John's gospel. There, the archetypal light shines in the archetypal darkness so that darkness and light, in a Gnostic sense, rely on each other at the beginning of *everyone's* ongoing, sacred narrative(s) of crucifixion and resurrection. To be creative in self-authoring toward individuation means living in paradox and the inter-structuring of light and dark.

This is why standardized approaches to education are death to existentially rich education. Rigidly sign-based corporate education allows only what is calculable and exists in the service of the bottom-line—the economics of hegemony, which powers and is powered by the increasingly "captivating" media as yet another form of corporate miseducation into what Marx called "false consciousness" (Marx and Engels, 1978). Corporate education operates in the psychospiritually vacuous service of *aurum vulgi,* vulgar gold.

But the existentially significant curriculum revolves around those consequential issues, foundational symbols, and revelatory *I-Thou* encounters that enrich the student's life narrative. In Education for Individuation, the student is set in a trajectory toward individuation, the *aurum* non *vulgi,* as that student makes the curriculum her own in subjectively relevant and potent ways.

The mystery of fruitful ambiguity, the interpenetration of light and dark in the individual's growth, the enrichment of cognition by subconscious and unconscious processes, and the nurturing of a creative life narrative—*these* are the elements of Education for Individuation. And it is the subtle, precious metal of the integrated student herself that is the final product of those many alchemical processes that are always at work in the archetypally dynamic classroom.

PART THREE

The Shadow Curriculum: The Seventh Dimension

We have looked at various points along the way at Eisner and Vallance's (1985) highly useful division of the curriculum into five categories:

1. the official curriculum, that which the state requires teachers to teach;
2. the operational curriculum, that which the teacher selects from the official curriculum to *actually* teach, sometimes with modifications, in addition to new things that the teacher in his (diminishing) freedom elects to include;
3. the hidden curriculum, the ideological message—invariably in the service of the governing discourses of the society in which the schools are embedded—that actually determines the official curriculum, no matter how "democratic" the rhetoric of the official curriculum;
4. the null curriculum, that which is *not* included in the curriculum because its presence would pose a threat to a present power structure that is encoded in the state-enforced official curriculum; and

5. the extra curriculum, that which happens outside of the classroom but still at a school site, and which may be just as educative, or miseducative, for the student as what goes on in the classroom.

To these categories, psychodynamic educational theorists have added a sixth category: *the subjective curriculum*. This refers to the student's individual *experience* of the curriculum in the classroom.

I would like to suggest another dimension to the curriculum—a seventh category. Let us call it *the shadow curriculum*. This grows out of Jung's idea that there is always a shadow side to things whenever archetypal dynamics are at play, and they are rarely as compact and intense as in deeply educational processes. The shadow curriculum involves the student's individual experience of the classroom, but it also incorporates sociocultural factors in a way that the subjective curriculum does not tend to do as explicitly or fully.

Seen from an archetypal perspective, one of the most important "places" the curriculum casts a shadow is from the realm of what Jung called an individual's "inferior function."

The Inferior Function and the Student's Shadow

What is the inferior function and how does it cast a shadow on the curriculum?

An example of the inferior function and its shadow casting is in the student whose interests and abilities clearly lie in physics and math. She might come to a required class in English literature with biases against the discipline if she had never done well in literature classes before, while some other students soared in it. These embarrassing and disempowering experiences have confirmed her in the notion that she has zero ability to study and enjoy novels, plays, and poetry. Why even try in this class? Science and math, in which she *is* a star student, exist in the realm of her "superior function," while such things as literature and art are probably in her "inferior function."

This is *not* to say that through the class taught by a wise teacher who was sensitive to this student's strengths and challenges, he could not help her make some progress—maybe substantial progress—in studying and enjoying literature, even though she might never excel in it. It *is* to say that English literature is something that the student does not feel good at, has not had success in, may indeed have limited abilities in, and therefore has simply written off as irrelevant to her—to her own holistic loss, of course, impoverishing her life narrative in shutting down much that would enrich her existentially.

Certain that literature is unimportant to her, and probably unimportant in life in general, she has *defensively* come to see it as not really a discipline at all but a waste of time messing around with airy-fairy notions that yield only flimsy, merely sentimental "results," which, being unmeasurable and result-ing in no practical "products," are simply useless in the last "analysis."

Conversely, a student who excels in reading and writing poetry might, with a sniff, discard the hard sciences as an exercise in tedium for unimaginative nerds who cannot see any farther in life than their pocket protectors and advanced calculus texts. He purposefully yawns through classes in physics or writes satirical limericks about the teacher while slumping in his desk, trying to look like the "bored artist." But this is just to mask his sense of inadequacy when his secretly frightened eyes rest on all those fearful (though also fasci-nating!) symbols and Greek letters that the teacher has written on the board, which so many of the other students seem to be having no trouble processing or producing.

Both the novice scientist and the budding poet are seeing each other's *superior function* in caricature and in a shadow. Helping her student catch, and *share,* a vision of the joy that the teacher not only *finds* in her discipline but *is* in her discipline is one of the greatest challenges and also most thrilling accomplishments that a teacher may experience with those students for whom her discipline lies in the shadowland of their *inferior function*, from which interior zone some of them are presently *externalizing* their own archetypal darkness onto her.

What a student casts into the disciplinary shadow is thus typically some-thing that he feels he is not good at so that there is not just an abstract dislike for the teacher's discipline but a personal dislike of the teacher herself, even before he has come to know her. This is because of the *archetypal force* of his shadow projection onto both the course, the entire discipline, and this teacher who represents it.

The student will then psychologically drape the teacher and her curriculum with that disowned, therefore shadowy part of *himself* because it is something that others may have criticized and even ridiculed in him throughout his life. This history of hurt the student carries on his back from the moment he enters the classroom on the first day.

To understand the superior function and inferior function better requires a brief look at classical Jungian "personality typology"—a categorization of personality types—which he laid out in his volume *Psychological Types* (1971).[1]

THE FOUR PERSONALITY TYPES AND THE TWO
PERSONALITY ATTITUDES

In Jungian psychology, there are two pairs of opposing personality types: thinking/feeling as one axis and sensate/intuitive another, which can be pictured as forming two axes of a cross. Before describing what Jung meant by these terms, however, it is necessary to stress Jung's warning that these terms only describe *tendencies* in each individual—a point that Jung's more simplistic interpreters and critics always seem to miss.

Jung never claimed that, say, a thinking type was that and *only that*—and that the person could be entirely understood by simply knowing that she was a thinking type. Far from it, Jung always made it clear that everyone had elements of all of the typological functions within herself, and that different ones might predominate at different times. However, *as a general rule*, a particular person will *tend to use* one particular type in her strategies and perspectives in interpreting and acting upon the world. Jung called an individual's generally preferred mode her *superior function.*

Such knowledge was useful to have about the person, of course, but it should never be employed to pigeonhole the person in what could only result in a caricature of her existential richness and complexity. A further point that Jung stressed was that no personality type was intrinsically better than the other three. Each was simply a different way of seeing, being, and acting in the world, and each had its own peculiar advantages and disadvantages, strengths and weaknesses.

"Thinking is the psychological function which, following its own laws, brings the contents of ideation into conceptual connection with each other" (1971, p. 481). The thinking type tends to be analytical, employing concepts, paradigms, models, and systems to comprehend and change his world. A thinking type would usually make a good engineer, for example.

At the opposite pole from thinking, feeling "is entirely a *subjective* process between the *ego* and a given content, a process, moreover, that imparts to the content a definite *value* in the sense of acceptance or rejection ('like' or 'dislike'). The process can also appear isolated, as it were, in the form of a *mood.*" (1971, p. 434). Feeling types see the world in terms of emotional preferences that are tied in to deeply held values. The political leader who is able to thrill an audience by the strength of her passionately held convictions might well be a feeling type.

The other paired opposites are the sensate and intuitive types.

The sensate processes her world—both internally and externally—in terms of how it presents itself to her in immediate, concrete *perceptions and sensations.* The sensate type relies upon "the psychological function that mediates the perception of a physical stimulus. It is, therefore, identical with perception.... Sensation is related not only to external stimuli but to inner ones, i.e., to changes in the internal organic processes" (1971, p. 461). Finely attuned to the physical functioning of both her internal and external world, the sensate type typically shines in roles that range from athlete to interior designer.

On the other end of this axis is the intuitive type. Intuition "is the function that mediates perceptions in an *unconscious* way . . . . In intuition a content presents itself whole and complete, without our being able to explain or discover how this content came into existence" (1971, p. 453).

The intuitive person always seems to have an uncanny sense of how or why a situation came into being and what direction it will probably take. Her hunches, neither off-handed guesswork nor detailed analysis, generally seem to be right on the mark, although neither she nor anyone else can tell you exactly why this is so. Intuitive types often make excellent therapists.

Since thinking and feeling are mostly conscious processes that involve comparing and contrasting things and situations in order to reach *evaluative* conclusions, Jung called them "rational functions." On the other hand, because sensing and intuiting rely on noncognitive processes to get an *experiential* hold on them, Jung called them "irrational functions." This latter term was unfortunate, however, for by it Jung did not mean that these functions were in any sense less adequate or valid than the rational functions. He merely meant to show that they resided more in the organic apprehension of a thing than in its cognitive assessment.

In sum, Jung called a person's basic type her *superior function* and concluded that the opposite pole would represent the person's *inferior function*—that is to say, the person's weak spot.

To complete his paradigm of personality, Jung added one more dimension, inventing terms which—like others of his terms such as *shadow* and *persona*—have become quite popular. These are *introversion* and *extraversion*—the two personality *attitudes*. Any of the four major functions could have either an introverted or extraverted attitude. Consequently, there are eight potential personality types. Since the terms "introversion" and "extraversion" are used so widely but often imprecisely, it is worth quoting Jung at length here. *Introversion* he defined as

> an inward turning of *libido*, in the sense of a negative relation to the object. Interest does not move toward the object but withdraws from it into the subject. Everyone whose attitude is introverted thinks, feels, and acts in a way that clearly demonstrates that the subject is the prime motivating factor and that the object is of secondary importance. Introversion may be intellectual or emotional, just as it can be characterized by *sensation* or *intuition*. (1971, p. 452f)

Conversely, *extraversion* is

> an outward turning of *libido*. I use this concept to denote a manifest relation of subject to object, a positive movement of subjective interest toward the object [an "object" in this case meaning not only a thing but also a situation, event, or person]. Everyone in the extraverted state thinks, feels, and acts in relation to the object, and moreover in a direct and clearly observable fashion, so that no doubt can remain about his positive dependence on the object. In a sense, therefore,

extraversion is a transfer of interest from subject to object. If it is an extraversion of thinking, the subject thinks his way into the object; if an extraversion of feeling, he feels himself into it. In extraversion there is a strong, if not exclusive, determination by the object. (1971, p. 427)

Just as each of the four major types must be thought of as a tendency only, not as a dictator governing an entire personality in all circumstances, so must introversion and extraversion be seen as ways of relating to the external world that are "habitual" to be sure but not exclusive (1971, p. 452f).

THE FOUR TYPES AND TWO ATTITUDES IN THE CLASSROOM—AND THEIR SHADOWS

The educational consequences of these ideas are many. Educational theory has mostly ignored Jung until recently—except for his typology, which has become quite popular, especially in its most famous product, *The Meyers-Briggs Personality Type Indicator*, or MBTI, which teachers sometimes use, or more popular color-coded variations on it, to develop an "instructional approach" to the student.

However, we must understand and use Jungian typology not just functionally. We must also grasp it archetypally—and always mindful of *the archetypal shadow of each personality type: its inferior function.* For, each personality type and attitude are not just instructional categories in the teacher's "toolbox of classroom strategies." Such things are beneficial. However, Jungian typology goes much more deeply than just these *ontic,* instrumental aspects. Each personality type is an archetype. It rests on an *ontological* foundation. And it thus comes bearing the full force of archetypal power, as does its shadowy flipside—the inferior function.

If a student is a feeling type, for instance, it suggests something not only about his observable "learning style." It speaks to his *archetypal way of engaging the world.* A teacher is not just looking at a person who favors this or that way of processing a unit of the curriculum. She is looking at a being whose very existence is to some considerable degree *founded* in that orientation.

Equally importantly, she also has standing before her a person whose opposite, inferior function (in this case, thinking) exists in his archetypal shadow, with all the primal negativity that the shadow can carry with it. The student may drench areas of the curriculum that are in his inferior function with this dark archetypal energy.

This shadowland is a vast area in the student's total psychospiritual makeup, not only an "instructional" issue. It is system wide in him. If the teacher is not alert to the profundity of this fact, she may not only damage the student at the level of his "learning ego" but in deeper psychospiritual ways as well. Additionally, she may receive particularly intense shadow projections from him since they are issuing from the primal realm of the archetype, not just the less intense and more considered realm of a "conscious dislike."

STANDARDIZED EDUCATION
AND THE INFERIOR FUNCTION

Standardized education poses a particular threat to a student in his inferior function if it is in one of the areas that a standardized curriculum is focusing on. Standardized education, being sign based, has little tolerance for ambiguity. Yet, despite his best efforts, a student for whom a particular class is in his inferior function will almost always be moving, and more often stumbling, through it in a great deal of ambiguity. Working with him effectively means gently helping him through that ambiguity and celebrating his victories, however small, in this problematic discipline.

However, in the thin air space of "the sign," the radar of standardized testing registers nothing but the binary of right or wrong. A student will not usually do well on a standardized test in his inferior domain regardless of his best effort. A below average score is often the most he can hope for.

However, a student simply *is* his test score on the emotionally sparse icescape of standardization. Enticing rewards await those who can negotiate that tundra, but humiliation is often the frozen bitter fruit for those who cannot. This student's depression, anxiety, and anger go unnoticed. They count for little or nothing—except perhaps as evidence of an "oppositional defiant behavior disorder." He is then forced to take the latest drug to "treat" him for his "negativity." There can, and in most cases will, be lifelong repercussions since one's narrative of himself as a student and his life narrative are tightly interwoven.

Can we really wonder at that student then acting out in class because of the unfeeling, or at least uninformed, manner in which he has been handled? And can we not suspect that what the Center for Disease Control calls the epidemic of "learning disabilities" is in considerable measure due not to a pathology in the student but in the standardized system itself (Almon, 1999)? A student may shut down or act out, out of sheer self-defense and as a form of protest—the only means of "empowerment" that remains for him.

Furthermore, it is almost always the case that he is in this class that exists in the shadow of his inferior function because he has been forced into it. This may increase the length and darkness of the shadow he will now dystonically project over the teacher and the subject matter.

Besides, no one gladly puts himself in the position of being made to perform in lockstep and then to be stressfully tested in areas where he feels he is weak. This is not to say that it is not growthful for him to be helped to learn to improve in such areas or that it is not legitimate to require him to take at least some classes in them. Indeed, improvement in one's inferior function will often be felt as a great triumph by the student and can positively affect his sense of efficacy in general.

It *is* to say, however, that for this to happen, the student's inferior function must be handled compassionately and creatively by the teacher, who must understand that she is not simply *tolerating* a student who is not particularly gifted in her domain. She must be aware that her response to him may be formative in his performance across the curriculum and throughout his life.

THE INFERIOR FUNCTION AND A PEDAGOGY OF CARE

The fact that the student is in this class "under duress" may close him down even more tightly to any appreciation of its subject matter—to consider its beauty and, if only in a small way, to venture into this valley, which, of course, another student might see as a sun-drenched mountain in the verdant landscape of his superior function. In a class in a student's inferior function, therefore, the teacher is called upon in a special way to practice what Nel Noddings' (1995) has termed a "pedagogy of care." As Nodding notes, a pedagogy of care ultimately leads to the student's enhanced performance not only in this particular class but also across the curriculum.

We all have stories of that time when we scored a victory—small to someone else, huge to us—in something we are not normally good at, the healing effect this had on us, and the bonding it created between us and the others who were with us at the time—they who perhaps helped us attain our small victory or at least cheered us on. This looms large in our life story.

The teacher who practices a pedagogy of care with an inferior-function student not only contributes to the student's even better *cognitive performance* in his superior-function areas. She also helps him pick up certain things of *existential worth* in the course of her class. These are lessons learned regarding persistence and focus, individual effort and communal support, humility and even an unexpected grace bestowed upon him by the universe in his *objectively* small but *subjectively* large victory. This may well become a sort of "moral exemplum" in his life story about an ultimate beneficence at work even in his weakest areas and maybe especially there.

To offer a personal example of a teacher's mishandling of a student's inferior function, if I may: I have been hounded all my life by a serious deficiency in my sensate function. It never ceases to astonish my friends how little I can do with my hands, my confusion navigating my car to a meeting place I have gone to meet them many times before, or arranging and then not appearing at an appointment made that week, even that day when I confirmed it two hours before and then simply and totally forgot.

This is a problem that was not only confirmed but (I am convinced) heightened for the rest of my life by a woodshop teacher in junior high school. Mr. Todd not only saw my inferiority but frequently held it up to ridicule it in class. Such masochistic treatment by a teacher of inferior-function students probably has its origin in the teacher's own "narcissistic wounds" (Kohut, 1950/1978), which the student, for some reason, is activating in the teacher, reminding the teacher of his own weakness in a certain aspect of his life and someone's failure to handle it well. Having been abused, he now abuses, as is of course often the case with victims-turned perpetrators.[2]

In any event, the unreflective teacher is unaware of why there is "just something about" a certain student or students that "rubs him the wrong way" and causes him to project *his* shadow onto *them*. Here we see again the point stressed in chapter 3 about the importance of psychodynamically and archetypally reflecting upon one's teaching to deal with subconscious and unconscious issues that may be affecting one's classroom practices (Mayes, 2002).

Different fields offer diverse but equally legitimate ways of knowing. It is, of course, cognitively rewarding and emotionally upbuilding for a student to at least become modestly acquainted with these other ways of processing reality, producing things in it, and the people who live in those worlds of discourse and action. Some of these areas may lie in the student's inferior function.

Moreover, acquainting students with a broad spectrum of areas of endeavor has, in fact, been one of the major purposes of K-12 schooling over the last 140 years (Cremin, 1964), the philosophical rationale for the core curriculum at the university (Brubacher and Rudy, 1997), and a central goal of schooling in and for a democracy (Dewey, 1916).

For a student to come into contact with areas that lie in her inferior domains—as going through a broad array of classes will inevitably entail—and for her to have some small successes in them creates in a student a justifiable sense of accomplishment that she now has a basic grasp of these fields. She does not have to live in fear or embarrassment of them anymore. Indeed, she now can, in a smaller but still significant fashion, appreciate them and even find pleasure in engaging in them, which can be enormously therapeutic in a person's life, especially in periods of stress.

In Buber's (1965) terms, a teacher's clumsy, even objectifying, way of dealing with an inferior-function student may cause an *I-Thou* rupture between him and the student that can easily flare up into open exchanges-of-fire between the teacher and student. These will disrupt the entire class—sometimes spoiling the tone, souring things in general, and limiting the horizons of the class for the rest of the term.

In a class led by a teacher with little or no understanding of the structure and dynamics of this aspect of the archetypal shadow in his class for his inferior-function student, he will cause her to grow even more prone to avoid people who are expert in this intellectual and professional domain, thus limiting her interpersonal and intellectual possibilities forever. The class will not have proven narratively enriching but impoverishing for her.

The emotional and ethical rewards of teaching are great. So are their emotional and ethical responsibilities. Psychodynamic and archetypal analyses of educational processes help the teacher teach in psychospiritual attunement with himself and his students. He comes to see all of his students more clearly as "Beings of Ultimacy" who, although at different ability levels in his scholastic domain, are evolving in many ways outside his domain. That evolution of each student will be impacted by how he handles that student in his classroom.

The Inferior Function and the Whole Student: Avoiding the "Local Pathology"

It is a basic tenet of holistic educational theory that any aspect of one's being which is not nurtured and developed will finally grow cancerous. The local malignancy then spreads until it has infested the individual's entire system. This is no less true of one's inferior functions. In fact, it tends to be *most* true of the inferior functions, for these are the functions that are most often ignored.

Unattended to, the inferior function metastasizes until it can consume the individual, who is now possessed and undermined at virtually every step by this now-toxic part of himself.

A feeling type, for instance, who ignores developing his thinking function piles up ignorance upon ignorance until he is just an ugly bunker of small-mindedness—a personal problem to those who know him and a political problem to the society that must cope with him. A thinking type who neglects the feeling world can, as the Self-object Theorist Donald Fairbairn (1940/1992) pointed out, wind up in a concept-encrusted, "schizoid-position" in life, with no emotional sense of the personal harm or social damage his wild theorizing is having upon others.

Standardized education, in contrast to the richness of holistic education and the health it promotes, only increases the problem of the inferior function by punishing the student for his objectively low scores. It not only ignores but also shuts down the possibility of his having rich subjective experiences in a certain area regardless of his objective ability in it. This further darkens the shadow the student casts on the curriculum and that the curriculum now casts on him. Standardized education again proves itself psychosocially pathogenic.

Jungian psychology and holistic education both insist upon the integration of a person's light and shadow side. Being able to heal the damage in a student's inferior function and tapping into its potential is the dual purpose of understanding the shadow side of the curriculum: its seventh dimension.

PART FOUR

Shadow Work and the Curriculum

The Multicultural Turn in Post-Jungian Studies

Over the last two decades, some post-Jungians have suggested that between the shadow and the collective unconscious there is a layer of psyche called the "collective cultural unconscious" where certain *cultural archetypes* are at play (Adams, 1996; Gray, 1996; Samuels, 2001). These cultural archetypes, *as* archetypes, would be more primary than culturally variable *archetypal images or symbols* but still not as foundational as the archetypes of the collective unconscious.

This proposed "layer" of psyche also opens up the possibility of *multi*cultural dynamics having archetypal dimensions. This is an important issue in Jungian studies, for it is becoming increasingly difficult, except for the most die-hard cultural conservatives, to consider culture as it was conceived by Jung and his generation. They, of course, saw it in a traditional manner that focused on the now-problematized idea of "race" and "ideal" of a more-or-less culturally unitary nation-state (Giddens, 1990, 2002). Jung may be seen as a precursor to postmodernism in some respects, but in many other ways he was quite conservative culturally (Hauke, 2000; Mayes, 2016, in press).

Jungian approaches to psyche—whether classical, developmental, or archetypal (Samuels, 1997)—must now take into account postmodern perspectives on the high degree of subcultural diversity *within* those traditional states and cultures. Indeed, some of those states and cultures no longer exist, and many of those that still do, no longer exist in their traditional form but are now transforming—often with internecine culture wars (Giddens, 1990, 2002). In its "multicultural imagination," post-Jungian theory is finding ways to engage multiculturalism in archetypal terms.

From physics to pharmacology, the humanities to the law, no discipline can consider itself as standing somehow outside the circle of the world-historical moment in which we all necessarily live, move, and have our being (Gadamer, 1980). It is one in which many of the grand narratives of what a human being is and what his or her relation to the cosmos might be must now be seen in light of how the panoply of subcultures—some of them ethnic, some of them intentional—that are now highly visible in many nations today have weighed in on these questions.

Multiculturalism must thus not be seen as some sort of *addition* to education in the 21st-century United States—a strategy for "dealing with" other cultures in order to assimilate them. The United States now *is* in this diversity, and multiculturalism is thus at the heart of U.S. education. I have examined this from a holistic standpoint in my book Understanding the Whole Student: Holistic Multicultural Education (Mayes et al, 2016). (Mayes et al., 2005; 2nd edition, 2016, in press).

The "Dominant-Cultural Conscious Mind"

What I would like to suggest is that one means of approaching multicultural issues from a Jungian educational vantage point might be to posit the existence of a *dominant-cultural conscious mind*—a kind of *collective ego structure*—of the dominant culture in a society. Here, we envision the ruling culture as if it were an individual. Jung himself implicitly offered a warrant for making such an interpretive move in rhetorically asking, "Does not all culture begin with the individual?" (1967, p. 205). And is not a hegemonic group's worldview to a large extent the combined ego interests of its members—its ideology the symbolic extension and self-legitimation of its combined ego investments?

In any event, the practical purpose of making this interpretive move would primarily be to examine the *archetypal shadows* that this collective ego structure casts onto subdominant groups within a society and on other cultures outside its boundaries—and, for the purposes of this article, to examine the educational implications of this for the postmodern classroom.

Note that I use the somewhat periphrastic "dominant-cultural *conscious mind*," not "dominant-cultural *consciousness*." The phrase "dominant-cultural *consciousness*" would imply that the dominant culture possesses a critical self-awareness along with a deeply welcoming attitude toward "difference" in subdominant cultures. But this is precisely what a dominant-cultural *conscious mind*, as I am defining that phrase, lacks in its toxic attitudes and oppressive practices toward subdominant groups.

As Jungian educational theorists and practitioners, our work in this area would then be to identify archetypal shadow projections of the dominant culture's conscious mind onto subdominant groups. We would look for those projections as they are: (1) *embedded in the curriculum* and (2) *at work in classroom dynamics.* As an extension of this, we could also (3) *interrogate in a classroom—sensitively, and in ways that are relevant and appropriate to the topic under analysis in classroom discourse—how members of subdominant groups may be introjecting this shadow, and then find ways to help students expunge the internalized oppressor who has psychologically colo-nized them.* We might also (4) *look into how certain members of subdominant groups might be projecting their own cultural shadows* onto other subdomi-nant groups or even, in acts of reverse prejudice, projecting their shadow back on to the dominant culture.

This is obviously a delicate undertaking in the classroom, but it is an important one. For the shadow is infused with archetypal energy and imag-ery that often go beyond those at the merely personal level. These can either drastically undermine or uniquely elevate classroom discourse and activities in a particularly potent manner.

This much seems certain. If we are to create "therapeutic classrooms"—in which the teacher is not a therapist but performs a therapeutic function (Elson, 1989; Shalem and Bensusan, 1999)—then, given the complex ways in which culture and psyche interpenetrate, dealing with cultural shadows will be a necessary component in creating an environment of care and growth (Noddings, 1995). For what we do not want is classroom environments char-acterized by knee-jerk defensiveness or cultural aggression.

Without finding ways to prevent such things, they can all too easily rush to the surface and take control of the multicultural classroom. As Salzberger-Wittenberg (1989) declared, teaching and learning are inevitably "emotional experiences."

But first, let us briefly look at U.S. curriculum history. This will contex-tualize a Jungian approach to postmodern multiculturalism in the classroom.

"Reconceptualizing" the Depths in Multicultural Education

With what is known as the Reconceptualist Movement in curriculum stud-ies in the 1960s under the stewardship of arguably the greatest Curriculum Theorist of the 20th century, Duane Huebner (1999),[3] the field of curriculum studies was set free to look at the curriculum as a "text" that could now be viewed from a wide range of hermeneutic lenses—not just in the discipli-narily uncritical and often politically subservient behavioral and cognitive modes that had come to dominate curriculum studies by the middle of the 20th century. Skinner's (1956) *The Technology of Teaching* and Bruner's (1960) *The Process of Education* exemplified this (Kliebard, 1986).

Despite heroic attempts in the Progressive Movement in U.S. education in the first half of the 20th century to take a wide-ranging view of the curricu-lum, this situation in curriculum studies had come to pass by the mid-1950s largely because of the perceived Soviet threat to U.S. geopolitical dominance since the end of World War II (Tyack, 1974).

Education was supposed to respond to this danger by delivering "expertly designed" curricula focusing on the sciences (to build machinery, factories, and weapons) and foreign languages (to carry on espionage). It was felt that this would produce citizens who would create a militarily and industrially invincible America in the Cold War (Spring, 1976). Cognitive-Behavioral educational theories and practices seemed to fit the bill perfectly.

But there was nothing fundamentally new in this strategy, although it did presage the advent of the "military-industrial-*educational*" complex, in whose totalist grip schools increasingly operate, and which, according to the Dean of U.S. Educational Historians, Lawrence Cremin (1988), would come to pose the greatest threat to democracy in the United States in the 21st century. Still, the oldest story in U.S. educational history has been the exporting of its most deeply entrenched socioeconomic, cultural, and ideological problems to the public schools in a futile attempt to get schools to "fix" those problems and then to blame schools when they do not (Tyack, 1974).

The Reconceptualist Movement of the 1960s liberated some curricularists to consider the curriculum again more deeply in order to critique such political agendas as Cognitive-Behaviorism uncritically served. Reconceptualism aimed at envisioning education more deeply in terms of the curriculum's psychosexual, political, aesthetic, ethical, and even theological possibilities.

In the almost half century since the beginning of the Reconceptualist Movement, it has largely been its *political* aspect—looking at the curriculum as a tool of ideological imposition and the perpetuation of social injustice along the lines of ethnicity, gender, class, and sexual orientation—that has survived to some extent and governs radical curriculum studies today.[4]

The work of these educational scholars has been vital in drawing our attention to the political biases of the *official curriculum*, the increasing constraints by the state on the teacher's autonomy in her personalized *operational curriculum*, the subtle but hegemonic messages conveyed in the *hidden curriculum*, and the exclusion of alternative voices and visions from the curriculum and their banishment to the scholastic Siberia of the *null* curriculum (Eisner and Vallance, 1985).

Nevertheless, what the post-Jungian Michael Adams (1996) has said of schools of social work is equally true of schools of education. In their almost exclusively political analyses of diversity and oppression, they have given no attention to what he calls a "multicultural psychoanalysis" that could reveal some of the more profound psychospiritual sources, mechanisms, and consequences of political and cultural violence.

This is not to say that the darker side of U.S. history has not been examined in the schools since the 1960s. It is simply to say that it has been done almost exclusively in political terms, as for example, in Howard Zinn's (1990) *A People's History of the United States.* There the author tells about American history from the point of view of those groups within it who have lost in its socioeconomic and culture wars and have been shoved to the margins.

Despite their many virtues, what is lacking in these texts are discussions of the psychodynamic and psychospiritual origins of prejudice and social injustice.

That is why I am suggesting in psychodynamic and archetypal terms the existence of a dominant-cultural conscious mind—or alternatively, a "dominant-cultural ego-structure"—and its archetypal shadow projections. Social injustice and educational colonialism may then be seen in depth-psychological terms as *the projection of the archetypal shadow of the dominant-cultural conscious mind onto subdominant groups.* This projection is then acted out as political, cultural, and economic aggression against those groups.

Looked at in these terms, for instance, Hitler enticed a humiliated Germany's shattered collective ego structure to project its archetypal shadow onto Jews, Catholics, Gypsies, gay people, and others. This is explicable in Jungian terms since it is typically the shadow that constellates and deploys as the ego's first line of defense whenever the ego perceives itself to be under assault and on a point of collapse (Jung, 1967, p. 66 fn. 5). This was certainly the case with Germany's riddled and ridiculed collective ego structure in the 1920s and early 1930s.

But all of this is just to state in terms of Jungian psychology something that we have all experienced personally. Have we not all sometimes felt the shadow in us arise and threaten to engulf us in poisonous, paralyzing waves of fear and doubt—to reduce to rubble the integrity of our ego structure—because the disastrous results of our choices or simply the accusations of another have put our cherished identity in question? Overwhelmed by the idea that we might be existentially inadequate, we deflect our emerging anxiety and guilt onto another person or group to blame them for our problem instead of owning it and working through it ourselves.

By this analysis, Hitler played on Germany's shadow in such a way that Germany could disown the darkness that had constellated within it after the shattering of its collective ego structure in its defeat in World War I and then economic collapse under the weight of unbearable reparation payments. This is typically the function of shadow projection—to enable an imperiled ego structure/conscious mind to maintain the illusion of its potency and goodness—its "unity" and "purity"—even, and indeed *especially*, in the midst of its actual traumatic rupture and then disintegration.

Herein lies the psychodynamic and archetypal core of Hitler's doctrine that the "pure Aryan" race should "unify" against all the "degenerate" cultures and subcultures that it could now point to as the cause of its world-historical humiliation—the international shaming of its collective ego structure.

Clearly, a psychoanalytic/archetypal analysis of the personal-egoic and transpersonal-shadow dynamics of oppression cannot replace political, economic, and historical analysis. However, it is a useful addition—one that can be applied to classroom discourse in ways that can have an immediate personal relevance for students in today's multicultural classrooms.

Before examining those pedagogical possibilities, however, we must first take a closer look at what is meant by a dominant-cultural ego structure/conscious mind. We will then explore some of the ways its shadow projections may have taken up residence in the curriculum and also be at work within students.

THE DOMINANT-CULTURAL CONSCIOUS
MIND AND ITS SHADOW

A dominant-cultural conscious mind primally originated—in a past shrouded in the mists of history—out of a unique configuration of archetypal impulses that grasped and united its founding members. Remarkable personages among that group are now enshrined as "culture heroes," the hallowed ancestors in a people's foundational narratives—some of those narratives scriptural in status.

A crucial factor in the "originating moment" of a culture is its language—which was and remains central to a culture's origination, subsequent organization, and ongoing maintenance. As the culture develops, its official language will, despite its changes, continue to be key in shaping the culture's understanding of the world, of other cultures, of patterns of relationship and exchange among its members, and ultimately of the cosmos (Vygotsky, 1986; Bernstein, 1996). A culture's founding myths, its recent updatings, the creation of new culture heroes, and its omnipresent language thus underlie and generate the *dominant-cultural conscious mind* as it is presently constituted.

This dominant-cultural conscious mind is made up of the dominant culture's: (1) secular and sacred rituals that commemorate its founding events and those mythic personages who embody its central commitments about "how things are" and "how they should be," (2) patterns and degrees of intimacy and association in a wide variety of interpersonal contexts from the boardroom to the bedroom, (3) guidelines about the significance of gender and how it might determine social roles, (4) normative paradigms of the individual's developmental lifecycle, and (5) daily practices of exchange of information, goods, and services.

Different cultures also apprehend, dwell in, and enact *time* in radically different ways (Bender and Wellerby, 1991). These have profound educational consequences for subdominant-culture students in dominant-culture classrooms, where assumptions and enactments regarding the pacing, patterns of participation, and purposes of classroom discussions and activities may be very different from their own (Mayes, 2016, in press).[5]

Naturally, all of these things determine how schooling is carried on in those spaces called "public schools," dedicated and set aside for the delivery of an official curriculum. This inherently privileges children who come from the dominant culture and tends to marginalize those from subdominant cultures, viewing them as a psychosocial "problem" that needs to be "fixed"—increasingly by state-sponsored cognitive-behavioral "therapeutic" and/or psychopharmaceutical means.

The collective-cultural conscious mind both generates and is in turn modified by the current state of the symbol systems of the dominant culture in a feedback loop that Giddens (1990) calls "structuration." For, a dominant culture's symbol systems are, although determinative, not static. They are ever registering and responding to the fierce force of countless dialectical tensions within by the greater culture (Hewitt, 1984).

Language, the most important of a culture's symbol systems, allows for various sorts of concrete and symbolic exchange, disallows others, and finally serves as a sort of hub for the vast structure of symbolic systems within which the individual finds himself positioned (Bourdieu, 1977). The registers and codes of the culture's language that one uses are key in determining a person's social positioning (Bourdieu, 1977; Halliday, 1984; Bernstein, 1996). This can obviously be a problem of the first order for the non-native-speaking student in the classrooms of the dominant culture—a problem not only linguistically but also psychodynamically, culturally, and even spiritually.[6]

In general, the collective-cultural conscious mind is constantly being expressed, legitimated, enforced, and reproduced at the workaday level in the culture's innumerable daily protocols and interactions (Blumer, 1969; Hewitt, 1984). And it is in force nowhere more clearly or powerfully than in a culture's "official curriculum" for its schools.

The media have also become a prime, if not *the* prime, mechanism for creating and controlling the collective-cultural conscious mind. And because of their seductive force, the media, as possibly the premier (mis)educational site today, may implant in members of subdominant groups the "false consciousness" that the worldview of the dominant culture is just the way things "are" and "should be." (Marx and Engels, 1978).[7] In this process, certain members of a subdominant group may internalize the worldview of the very group or groups which are dominating them.

Having internalized the dominant culture's view of things and thus possessed by false consciousness, victims of oppression—ranging from sexual abuse to political abuse—then blame themselves for their eviscerated condition instead of critiquing and confronting their oppressors.

Of course, an individual may not just haplessly succumb to all of this. She may also interpret, internalize, and give voice to the dominant-cultural conscious mind in many different ways, but doing so in a manner that finally depends upon the degrees of freedom that the dominant culture permits—that is to say, as long as she does not substantially challenge present arrangements of power.

Others may choose to adapt to the dominant-cultural conscious mind for strategic reasons of social positioning. This is sometimes the case with third-generation citizens of a country, for example, who are more intent on succeeding in the culture of their birth than in maintaining the culture of their immigrant grandparents.[8] Indeed, they may even be trying to minimize or even erase that culture of origin in their lives for purposes of more prestigious inclusion in the culture of power. This can be a source of painful intergenerational conflict.

Yet others may drastically alter or even outright reject a dominant-cultural conscious mind in how they choose to narrativize and enact their lives—again, depending upon the "freedom" to do so that the dominant culture permits. How much a subdominant group may choose to reject the dominant-cultural conscious mind also depends on the extent of the subdominant group's willingness to suffer exclusion for "difference"—as in the case of the religiously conservative Amish in Pennsylvania—or to hide its "deviant" practices in the depths of dark closets—as used to be the case more than it presently is with subcultures of alternative sexualities, but which still sadly exists.

As   went to great length to show, *every conscious attitude has its flipside*. This is the archetypal shadow. The dominant-cultural ego structure is no exception to the general rule that excessive commitment to a conscious attitude and posture constellates the shadow as that which it does not wish to be aware of, indeed, that which it is terrified to be aware of (Jung, 1978, pp. 47, 71). It will then look for a hook on which to hang its disowned darkness—and, of course, marginalized groups make excellent hooks (Gray, 1996, p. 225).

It is important to recognize, too, that a person's radical entrenchment in his *subdominant*-culture's conscious mind has its own shadow, too, which it may then project onto other subdominant groups. Indeed, even *within* a particular subdominant group, some groups—subcultures within a subculture—may cast their shadows onto each other in an injurious instance of "intragroup variability" (Devine, 1995).

These things being the case, the dominant-cultural conscious mind and the projection of its shadow have important educational implications that involve every student and span the curriculum.

CHALLENGING AND BEFRIENDING THE SHADOW IN THE CURRICULUM

In the act of what Paolo Freire (1970) called "conscientización," "bringing to consciousness," the teacher helps her class examine the dominant culture's conscious attitudes that have led, or *compelled*, them to study these particular texts (Apple, 1990). Why these texts and not others? What does this choice of *these* texts, situated in *this* curriculum, say about the dominant culture's conscious worldview?

What Freire later (2001) came to realize is that these important questions still remained within the sphere of the political and did not yet extend to the more broadly and deeply existential. For as Fay (1986), critiquing critiques at the merely ideological level that standard "critical social science" proffers, observes that the liberation they aim at has its limits. But we must go deeper than only that.

For oppression is not only ideological. It is system wide in an individual. It has planted its flag not only in her cognition but has also established its influence in her body, her emotions, her ability to value and evaluate her *own* experiences, and her willingness to believe in something transcendent to or immanent in her life. Additionally, says Fay, any approach to liberation must reckon with the fact that the individual is "embedded" in all sorts of local affections and affiliations, which the decontextualized "ideological critiques" of critical social science cannot touch. We must honor political and economic analyses of oppression. But they alone will never set the prisoner free.

There is no curriculum that does not impinge upon every aspect of the student—whether she is a member of a dominant or subdominant culture—in the assumptions that the official curriculum is making, and imposing, about what reality "is" and the uses to which "knowledge" shall be put (Foucaer, 1980). This is as true in a home economics class as in a philosophy class (Mayes, 2016, in press). And contrary to popular opinion, it is no less true in a "hard sciences" class (Kuhn, 1970).

To work in the service of our students' liberation thus requires that we invite them to probe more deeply into the curriculum and its shadow—and also their own. As they do so, further questions about the curriculum and themselves—queries rooted in the soil of primary subconscious and unconscious processes—will naturally emerge and call out to be recognized (Mayes, 2009a, 2009b).

For instance: What is the dominant culture as a collective ego structure not only not seeing but is—as is often the case with a refractory analysand in therapy—straining to *resisting seeing* because it is finally terrified to acknowledge, confess, and repent of the truth about itself—its shadow?[9] (Jung, 1978, pp. 47, 71)

Having asked ourselves and each other in a classroom to what degree we are being shaped by the dominant-cultural conscious mind, and to what extent, if any, each of us may consciously go on to *choose* for this to happen, we then proceed to ask even deeper questions.

That is, now that students through a reflective process have arrived at a place where they are *consciously* consenting to or dissenting from this curriculum, are there new shadows that are even now starting to *unconsciously* constellate within *them* as members of a dominant or subdominant culture that we need to surface and examine—shadows born of anger, resentment, guilt, or fear? Why have *those* shadows now begun arising? What are they? How prone might all of this make students to now cast *these* shadows onto another? And what can we in the course of a term or an academic year do about *that* as a community of discourse?

And more generally, how has our shadow casting led us as individuals and members of particular groups, dominant and subdominant, to even further cast the Other (Levinas, 1996) into the shadow, judging him "strange" and "inferior," even "deviant" and in need of "curing," because he sees things differently and thus holds views and engages in practices that are life giving to him but that we, both as individuals and members of a (sub)culture, might inhumanely condemn?

This kind of "psychospiritual reflectivity" (Mayes, 2001) on the shadow in the official curriculum as we experience that curriculum, *both* before *and* after reflecting on it, raises emotionally electric psychospiritual issues that political analyses do not reveal and by their very nature cannot address.

And extending that reflectivity in a sobering way, the student also asks himself if he, without such reflectivity, might have become so possessed by his own shadow that he was projecting onto the Other (Levinas, 1996) that he might someday have felt "justified" in doing symbolic or actual violence to him? Where is our inner, archetypal "Nazi," no matter how "virtuous" we might think we are or where we are socially positioned— high or low?

The Jungian Erich Neumann summed it all up nicely in writing that a collective shadow is, without reflectivity on and withdrawal of that shadow, "transferred to the outside world and experienced as an outside object. It is combated, punished, and exterminated as 'the alien out there' instead of being dealt with as one's own 'inner problem'" (Neumann, 1969, p. 50).

Albert Camus wrote, "The jailor is bound to prisoner." How could it be otherwise? The jailor, objectifying the Other, thereby strips himself of his own humanity. Thus self-abased, self-abused, and self-imprisoned, he ultimately objectifies himself.

As she reflects psychospiritually on both the curriculum and herself, yet another cluster of questions forms in the student, having now to do as much with *repression* as *oppression*. They boil down to this central question: How may she have *introjected* an oppressor's shadow projection onto her? "What anger, depression, guilt, or anxiety has my internalizing of the oppressor's shadow bred in *me*—and not just politically and culturally, although it includes that, but in my entirety—as an existential being? How have I turned off, shut down, gone away, and given up throughout my being? How has it come to pass that my *mana,* my power, my birthright, has been sucked out of me—or rather, how is it that I have learned to *repress* it?"

This reflectivity occurs at both psychodynamic and archetypal levels as these issues are constellated by the shadow of the curriculum, on one hand, and the immediacy, richness, and relevance of classroom discourse, on the other hand. They are obviously difficult. However, they are presenting themselves in the lucent spirit of Jung's *hermeneutics of hope* (Ricoeur, 1991; also, Homans, 1995)—looking for the resurrected possibilities of growth, even in the agony of a present crucifixion.

Despite its inevitably darker tone, such reflectivity is ultimately healthful and bright. But this should not surprise us. For as Jung declared, "Wholeness is perforce paradoxical in its manifestations" (1969, p. 145). And it is the student's wholeness that must be the paramount consideration in what I have elsewhere called "Education for Individuation" (2005b, 2007, 2009b, 2016, in press).

In education for individuation, the pedagogical paradox of individuation in the classroom is always presenting itself to us as Jungian educational theorists and practitioners.

This is because the cultivation of the shadow—as the student encounters it in the curriculum, recognizes it as what has violated and colonized her, and then, in growing empowerment, expunges it from herself—is precisely what is necessary to accomplish what Jung was always calling for; namely, the mining of the shadow for its hidden gold. This, said Jung, in his crowning labors on alchemy in the last phase of his career, is the psychospiritual analogue of the alchemical project: the transmuting of the wretched, tortured, and tenebrous *nigredo* into the paradisiacal sum and substance of heaven: the *lapis philosophorum,* the Philosopher's Stone.

And in this process, the student has learned (or is learning, since individuation is an endless, recursive process) to resist unleashing the full fury of her counter-shadow-projection onto the oppressor. Left unbridled, such anger becomes obsessive and excessive. Self-destructively vituperative, it could leave the student awash in bitterness, that corrosive psychic acid that eats its host alive. For as in psychotherapy, it is not good for the patient to stay stuck for any longer than is necessary to locate and express her grief and anger—and then move on. The wound must be staunched at some point and permitted to heal in the form of a scar—its jagged shape symbolizing the wisdom gained through suffering.

Further, having put to a halt her own cultural aggressing in the projection of *her* culture's shadow onto another culture, the student now sees clearly enough to ask herself a visionary question: "What can I adopt or adapt from that previously feared or despised culture in order to enrich my own life-narrative towards individuation, and, in the process, also restore my battered, violated people?" This is the role of the culture hero as he or she returns from the spooky forest of psychospiritual adventure to bring her culture saving knowledge (Campbell, 1949).

It must be stressed again that the teacher, filling a therapeutic role but not "playing the therapist," sensitively poses these questions to his students, emphatically witnesses their engagement with them, and skillfully assists them along the way—but that he does so *always* and *only* in a manner that is relevant and appropriate to the age of the students and the topics under analysis in the classroom.

In classroom discussion, research and writing, group work, dyads, individual reflectivity, and student activism in the community—the teacher shepherds his students through these rocky highlands and swampy lowlands. And this he can do credibly and efficaciously only if he has also engaged in his own psychospiritual reflectivity and continues to do so in his *own* ongoing approximations of individuation.

This is hard work and risky business for the teacher. Like Winnicott's (1992) "good-enough mother," he must *contain* the process by creating and maintaining a "good holding environment" for his students in the therapeutic classroom (Elson, 1989) throughout the ups and downs of "teaching and learning as emotional experiences" (Salzberger-Wittenberg, 1989). It is understandable why a teacher would choose not to do so. But this does not make the loss any less to his students and to himself if he opts out—indeed, if he never really bought in.

I have tried to offer models and modes—drawn primarily from Jungian psychology but also from contemplative practices from Eastern and Western wisdom traditions—that the teacher might employ to accomplish this (2001, 2002, 2004).The goal is for the teacher and student to be fellow travelers—with the teacher, of course, farther along in the process and at a higher level of *conscientización*.

Both the teacher and the student thereby come to better appreciate the personal and archetypal dynamics of the shadow in the curriculum so as to promote a vision of the shadow in themselves. They move more purposefully into an apprehension of what it means to be both the oppressor and the oppressed, the jailor and the jailed, and, in knowing this, never to be either one again. The classroom thus becomes a site of growth in compassion as well as the alchemical laboratory in which opposites are unified within oneself—these being the hallmark of the individuating process.

DOING THE DIALECTICS OF THE SHADOW IN THE CLASSROOM

The German Existentialist Theologian Reinhold Niebuhr (1986) said that we are all "the children of light and the children of darkness." We need not await some final apocalyptic sorting of the two into "The Good" and "The Evil" at the end of time. The Apocalypse is taking place every day in the individual who is sorting out the two in himself in order to live a more realistic, less judgmental, and thus creative and productive life. This should be true of the student too, whatever that student's "occupational path."

For, a student is not "human capital" as he is now often so reductively, indeed grotesquely, conceived in a great deal of current educational theory and practice. A student is, rather, a hero on an archetypal journey. He can, with our help as the archetypal "wide elders"/teachers, seek out the Holy Grail of individuation—the sacred container of the Blood of God, which is, finally, none other than the student's own psychospiritual lifeblood in the chalice of his heart. This will allow the student to return to his people after his trek through the forest of the curriculum to proffer saving wisdom to his culture (Mayes, 2009a).

In insisting that every archetype has a light and a dark side, Jung often wrote in psychospiritual terms about the individual as the ongoing site of an ethical apocalypse (1969a, p. 183). Individuation largely consists in seeing the Apocalypse in oneself, withdrawing projections onto others, refusing to introject another's darkness, and finding a way to uniquely reconcile the light and dark within oneself in order to live a life that is endued with power but oriented in compassion.

Reflectivity on the shadow within oneself—and, again, always in the context of the curriculum in order to remain relevant and appropriate to the educational endeavor—helps students along this path. In this way, education reveals itself as ethical and even spiritual project. Without this, education too easily degenerates into mere training in the service of the state.

Historical, political, and economic analyses of oppression are not abandoned in all of this. Indeed, they may now go hand in hand with a "multicultural psychoanalysis" everywhere from the public schools to professional schools (Adams, 1996). This not only enhances the students' understanding of oppression and repression—both historically and presently—but it does so in a way that empowers his students' lives as cultural beings, who now possess archetypal lenses through which to see the sacred endeavors of teaching and learning.

Therefore, "every individual," and this includes every teacher and student, "needs revolution," as Jung wrote:

> inner division, overthrow of the existing order, and renewal. Individual self-reflection, return of the individual to the ground of human nature, to his own deepest being with its individual and social destiny—here is the beginning of a cure for that blindness which reigns at the present hour. (1967, p. 5)

There are already excellent tools at hand for shedding the light of reflectivity upon the cultural shadows of the official curriculum as it is both *cast by* and *cast upon* each student in the classroom in multiple ways.

For instance, in Heath's (1983) idea of students as "ethnographic detectives," they examine each other about their own cultural perspectives on issues under analysis in the classroom. There is also Spindler and Spindler's (1992) idea of "cultural reflectivity" for teachers and students.

In these two forms of reflectivity in the classroom, one examines himself about the deep-seated, often shadow-laden, psychosocial commitments that make up his own view of topics under discussion in the classroom. He then works with that material in personal reflectivity, dyadically, in small-group processes, and with the class as a whole to surface those commitments and decide whether to celebrate them now in a more conscious and directed way, to change them if they are not serving him in his narratival growth to wholeness, or even to reject them if they now show themselves in the light of day to be unproductive and even hurtful to oneself and others.

CONCLUSION: THE LIBERATING CLASSROOM

We must become free of that is in us which has made others unfree because of our shadow projections onto them. We must withdraw the projections of our own weaknesses and wounds onto others and then go about the business of facing and healing ourselves. We may find, as we look into that darkness, that there is light.

We must also expunge that which we have psychosexually, politically or even spiritually internalized from an oppressor, lest it cause us to condemn and consume ourselves in fruitless flames and thereby foreclose our creativity. And in expunging the oppressor, we must not let the driving force of anger, that is initially necessary to expel him from our inner sanctums, then *stay* in those sanctums, merely to drench them in a new type of toxicity.

The psychodynamically and archetypally sensitive classroom can be a special site, a sacred zone, archetypally abundant. It can be a *temenos*—personally and culturally therapeutic in both our postmodern condition and our perennial one.

But this can only happen when liberating shadow work is done by profound engagement with that very curriculum which, although often a political bane, can also be worked into a mythical boon.

COMMENTARY BY DANIEL H. ANDRUS

Daniel H. Andrus, M.ED., is presently the principal of Serrano High School. Previously, he was a teacher of English Language Arts and Spanish in the public schools, most notably at Paso Robles High School. He has been a high school administrator for 11 years.

In my 22 years as a teacher and administrator, I have heard many metaphors attempting to explain the teacher-student relationship. Students have been compared to: seeds, blank slates or canvases, boats on a river or a sea, lumps of clay, products of an assembly line, economic assets, and sponges. In each of these examples, students are objects to be acted upon by teachers. Most recently, students have simply become data points to measure how well we can standardize who they are and how they learn.

All of this stands in stark contrast to the Jungian ideal of "education for individuation" presented by Cliff Mayes. This approach recognizes students as individual heroes and heroines on an archetypal journey aided by teachers who are Wise Elders in a profound *I-Thou* relationship with them.

Before *No Child Left Behind*, I was educated as a teacher to understand and appreciate Jungian personality typology and to adapt my teaching to fit the learning styles and the superior and inferior functions of my students. However, the advent of standardization and high-stakes testing has pushed us back into objectifying our students and ignoring their individuality.

Not only have many teachers reacted to standardization by falling back into an *I-It* pedagogy. Administrators have treated teachers in the same way.

A trap has been laid in which teachers are seen as a function of their certification, degrees, and data. For some elementary teachers, math is in their inferior function even though their certification may say that they are highly qualified. *Common Core's* renewed push for school-wide literacy instruction challenges some secondary math, science, art, or music teachers in the same way. In desperation, administrators use standard teacher evaluations in the same way that teachers do with students. At all levels, the more we push the official curriculum, the deeper some become entrapped by the shadow curriculum.

Mayes offers a solution. By accepting teachers and students as individuals with distinct abilities, knowledge, and understanding who must undertake a personal journey to transform and discover hidden potential, schools can move from being sites of *I-It* to venues of *I-Thou*. All will fill, and should be instructed about, their now dual archetypal roles as Hero and Helper once they have been beckoned to cross the threshold and not only accept but embrace their journey.

This entails teachers and administrators understanding our role as Alchemists (the archetypal Wizard or Magician) and as Wise Elders (or mentors). This new relationship requires a new "cultural consciousness" within a school that must be constructed purposefully and jointly. It helps transform both teacher and administrator into partners on the learning journey. Mayes declares that "every profoundly educative process is in this sense an archetypal call to adventure" and that "much depends on how convincingly the teacher (or administrator) is able to give voice to the summons . . . throughout the journey."

In discussing Jung's idea of the shadow, Mayes asserts that "the essence of education for individuation is self-realization of buried potential." Self-realization through the epic archetypal journey, however, is frightening because it will require parts of us to die away so that we can become something greater—the archetype of crucifixion-and-resurrection, which Mayes also explores in educational contexts. Fear, which comes from the dark side of our archetypes, weakens trust and compels some to retreat from the challenge. This is all the more reason that standardized teacher evaluations must give way to *I-Thou* interactions.

Teacher development needs to guide teachers back to an acceptance of their journey as both guides *and* learners. It needs to focus on the school transforming as individual students and teachers move beyond the shadow of fear and doubt and embrace a new kind of *consensual reality*, but this a productive one: a *mutually constructed* ethos that also honors the *I-Thou* status of *individuals*—one of those generative paradoxes that Jung wrote about and that Mayes calls for across the spectrum of educational settings and purposes.

NOTES

1. This discussion of the four personality "types/functions" and the two personality "attitudes" in the following several pages is taken from my (2005a) book, *Jung and Education: Elements of an Archetypal Pedagogy* (Rowman and Littlefield Press). That section ends where the discussion of educational implications is again picked up.

2. I will be forever grateful to the late Professor Edward Pajak of Johns Hopkins University for our discussions about psychoanalysis and education—a field that he advanced—especially his thoughts about the effects the teacher's, student's, and parent's narcissistic wounds on educational processes. I wish to acknowledge the effect of Professor Pajak's groundbreaking thinking on me and others regarding this and many other topics in psychoanalytic pedagogy in both his books and in conversation. His kindness in freely sharing his always compelling thoughts with me in our chats was unfeigned. His searching intelligence and warm wit made him not only a great scholar but an even greater person. The absence of Ed's theoretical insights mixed with his unerring practicality—and even more, just his wise presence—is a loss in our current conversations that nothing but Ed himself could ever fill.

3. See Pinar (1975, 2000), Huebner's most important student and now the ongoing standard bearer for Reconceptualist approaches to curriculum studies.

4. For prominent examples of this, see: Apple, 1990; Bowles & Gintis, 1976; Grant, 1995; De Castell and Luke, 1983; McLaren, 1998; Morrow and Torres, 1995; Nieto, 2000; Pinar, 2000.

5. See also: Mayes, 2009b, 2007.

6. This, of course, is an enormous problem for the student whose native language is not English. For, not only is there the obvious fact that she must learn a new language, daunting enough in itself. She must also find ways to bridge the "cultural discontinuity" between the patterns of meaning and modes of interacting embedded in her language and those (which may be quite different) in the new language, In her life as a student, this especially involves those patterns of meaning and ways of interacting regarding teachers and peers in a school setting, for these will also differ, sometimes dramatically, in her linguistic-cultural tradition and those in the linguistic-cultural tradition of the culture of her new classroom. This goes to the very heart of how a student interprets the world and acts in it and points to the moral obligation—not to mention the social and economic wisdom—of responding to the needs of L2 students with a maximum degree of skill and compassion (Grant, 1995; Nieto, 2000; Mayes, 2016 et al., in press). One does not merely *speak* one's native language. One's language is not an incidental but a defining characteristic of a person. Herein lie the political, economic, sociolinguistic, psychodynamic, and ethical foundations of the need for bilingual education.

7. How much the web is also a site of contesting and even subverting dominant worldviews is an important question but one that goes beyond the scope of this study.

8. Interestingly, there is a tendency among third-generation members of a culture to rediscover its roots and reestablish some of the great-grandparents' cultural practices.

9. See Kirschner (1996) for a seminal study of the roots of psychoanalysis in the Judeo-Christian narrative of Fall from Edenic Innocence (neurosis), Repentance (the therapeutic process of self-examination), and Restoration/Redemption (the New Jerusalem of the healed psyche).

Chapter 6

The Hermetic Teacher

The Greek god Hermes is one of the earliest and most captivating embodiments of the Trickster archetype in Western culture. Not incidentally, he is also one of its most colorful teachers. It is in his simultaneous roles as a trickster and teacher—a master of paradox—that I wish now to explore Hermes as a pedagogical archetype.

HERMES: TRICKSTER AND "SPIRITUS RECTOR"

The *Homeric Hymn to Hermes*, the primary source of our knowledge about Hermes, introduces us to him on the eventful day of his birth.

We learn that he was the product of a union between Zeus and the nymph Maia, who gave birth to their love child in a cave. Hermes, the child of the Author of the Law that is handed down from the top of Mount Olympus, is equally the offspring of a watery nymph who goes with the flow of cavernous passions.

In Hermes, we thus see at the outset how archetypes: (1) already contain their opposites within themselves, which is why they are paradoxical; (2) actually *turn* into those opposites given enough time; a process Jung called *enantiodromia*—something each one of us knows at some point in our lives in our own transformations from one idea or state of being into its opposite; and (3) strive toward synthesis and a durable, dynamic balance within themselves and with the other archetypes in our psychospiritual economy. This integrality is key to individuation.

All of this is so because archetypes are not entities, not things-in-themselves. Rather, they are more gracefully and usefully imaged as loosely held together force fields—employing that term metaphorically—around centers of universal persistence and existential moment to us as human beings. They are always themselves in flux, as life itself is always in flux, and "the archetypes" are just an attempt at an identification and categorization of "elements" of the unknowable. They move in and out of other such force fields in a constant interpenetration of aspects of the Self in pursuit of itself as a unity: individuation.

Individuation is an existential project—indeed the fundamental existential project—never to be fully accomplished once and for all in this life but always to be more adequately known in experience and realized in action. Pursuing this interior knowledge and acting on it in the world is, Jung asserted, what it means to live ethically. "Morality is not imposed from outside; we have it in ourselves from the start" (1967a, p. 27). The characters and motifs in myths are ethical dramas emblematic of aspects of the Self in search of itself in resolution and balance.

Hermes was not a god but a demigod, making him a bridge between the mortal and the immortal and thus particularly relevant to the human condition—we, creatures of time longing for the timeless.

On the very first day of life of this supremely clever infant named Hermes, we discover he not only invents the lyre but manages to rustle the cattle of Apollo, his half brother. From the outset, Hermes, creatively engaged with the arts, is also given to upsetting convention. For his brother Apollo can be tiresomely legalistic, and one indeed suspects that Hermes' energy constellates in such incendiary ways partly as a reaction against his brother's more stolid nature. Hermes puts on the garb of the revolutionary, the arch disturber of the ordinary order of things, because it is his nature, of course, but also because it is his strategic position in the drama of individuation.

This reaction constellates, in the figure of Hermes, as a psychospiritual statement against those routines and regulations that so easily hypnotize the culturally overly determined individual, who is not really an "individual" at all. Consensual reality lulls him day after day into what ultimately amounts to little more than a slavish quasi-existence that has grown smug and lazy on whatever unexamined dogma the person happened to be born into. This is perhaps hinted at in the myth by the presence of the cows—an archetypal symbol of pleasant domesticity but one that may devolve into the mindless conformity that excessive social control breeds, what Freud and Jung both called "the herd mentality", and what psychoanalytic pedagogues for the last century have warned against as contrary to democracy and prime for totalitarianism (Mayes, 2009b).

But such things will not come to pass on Hermes' watch, not with *him* as the *spiritus rector*, the "teacher spirit," in a situation. It is obvious that he detests control but only when it is excessive. After all, Hermes will grow up to become famous for how he always pays due reverence to his superior gods.

But when control no longer is serving the metabolic function of keeping things in dynamic working order but exists for its own sake and for the self-aggrandizement of those who exercise it over others, he suddenly materializes on the scene and disrupts things. But Hermes does not do this to promote anarchy. Hermes is no anarchist.

Rather, he disrupts positively—to prevent entropy caused by totalitarianism, which is death to the individual. It is also death to educational processes—pedagogical and curricular stasis in the form of objectified teachers, students, and curricula. Standardization in education is antihermetic, entropic—"anti-education," in fact. The archetype of Hermes stands in revolutionary counterpoint to such things, the patron saint of authentic educative processes, a champion of education in the spirit of the symbol against training in the service of the sign, as I made that distinction in chapter 4.

It is in the context of excessive control that we may, at least in part, understand why it is that the firebrand Hermes holds Apollo's shepherd's staff in the images of him that were found all over the cities and country sides where he presided. This curious image (Hermes with the staff of control is like Thomas Paine wearing an icon of the king!) bespeaks the fact that, although the cause of Hermes is freedom, freedom itself must be guided by a stabilizing purpose.

The staff thus also symbolizes the hermetic teacher's own growth in individuation, his own transcendence into higher types of unity, his own progress in his pedagogical calling, which, as we saw in chapter 4, he must exercise with authority but also humility, the antidote to psychic inflation and self-indulgence, in order to guide his class in health.

And note how it is in a melding of the archetype of *the teacher as Hermes* as well as in *the teacher's role as a Wise Elder* that the bivalent teacher issues the call of adventure to the student. This evidences again how permeable archetypes are, how constantly they move into and out of each other, and how basically inscrutable their operation is in the economy of the soul. Goethe's lines at the end of *Faust* about "Formation, transformation, the Eternal Mind's eternal recreation" appealed to Jung, no doubt because of how it captured the structure and dynamics of the archetypes and the collective unconscious.

Brought before Zeus for stealing the cattle, the infant Hermes denies having even been able to commit the crime because he is still so young. This enrages Apollo, who knows full well what his brother did. Seeing that it is now useless to try to defend himself on evidentiary grounds, Hermes, ever the charmer, changes tactics and begins to masterfully play his lyre.

This enchants Zeus, who, although not for an instant hoodwinked by the child, is delighted at this precocious, witty son of his. So total and tidal is Hermes' charm that even Apollo gives up his grudge about Hermes' theft and comes to his brother's side, letting Hermes keep the livestock. To seal the deal a trade is made: Apollo gets Hermes' lyre and Hermes gets Apollo's shepherd's crook.

In this turn of the story, Apollo's insistence upon *Logos-clarity* and legal exactitude is coming to be tempered somewhat, as suggested symbolically in his acquisition of the lyre, an instrument of love in the allure of art. *The mathetic realm is learning to give the poetic its due.*

On the other side of things, Hermes' excessive *Eros-impulse* to jump head first into the waters of passion (his mother was a nymph, after all) in libidinally possessed and archetypally imbalanced acts of rebellious emotion is toned down to some degree in his acceptance of Apollo's staff—a symbol of soberness and duty, the pastoral tool of the guardian of the flock. *The poetic realm is learning to give the mathetic its due.* The archetypes strive, each within and all among themselves, toward creative synthesis, the goal of the archetypally balanced classroom.

The archetypally wise teacher knows when to actively position herself authoritatively in the process, and always on her students' behalves, to help things along, never to vaunt her own importance. Of equal importance is that she also knows when to get out of the process' way, which is *not* the case when the teacher's narcissistic wounds, counter-projections, or other problems are muddying the teacher's judgment, who now tries to take charge when she should not, or some other variation on the theme of a teacher power-tripping her students (Mayes, 2007).

When this happens, the teacher's issues will inevitably spill out of her cracked personal psychic ship, which now toxically lets loose its load of issues into a now compromised educational flow and poisons the psychodynamic and archetypal rivers running through the classroom. Again, personal, cultural, and archetypal reflectivity, as discussed in chapter 3, are a must for the teacher who strives above all else in the classroom to meet the moral imperative of carrying out her role in health and in the service of her students.

Even from this brief account of the genesis of Hermes, it is clear that his sudden, full-blown emergence onto the scene as portrayed in the Homeric epic, and indeed his total psychospiritual constellation in *any* situation, particularly one so emotionally and archetypally charged as a classroom, sets in motion an archetypal dialectic between Logos and Eros, order and spontaneity, program and passion—in short, the creative tug-and-pull between the Kantian poles of the mathetic and poetic domains, which is key to Jung's vision of the structure and dynamics of the psyche and integral to an archetypal view of education.

It is the teacher as Trickster, the master of *play,* who, despite his occasional seriousness, switches on this electric *play* of opposites in the classroom, the local actor evoking the universal dialectic in the classroom.

Or, perhaps it is the other way around. Perhaps it is the archetypal play of opposites, the dialectical energy that sets the collective unconscious aglow, which is electing to incarnate in *this* particular teacher, in *this* moment, in *this* class. Perhaps it is a universal energy visiting and infusing the local actor in an instance of psychospiritual grace—a pedagogical incarnation in the classroom.

Whatever the case—whether we invoke the archetype, whether the archetype somehow autonomously visits us, or whether both are going on at the same time—the classroom becomes a *temenos* when Hermes, the *spiritus rector*, manifests within it. And when he does, the existentially authentic classroom turns into a psychospiritual container, an alchemical retort, itself a living thing because it is part of the sacred alchemical work in which deeply educative processes go on, from transformative stage to stage.

HERMES AS SHAMAN
AND THE TEACHER AS SHAPESHIFTER

Since his origin in the mists of history, Trickster has been endued with shamanic powers, and this was certainly a part of Hermes' identity. Like a shaman—the "medicine man" of First Nation cultures—Hermes is ultimately a healer despite (or better, because of) his sometimes shocking behavior. It is in the service of his patient's well-being that the shaman moves at will among various planes of existence. He is a traveler from one sphere of being to another, brokering between incommensurate realities, to find a cure for his patient's problem (Eliade, 1974). To accomplish this, the shaman must often be a shape-shifter, as Hermes was.

In his shapeshifting, the shaman's very presence is instructional. Just to know something of the shaman's many metamorphoses is to catch a vision of how many identities can be embodied in just one person's existence, how many perspectives, each one valid, can be included in an individual's composite understanding of things, and what experiential and intellectual abundance this may offer.

This is why a "shamanic teacher" (Mayes, 2007) can so often help the student experience things differently—so much so, indeed, that the student feels empowered after a while under the tutelage of a hermetic teacher's multiplex presence—to see that one need not be just a single, static "thing," a diminutive ego, a pawn in someone else's game, but that "each of us is a crowd," and that, far from a problem for the ego, this can be an empowering psychological and ethical fact (Ferrucci, 1982, p. 47f).

This recognition allows the student to see things from many different angles in a much more nuanced manner—as does the viewer of a cubist painting. Thus, did Maxine Greene (1974) advocate for the idea of "the cubist curriculum."

Here the curriculum, assessed from many perspectives *among* the students, allows *each* student to view not only the curriculum but also ultimately her life as one of multiple possibilities, varied roads to freedom. This evidences to the student that she does not have to be a static "thing" to be programmatically used by others, but a living unity-in-multiplicity, to be honored in her own right, gathered up unto herself as an organic whole, and then set free in search of ever higher states of synthesis and potency.[1]

This is the way of individuation. It is education for liberation. It is the curriculum not only in a pedagogy of the symbol but also the curriculum itself *as* a symbol of the students' waxing freedom.

Now, it is often a tricky thing for the hermetic teacher to know how much of his multifarious life to share with a class, but it is an inevitable question for a teacher such as he is, and is endeavoring to ever more abundantly become.

Of course, this is not a problem for the cautious, uninvested practitioner, who never shares himself with his students. But living and teaching from such a frigid position in such nonrelationship with one's students is not "risk-free"—as he might imagine. Indeed, the danger has already come, conquered, and consumed him. For either now, as he looks out onto the lunar landscape of his now-defensively-camouflaged students, or later, in the vacancy of unpopulated memories, his self-exile will be confirmed.

Such emotional emptiness, the cause and consequence of training in the service of the sign, will never do for the passionate practitioner since what that teacher teaches is not ancillary to his life but essential to it. He will probably have taken on many "shapes" in the course of his life regarding what is presently being discussed or done in class and which have brought him to the head of this classroom. These transformations are integral to his life narrative. Disclosing some of this to the class may serve the dramatic purpose of exemplifying for the student various points of view on a topic and how this multiplicity may exist in and enrich the life of a single individual.

Of course, nothing overly personal or growing out of an excessive wish to be loved by one's students should be "shared" by the teacher. If a teacher does this, it is cause for personal and archetypal reflectivity in the teacher, and possibly even psychotherapy, to deal with a possible wound or need he is wrongly trying to get healed or filled by students.

It was precisely the potential for this kind of thing that moved Caroline Zachry, a leader in the psychoanalytic wing of educational Progressivism in the early 20th century, to issue call for all teachers to undergo psychoanalysis during their student teaching years. For, in addition to what is contained in the curriculum, the teacher who is emotionally invested in both his subject matter and his students will to some degree not only be *sharing* what he knows but *showing* who he is.

And students are typically interested in, sometimes even fascinated by, not only what the teacher knows but how he has come to know it—what in his life has led him to now be standing before them in this classroom, clothed in a certain power. The students' interest in the teacher and the chronicle of the shapes he has assumed to get to where he is now is natural. It likely has various causes. And it is part and parcel of what Salzberger-Wittenberg (1989) has identified as "the emotional experience of teaching and learning."

One of the causes for a student's interest in her teacher is clarified by the post-Freudian idea, discussed in chapter 2, that the teacher is a pedagogical "self-object" for the student.

In this process, the teacher becomes in the course of the term an introjected figure for the student, a self-object. The student's interior relationship with this self-object, often colored by his earlier relationships with his primary caregivers, will now become significant in his own understanding of who he is as a learner (i.e., his "learning ego") and who he might even become one day as a practitioner in this particular field, whether it is modern dance or chemistry, auto-shop or French literature (Wool, 1989; Appel, 1996; Barford, 2002).

At a transpersonal level, students' interest also stems from the fact that the archetypes of teaching and learning have been constellated in them at primary psychospiritual levels simply by virtue of the fact that they are now in a classroom. The teacher stands in the center of that *temenos* in his archetypal role and is thus already endowed with *mana,* which Jung interpreted as the archetype of psychological energy itself (1969c, p. 251, fn. 88).

Finally, students want to know something about the personal nature of their teacher's intellectual journey because educative processes stimulate *I-Thou* instincts and call out for *I-Thou* responses in a way that few other relationships do (Buber, 1985). Relationship is the primal language of true education.

By sharing with his class something of the story of the shapes that he has assumed in his lifelong journey to *this* class, at *this* time, with *these* students, the teacher may, in a present and specific care for precisely *these* students, expand and multiply their future horizons.

And in yet another instancing of the healthy symbiosis of the archetypes of Hermes and the Wise Elder, the teacher, having passed through so many more transformations than his novice-hero students could have yet done, *models* for his students—in an example of the "idealizing transference" discussed in chapter 2—the kind of person each student might in his own way become farther down the archetypally heroic educative path. The teacher thereby becomes at once more human and more spiritual for the student, just as Hermes lives in both of those worlds in a special way.

Just as Hermes as a demigod was human and divine, moving between both the mundane and transcendent worlds, so the hermetic teacher bridges two worlds, establishing an ego-Self axis in himself by means of his own academic work, which also involves what is contained in the curriculum.

By relating to his students something of the shapeshifting states and stages this journey has entailed for him, and is *still* entailing for him, in his own chronicle of individuation in education, the teacher becomes a living *exemplum* for his students to consider as—each student in his or her own way—they write *their* stories of the multiple transformations that may make them (indeed, in this classroom, even now *are* making them) more whole and free.

THE TEACHER AS "HERMENEUT"

Despite the many contradictions and inconveniences that he was famous for creating, Hermes was paradoxically (but then again, "paradox" is his other name) known and loved as a religious figure by many. Of course, with his antics, he could hardly be called "pious" in any conventional sense, but he was nevertheless associated with the performance of sacrificial rites and entrusted with the high priestly role of carrying messages for the gods.

And it *would be* such a many-faceted being as Hermes—who, like all Tricksters, rocks people's simplistic assumptions and identities—whom the gods would choose to report the typically cryptic and sometimes shattering declarations from heaven to humanity.

So it devolved upon Hermes' to fill the pedagogical role of not only *delivering* these divinely vexing lessons to man but also of *interpreting* them for him—showing man in the balance how such interpreting was done. This is why Hermes' name is the base of the word "hermeneutics"—the theory of interpretation. Hermes thus adds to his impressive, if confusing, resume the fact that he was a *hermeneut.*

Understandably, most teachers have the hermeneutic wish to be the most important person in making their own curriculum. They naturally dislike laboring under the excessive influence of: (1) an official curriculum determined by the state; (2) state monitoring all along the way, through both concrete and symbolic means, to determine how "well" they are doing in "delivering" this official curriculum; and (3) high-stakes, standardized tests at the end of the year, the basic purpose of which is to put a final stamp on how obediently teacher and students have conformed—and then to reward or punish them accordingly.

Such delimiting factors will always play some sort of role in what is going on in the American classroom, of course, especially in light of various U.S. Supreme Court rulings that have established the state's "compelling interest" in education. But when, as is currently the case, such factors are hegemonically in force, constituting what is becoming the state's almost total control over what goes on in a classroom, Hermes is being driven away and the hermetic teacher is being pinned down, like Prometheus to the face of a cliff by outraged gods who will not stand for any challenge to their control over the spirit of man.

As a *hermeneut,* the teacher models for the class how one may interpret a text from many different planes and points of view, highlighting the strengths and weaknesses of each interpretation. And "text" is being used here in the post-Structuralist sense to mean just about anything or anyone at all being interpreted through multiple lenses (Lyotard, 1988). A person can be a text just as much as a book can. So, for example, can a classroom, a school site, or an entire school system be.

The Hermes teacher's aim in such interpretation is two-fold.

The first is to encourage the student to appropriate whatever interpretations of a "text" that is being discussed in class in the ways that best suit her in clarifying and carrying on her own life journey. This aids the student in "composing" her own narrative in increasing degrees of freedom and hope (Freire, 2001). This is the teacher's premier wish for all of the students under his care.

The second is to help the student become a *hermeneut* herself so that she may become ever more adept in generating ever more creative life narratives, both in this class and after it. This is the existential project of being an *etre-pour-soi,* a being for oneself—but not in the sense of selfishness. To the contrary, such a person is of great service in many ways. Rather, it is in the cause of an authenticity—a clearer awareness of herself and others (Sartre, 1956).

The hermeneutic project is one that, for all the analytic skill it requires, is primarily *subjective* (Heidegger, 1964). In educational contexts, the hermeneutic endeavor is fundamentally subjective, not objective, in that it invites the student to discover and live out what she *values,* or in this very process is *coming to value.* In this, it is the heart, not the mind, that must finally be calling the shots. For as Jung pointed out, "The intellect is undeniably useful in its own field, but is a great cheat and illusionist outside of it whenever it tries to manipulate values" (1969c, p. 32).

Subjectivity and value (in many ways the same thing), nonmeasurable (because immeasurable), are anathema to a standardized, or any overly determined, approach to education. However, the teacher who works in the archetypal light of Hermes stands within a pedagogy in the spirit of the symbol. He is a *hermeneut,* and what he wants for his students is that they become *hermeneuts,* too.

THE HERMETIC TEACHER'S PEDAGOGY OF "LIMINALITY"[2]

Hermes was the god of language—and of its limits. His sponsorship of literature and rhetoric made him the patron saint of metaphors and all manner of literary devices. He was thus the lord of linguistic *in*-direction, presiding over intuitive *in*-sight and poetic *ex*-pression as the best means available to human beings of approaching and voicing their most important commitments—which, involving reason, finally go so much deeper than reason, and higher than it, too.

For, all of those personal truths, in constant quest of ultimacy, transcend the limitations of our propositional discourses, the limits—that is, the "liminality"—that our propositional discourses *themselves* generate by creating some "horizons of possibility" but, in so doing, blind us to others (Gadamer, 1980).

The hermetically inclined teacher therefore *employs* the terms of his field with his students insofar as they are empowering. But he also *problematizes* them for his students in the potential those terms have to do harm if they are reified—treated as being "really real."

Every term on the first day of class, therefore, I say to my students: "Every 'solution' to the problems that we will be discussing in this class will—as you will see over and over again—give rise to another kind of problem, even a complete set of new ones. Let us never forget that there is a mystery at the core of everything and it will not yield to our languages, however subtle.

"Our task is not to find 'the perfect solution' to a problem. It does not exist. Our task—*your* task, each one of you in your own way—is to forge an *approach* to any given problem we happen to be discussing, an approach that will hopefully address the problem creatively and humanely, but it is one that will inevitably generate a new problem or set of problems for you to consider and, again … to *approach*!

"No one has a monopoly on the truth, although many claim to. They are either fascists or lunatics. So let us always be *approaching* problems, and all of this in intellectual humility and in the service of our fellow human beings, not imposing our 'perfect' answers on them. For if history shows one thing, it is this: the road to death camps is paved with 'final solutions.' We must appreciate what the tools and techniques of our discipline allow us to do. We must also be aware of their limits. And this means, above all, that we must aware of *our* limits."

This makes sense to the teacher who works in the spirit of Hermes, recalling that one of Hermes' most important roles was as the god of limits and of the intersection of worlds, seen and unseen, mundane and eternal. He presided over both the maintenance and crossing of partitioning lines. This is why traders and thieves alike honored Hermes as their patron. What joined respectable businessmen and unrepentant rogues in their veneration of Hermes was that Hermes was the god of roads and crossroads, of both passable and impassable borders, of moving forward in enrichment.

And he was true in his dual role of enforcer and overcomer of limits, generously protecting those who paid homage to the stone shrines that commemorated him at crossroads while showing his disfavor to those who did not. Such selfish people were those most prone to ignore others in their hours of need at their *own* dire limits. Though the consummate comedian, Hermes showed compassion.

But then again, humor often rests upon, and offers rest from, our contradictory condition. The two masks of ancient Greek theater, one tragic, the other comic—the dialectical personas that the actor put on—cover the same human face, now anguishing, now aspiring, and sometimes both at the same time. And this also means that the hermetic teacher sees, empathizes with (for he has his own many limits too—even in this present field in which he excels), and builds up a student when he sees her coming up against her own limits—a point discussed in chapter 5 regarding "the inferior function."

Because he was the prince of paradox, Hermes, known to Roman culture as Mercury, was the patron god of the Christian alchemists of the Middle Ages and Renaissance. And it is understandable that they conferred this role upon him. The spiritual alchemist's project was paradoxical through and through: the transformation of the basest of matter—rejected stuff that had been tossed away into the hopeless reaches of the weary streets where the outcast trudged—into the heavenly substance of salvation.

What the alchemists drew upon as the light to guide their often shadow-strewn work was the dream of producing the *medicina catholica,* the catholic ("universal") medicine, which would transfigure the baseness of the material world into the rarefied matter of heaven. *Mercurius duplex* the Christian alchemists called him, also *Mercurius Trismegistus,* the dual-natured- and thrice-great Mercury.

They labored under the astrological symbol of Mercury next to the religious symbol of the Cross—the polytheistic and the Judeo-Christian traditions brought into harmony in what Jung felt was a sort of world-historical example of individuation as *coincidentia oppositorum*—the coming together of opposites (1970a, pp. 166–167).[3]

For all the tricks he plays upon mankind, Hermes was widely celebrated as the friendliest of all the gods to humans. Perhaps this is because Hermes is the god whose nature and deeds exhibit to man—to both man's wonderment and woe—the story of man himself, how he lives in the middle of an ineradicable tension.

This fundamental human tension is embodied in the sheer paradox that Hermes not only *enacts* but *is*—his many-faceted physical and ethical possibilities, his sublimity yet earthiness, his grounded compassion at one moment followed by Olympian detachment at another, his multiple identities that somehow form a unity, and above all his talent for transcendence while also being all tangled up (and tangling everyone else up) in paradox.

All of these things existed simultaneously in Hermes, a subtle teacher whose final lesson to man on the classroom of Planet Earth is this: *There is transcendence even in contradiction, and there is contradiction even in transcendence.* This is the lesson-within-the-lesson in every classroom where Hermes presides.

THE HERMETIC TEACHER: DANCING THE
DIALECTIC BEYOND THE BINARY

The figure of Trickster has had "a special and permanent appeal and an unusual attraction for mankind from the very beginnings of civilization" (Kerényi, 1956, p. 9). Trickster's historical persistence, according to the great philologist and mythologist Karl Kerényi, stems from the fact that he is a *speculum mentis*, a mirror of the mind, "wherein is depicted man's struggle with himself and with a world into which he had been thrust without volition and consent" (1956, p. ix).

This being so, and since, as Hyde (1998) has put it, "Trickster makes this world," it is important to ask what, finally, this internally contradictory but supremely important character—businessman and thief, interpreter and confounder, comforter and disturber—has to tell us about our condition, and how we can as teachers use this knowledge skillfully in our and our students' growth.

The answer to these questions lies in the necessity of getting beyond the all-too-human inclination—which was discussed in chapter 2 and now comes into clearer archetypal focus in the figure of Hermes—to think in binaries, black-and-white terms. "Choose just one!" our minds seem hardwired to demand of us: *Up or down, healthy or unhealthy, good or bad, beautiful or ugly, powerful or weak, correct or incorrect, this or that.* We yearn for a simple, safe, fixed ground upon which to plant the flag of our ego. But that is *maya,* as Buddhism calls it: sheer illusion. Life is not like that.

Perhaps there are evolutionary bases for this need for the highest and most secure vantage point above any threats or competitors (Renfrew, 2007). We crave the answers that are *truly* true, while others' answers are (of course) only partially true at best—and probably wrong!

The compulsion to be certain of things and superior to others in our understanding is natural. We can hardly be blamed for it—up to a point.

But we must also grow up, cast off the *puer* or *puella* archetype that is possessing us, assume the mantle of the Wise Elder, and show mercy in how we assess others—and, hardest task of all, in how we judge ourselves—in negotiating the many moral mazes of our misty existence.

For life's most pressing issues are undented by the crude hammer of our dualistic "solutions," however hard we pound. As H. L. Mencken famously observed: for every complex question there is a simple answer—and it is wrong. The universe seems designed to problematize *our* designs.

Indeed, Heraclitus laid it down as a fundamental principle that everything is in constant flux and ultimately turns into its opposite anyway. This tendency of things to change into their opposites Jung used the Greek term *enantiodromia* to denote (Jung, 1967, p. 72). He reckoned it a psychodynamic law that accounted for many of psyche's mysterious motions. It is a pedagogical principle, too.

Enantiodromia highlights the untenable nature of the simplistic dichotomies that we reify and then rely on to define our worlds—and in ways that usually render "us" the heroes, "them" the villains or fools. But such pseudologic makes for bad theater and does nothing to confront in good faith the big questions of our existence, which sometimes have very different but equally plausible answers. As with the Hydra-beast that grew two new heads each time one was cut off, our answers engender new dilemmas of equal or even greater complexity than the ones we started with.

Robert Bolt (1988) summed up "man's struggle with himself" and his universe in the play *A Man for All Seasons*. Sir Thomas More, who was later enshrined as a saint by the Catholic Church after being martyred for his supremely subjective faith, declares: "God made the angels to show Him splendor, as He made animals for innocence and plants for their simplicity. But Man He made to serve Him wittily, in the tangle of his mind."

Those tangles, thick with puzzles, thorny with paradoxes, are Hermes' natural habitat and the archetypally resonant teacher's natural habitat too. Although his pranks are sometimes irritating, Hermes is finally the friendliest of gods to men because his goal is to teach humankind its most important lesson: To live intelligently and compassionately, we must realize that we are, in the last analysis and indeed beyond every analysis, always *feeling* our way forward in the labyrinthine passages of slippery experience between the icy walls of simple opposites.

Trickster's humor parodies—and in so doing, strips away—our certainties, our high-sounding proclamations that finally prove to be paltry oratory, our narcissism strutting around as virtue, our dogmas that we cling to so fervently and proclaim so piously precisely because of how uncertain of them we really are—truth be told.

Hermes problematizes our simplistic notions of who we are, our over-estimation of ourselves and our theories. He demands of us constant reflectivity, confession, reparation, and reconstruction. He is indeed "the funeral of the self" (Belmonte, 1990) as symbolized by the fact that Hermes was one of only four gods allowed to guide the souls of the dead to the underworld—a *psychopomp* as those four were called.

So if the Trickster offends in holding the mirror up to us, it is only because he is really just showing us how *we* have offended. And similarly, his pranks reveal just how tenuous and tiny our lives are, how necessarily provisional our conclusions, and how all of this obliges us to be tolerant of others and humble within ourselves in seeking out ever more nuanced responses, humane and humorous, to our existential situation.

Generously applying the soul-soothing lotion of laughter, the hermetic teacher obliges us to face the not-so-funny fact that many of our cozy social conventions and ideological allegiances—our "consensual realities"—are only conditional, largely just locally shaped, and potentially of great harm when pushed to the limit and forced on others. Consequently, wherever consensual reality holds excessive sway, making people too certain of themselves and too quick to judge others, the trickster is prone to appear and upset the normative apple cart.

True, trickster's outlandishness is political. But it is much more than that. It is thoroughly existential. It reflects the myriad contradictions that each of us ultimately *is*, for that is simply the human condition and no one is immune to it. Trickster is indeed the *speculum mentis*—the reflection of our contradictory souls in the face of a puzzling world.

By means of the living curriculum and in the sacred space of the classroom—exploring all the existential possibilities but also mindful of the institutional constraints inherent in that official setting—the hermetic teacher's calling is to help his student work with the internal and external complexities of her life, while he is simultaneously doing the same thing in his own life, albeit at a higher hermeneutic level.

By resolving contradictions and transcending binaries into ever higher unities, which will draw the student on to ever more refined polar tensions to discover and resolve, the student internalizes the curriculum, makes it her own, and grows.

She is "authoring" herself, in a series of open-ended narratives of expanding efficacy and compassion, into more valid ways of knowing—in both this specific field of inquiry and in her existence as a whole. This is the work of Hermes. It is also the pattern of individuation. And it is the dialectical dance of deeply educational processes.

Hermes duplex. Hermes trismegistus. He was the patron saint of all spiritual alchemists. He continues to be the patron saint of all alchemical teachers.

Commentary by Darryl Denhalter

Darryl Bond Denhalter is an elementary school principal and is pursuing a doctorate degree from the Educational Leadership and Foundations Department at Brigham Young University. He began teaching in the Garden Grove Unified School District.

In this chapter, Mayes draws a parallel between Greek mythology and the craft of effective teaching in order to not only promote reflectivity in other teachers but, one senses, to reflect on his own teaching as well.

Legend has it that Hermes was "the protector of travelers, thieves, and athletes. He occasionally tricked the other gods for his own amusement or in an effort to protect humans."[4] As Mayes points out, Hermes, a scoundrel, was free with his noble deeds, too. And in the story of his genuine charm before Apollo and his kindness in giving his brother a lyre, it is clear that Hermes had social graces and an inherent goodness—in addition, in an *enantiodromia*, to a certain naughtiness.

And although Apollo has a *more* stolid nature than Hermes, he still displayed irritation when he tattled to his father on his brother. We see an *enantiodromia* in the very proper Apollo, a dark side in even the archetypal figure characterized symbol is the sun.

With a teacher who is brave enough to reveal—always in a deliberate and controlled fashion—her own Hermes-like contradictions, the classroom may become a *temenos*, or a sacred place for learning. Skillfully executed, hermetic instruction can lead her student to self-discovery, individuation, and liberation. In recognizing his *own* contradictory nature by seeing the teacher skillfully contain hers, the student, in a paradoxically idealizing-transference, sees a model to emulate. This should cause the educator to reflect on her own role as teacher. Is she sharing herself with her students? Or, is she staying aloof? Is she doing this because she cannot contain her own contradictions in a growthful way? If so, why is this?

An obstacle educators face is the dilemma of being forced to use mandated curricula, even mandated ways of teaching her curriculum, in what she had dreamed would be *her* classroom to nurture and guide. Increasingly, teachers are being compelled to abandon their *individual* instructional styles to adopt a scripted "standard" of "instruction." For some teachers who may be new to the profession, or for others who lack the ability to inspire students, this shift toward such compulsivity in the classroom may be welcome, even temporarily helpful. But it will grow boring soon enough.

In the course of term after term, year after year, of mandated curricula, the ethical purpose of education, to learn and discover one's deepest self (individuation) becomes overshadowed, perhaps even completely, for dubious purposes: to perform well on a high-stakes test, to win an award, to gain parental approval, or just to attain a diploma, etc. As Mayes writes in chapter 4, "The student who receives the message that he is good and important because of all the rewards he gets for scoring well on such tests will soon learn to forfeit the pursuit of his real self in order to 'be' and do whatever is necessary to get a high score on the next test." Are we beginning to sense here the importance of hermetic instruction—and the danger of destroying the archetype of Hermes at play in the classroom?

Mayes is encouraging us to teach and lead at a school site in a way that inspires learning through reflection and discovery. We must cut through prescribed and mandated curriculum and testing and seek to develop the craft of inspirational instruction. It is inspiration that the archetype of Hermes as a teacher provides the teacher, who may then go on to provide a safe haven in which students may begin in earnest to individuate.

NOTES

1. See also Assagioli, 1973; Ferrucci, 1982, and the idea of *Psychosynthesis* for a similar conception of psychological wholeness.

2. I owe the phrase "pedagogy of liminality" to Dr. Sylvia McMillan, with whom I spent many fascinating hours discussing this idea. Her use of Kierkegaard's thought as a basis for resistance to corporate education is groundbreaking and merits a great deal of further research. (McMillan, 2014).

3. See Tarnas (2006), *Cosmos and History: Intimations of a New World View,* for an archetypal interpretation of history.

4. www.greekmythology.com, "Hermes," accessed on 7/10/15.

Conclusion

"Teleos" in Education

THE PIONEERING PSYCHOANALYTIC THEORISTS

We saw early in this study that the depth-psychological approach to education began with psychoanalysis in the early years of the last century with Freud himself and some important members of his inner circle writing about it, especially those who had been teachers before becoming psychoanalysts.

Prominent in the early psychoanalytic literature on education was the epistemological point that secondary cognitive processes emerge out of and are shaped by primary subconscious dynamics.

This suggests that what the teacher sees as a "scholastic problem" in a student might actually be stemming not from a cognitive "incapacity" but an emotional process. Whether that psychodynamic was "pathological" and thus in need of "treatment" or essentially a healthy impulse in the student that needed only to be identified and nurtured into fruition, it was important for the teacher to be aware that something deeper than the child's cognitive abilities might be at play in his academic performance.

The teacher also needed to know that a student's problematic academic performance might be stemming from a healthy impulse to resist instruction for one valid personal, cultural, or ethical reason or another. It also meant, somewhat counterintuitively for some teachers, that positive, even stellar, academic performance might be unhealthy.

This was the case when academic success was the bitter fruit of a student's neurotic need to perform well for others, which was "learning for love, not love of learning" as later psychoanalytic educational theory would put it (Ekstein and Motto, 1969). Although doing well in scholastic terms, such a child would be living in the agony that comes from trudging through a false life—creating an educational problem that would permeate his entire psyche and finally prove destructive of his psychological health, even into adulthood.

Relatedly and of equal importance in the early psychoanalytic literature on education was the therapeutic notion of the transference—the patient projecting images and issues from his early relationship with his primary caregivers, usually the mother and father, onto the authority figure of the therapist.

Knowing that something similar—the student projecting his parental issues onto the authority figure of the teacher—not only *could* happen but was probably quite common in a classroom, and then learning to work with it, would help the teacher respond skillfully to the student's transference so as to benefit the student emotionally and academically. It would also protect the teacher against the potentially alluring or combative energy coming from the troubled student.

In the second half of the 20th century, the self-object and object-relations theories of the neo- and post-Freudians added another set of potent ideas to the store of what psychoanalysis had already given educational theory and practice.

Object-relations theorists noted that just as a parent is the primary psychic object which a child introjected in forming his image of himself—healthy or unhealthy, depending on the nature of how the parent related to the child—so too might the teacher loom large in a contingent but consequential way in the student's psyche. And when it came to how a child saw himself as a person who is capable of learning—so integral in anyone's overall vision of himself as an efficacious person—the teacher was crucial in the formation of that child's "learning ego" (Anthony, 1989).

A teacher who created a safe holding environment for a student—one in which failure was not catastrophic or evidence of the child's lack of worth but something to be compassionately and creatively worked with—communicated to the student the growthful message that it was not only acceptable but optimal to be good enough (Winnicott, 1992). This would bolster the child's learning ego.

The purpose was not to encourage lackadaisical academic performance—if only because that would finally serve to diminish the student's learning ego. Rather, it was to guard against the anxiety and depression that perfectionism breeds, such things actually working against the child being all that he can be in ways that are most satisfying to him and most productive for the communities in which he lives.

THE JUNGIAN TURN IN EDUCATION: APPROACHING WHOLENESS

At the core of Jung's writings is the notion of the collective unconscious. This is nothing other than the mystery of human existence itself—"not this thing or that but the Unknown as it immediately affects us" (1969b, p. 68). Jung's engagement with that Mystery—in interior vision, therapeutic practice, and scholarly research and writing—generated certain terms we may call his *psychospiritual lexicon.* In a sense, the major terms of Jung's psychospiritual lexicon expresses a different aspect of his multiple and multivalent experiences of the inexpressible Mystery.[1]

In this study, I have thus not tried to devise a "Jungian theory of education" but rather to tease out certain educational implications of some of the most important terms in a Jungian psychospiritual lexicon.

Most of these terms were Jung's own, a few were taken from psychoanalysis but lent a richer sense by Jung, and some were implicit in his work but explicitly formulated by later Jungians: the archetypes and archetypal images, the shadow as both a personal and social phenomenon, transference, and counter-transference, *enantiodromia* and the transcendent function, the ego-Self axis, and individuation. I also put special emphasis in this study on the archetypal narrative of the Hero's Journey and the archetypal figures of the *puer and puella,* Logos and Eros, the Wise Elder, and Hermes as having special educational relevance.

Jung's purpose was not to offer a grand theory and empirical *model* of psyche as Freud had done in the positivist and "grand narrative" spirit of the times. Jung strove rather to give voice to his most significant experiences as a man and as a psychotherapist—doing so in a clinically situated but poetically motivated manner (Rowland, 2005). As we have seen, Jung appreciated the utility of theories and was a formidable theorizer himself.

Ultimately, however, he was suspicious of theories because of their tendency to get reified by their adherents and enshrined as a dogma. Then, in the pretentious, even perilous illusion that they possessed a unique "fix" on what is "really real," these "true believers" would set out to impose their views on others, sometimes to disastrous effect.

Rather, Jung, whose focus was ever on the individual, wished to encourage each of us to travel his or her *own* way within the Mystery on the path of deeply educative processes toward the goal of individuation. It is this, much more than a theory of psyche, that Jung offers. One suspects this is the kernel of meaning in his statement, "Thank God I am Jung and not a Jungian!" (as cited in Stein, 2005, p. 4).

Accordingly, in exploring some of the educational consequences of prominent terms in Jung's psychospiritual lexicon, my goal has been to aid the *individual* educational scholar-practitioner in her *own* envisioning of educational processes and in her *own* incarnating of that vision in her classroom practice. The classroom may thus become not only a site of cognitive growth for students, and all the more so because of its psychospiritual sensitivity, but a vital part of that never-ending process called "individuation."

This is, to be sure, in considerable measure a joint project for the teacher students in that "community of discourse" known as a classroom (Brown, Collins, and Duguid, 1988). But it is an endeavor that is necessarily experienced and actualized individually as it figures into each person's ongoing authorship of self in a larger life narrative.

The Individual: "That delicate plant"

Given Jung's belief in the sanctity of the individual in dialectical progress toward ever higher degrees of integrality and creativity, it is easy to understand his philosophical and psychotherapeutic maxim that "morality ... rests entirely on the moral sense of the individual and the freedom necessary for this" (1967, p. 153). And it was precisely this individual who, Jung warned, was imperiled by the 20th century's growing enslavement to corporatist and collectivist philosophies.

Jung saw collectivism on either the Right or Left as an almost demonic force in the modern world. "Who would suspect [the devil] under those high-sounding names of his, such as public welfare, lifelong security, peace among the nations, etc.? He hides under idealisms, under -*isms* in general, and of these the most pernicious is doctrinarism" (1969b, p. 86). He saw these -*isms* as now all but dominating the major industrial societies, and, although he did not write a great deal on the subject, what he did write made it clear that he feared that programs of social control, on the Right and Left, were beginning to govern what went on in classrooms in the name of an -*ism*.

He observed that corporatist education "blots out" the individual across the span of the person's formal education: it "begins in school [and] continues at the university" (1967, p. 153). This is dangerous, said Jung, because it creates the "mass man" of a society awash in what Donald Schön would later call "technical rationality" (1987).

Technical rationality robs the individual of his uniqueness by operationalizing what the U.S. education historian Herbert Kliebard calls the "social efficiency" agenda (Kliebard, 1986). Naturally, this does violence to teachers' and students' unique existential needs, which are neither registered nor responded to by the demands of social efficiency. The net effect of this impingement upon the delicacy of the archetypal relationship between teacher and student is to take us a step farther down the road of psychological, social, and moral disorientation.

Jung's anxiety about the course of Western society and its schools has turned out to be justified, as evidenced in the growing corporate-capitalist agenda that permeates U.S. education as students are not so much *taught* as they are *taught where they will fit* in the corporate political economy (Morrow and Torres, 1995). This would not have surprised Jung. Although he in principle admired

America's *ideological* commitment to the sanctity of the individual, he felt in fact that its *actual* commitment to capitalism was excessive.

Capitalism's 18th-century positivist assumptions and its rampant materialistic appetite would lead America astray, Jung feared—the individual being eaten up at last by the profit motive of impersonal, voracious corporate entities that demanded conformity. And they were growing with such speed and in so many symbolic and concrete areas of America, Jung observed, that they were already well on the way to ravaging the individual, vacating him politically and psychologically of what should be his privileged status.

Like the physician he was, Jung's finger was always perceptively positioned on the cultural wrist to monitor its health. What he diagnosed was a world-historical disease—the consumption of the individual by malignant, depersonalizing forces. The prognosis, he felt compelled to report, was not good (Jung, 1970b).

But this made it all the more crucial to focus on the primacy of the individual and minister to his deepest needs! Only this ran any chance of countering the present pathological course of things by means of a psychoeducational antidote that might not only rehabilitate cultures but renew them. For after all, he asked, "Does not all culture begin with the individual?" (1967, 205), which is not only a cultural truth but an ethical one, which is why "special attention must be paid to this delicate plant 'individuality' if it is not to be completely smothered" (1967, p. 155).

Education and the Cultural Shadow

When it comes to the cultural aspects of education, Jung's vision is a complex blend of a conservative spirit and a progressive one (Mayes, 2005).

On the conservative side, Jung advocated a traditional humanities curriculum as part of the student's schooling in the higher grades.

> The school curriculum ... should never wander too far from the humanities into overspecialized fields. The coming generation should at least be shown the doors that lead to the many different departments of life and the mind. And it seems to me especially important for any broad-based culture to have a regard for history in the widest sense of the word. As important as it is to pay attention to what is practical and useful, and to consider the future, that backward glance at the past is just as important. Culture means continuity, not a tearing up of roots through "progress." (1954, p. 144)

True to his conservative inclinations as a dedicatedly independent Swiss, Jung warned that "anything new should always be questioned and tested with caution, for it may very easily turn out to be only a new disease" (1954, p. 145).

Besides, it is only by honoring the tried and true standards that have developed over time, felt Jung, that we can rein in our animal instincts, many of which may be—as Jung the psychiatrist well knew—psychologically and morally devastating to self and others (1969a, p. 80). Those who see in Jung's fascination with archetypes and ancient cultures a call for a return to primitivism grievously misread him. Such traditionalist statements as the above abound in every volume of *The Collected Works.*

Jung saw education as one of humanity's best hopes to rein in our constant potential for bestiality and promote social and spiritual evolution. He detested "the present tendency to destroy all tradition or render it unconscious," for this must "interrupt the normal process of development for several hundred years and substitute an interlude of barbarism. Wherever the Marxist utopia prevails, this has already happened" (1969b, p. 181). Our personal identities are so interwoven with our individual and collective histories that we cannot know ourselves if we do not know our stories (Henderson, 1991, p. 247).

Although Jung had no quarrel with the idea that education can transmit practical knowledge and promote workable skills, it should never be *primarily* a matter of technical rationality.

> Man is not a machine that can remodeled ... as occasion demands, in the hope that it will go on functioning as regularly as before but in a quite different way. Man carries his whole history with him; in his very structure is written the history of mankind. This historical element in man represents a vital need to which a wise psychic economy must respond. Somehow the past must come alive and participate in the present. (1971, p. 338)

We can know ourselves only by being rooted in an informed appreciation of our past, which is an abiding bulwark against superficial programs in the present for some utopia or other in the hazy future. This is why "loss of roots and lack of tradition neuroticize the masses and prepare them for collective hysteria" (1969b, p. 181). Education has a culturally conserving role to play for Jung.

However, unlike many who in our postmodern world naively advocate for a culturally conservative curriculum that insists that schools only teach and celebrate the history, ideologies, and language of the dominant group, Jung did not do so out of a sense of cultural superiority or xenophobia.

Jung was a great student of cultures. He traveled from the depths of Africa to the deserts of New Mexico (sometimes with such reckless courage as to put himself and members of his party in peril) to gain firsthand experience of First Nation peoples, about whom he wrote with lucidity and admiration. Hence, there is a world of personal and intellectual authenticity in Jung's pithy observation (not a particularly popular one in his day) that "the white race is not a species of homo sapiens specially favored by God" (1966a, p. 82).

It is decidedly not only the white European or the Protestant North American who needs to know about his history. Everyone must know about the great ideas, hopes, triumphs, failures, and, above all, sacred narratives of his *own* culture(s), for at their heart lie those symbols and systems that can bring out the best in him as an individual and a member of his culture(s). This is necessary in the radical differences, and blends, of various cultures in which many of us now live, and which many of us *are*.

These culturally foundational narratives, for all their diversity, are similar in their effect. They make up "the body of lore concerning the things that lie beyond man's earthly existence, and of wise rules of conduct" (1966b, p. 96). The so-called "advanced" cultures are no better or wiser in this respect than so-called "primitive" cultures—and in not a few instances, Jung often emphasized, the former can learn a great deal from the latter.

As Jung saw the Westerner's faith in its foundational cultural narratives eroding, indeed degenerating, he noted that "the old myth needs to be clothed anew in every renewed age if it is not to lose its therapeutic effect" (1969b, p. 181).

Often, studying and incorporating elements from other cultural traditions is just what is needed to provide a society with its new cultural "clothing." Jung's view of "the social construction of reality" (Berger and Luckman, 1967) and the inherent value of cultural diversity is therefore quite topical and useful—a blend of political and cultural conservatism and progressivism—that evinces the immense scope of Jung's thought and work. And after all, such cultural eclecticism is what one would expect from a thinker and practitioner whose focus was always on the blending of opposites.

And in this cultural, indeed existential, project, Jung believed that his idea of the shadow and projection could help us reveal and reform the darker side of our own cultures. In Spindler and Spindler's (1992) idea of "cultural reflectivity"—deep reflection on one's own culture to discover both the liberating and limiting influences it exerts within oneself and on one's actions—and Heath's (1983) notion of the classroom as a community of "ethnographic detectives"—students inquiring into each other's cultural views on topics under discussion in the classroom—we have observed some ways that this can happen in the classroom.

For just as individuals have subconscious and unconscious sides, nothing lacking in darkness, which they tend to project onto others, so do societies. A (sub)culture's shadow can be discerned in who it perceives its enemies to be, for it is onto those enemies that it will heap projections of what it most fears in itself. In this sense, the collective shadow is the flip side of a culture's conscious values (1969a, p. 26).

And insofar as families, communities, political parties, and ethnic groups have normative values, they also possess, and are sometimes possessed by, the darker underside of those values, which they then easily project onto other families, communities, political parties, and ethnic groups.

Education can help students explore such projections. When education assists the individual in casting light on the shadow in himself and his culture, then, guarded against the seductive prejudices of groupthink, he can become an agent in making his (sub)culture more dynamic and clear. Jung wrote:

> Every advance in culture is, psychologically, an extension of consciousness, a coming to consciousness that can take place only through discrimination. Therefore an advance always begins with individuation, that is to say with the individual, conscious of his isolation, cutting a new path through hitherto untrodden territory.... If he succeeds in giving collective validity to his widened consciousness, he creates a tension of opposites that provides the stimulation which culture needs for its further progress. (1969c, p. 59)

Education for Ultimacy in the Temenos Classroom

At the heart of both an individual's and a culture's narratives of hope—and if a classroom is not a zone of hope it may quickly turn into a pit of despair—is the need to connect with the transcendent and to live in its light. This is a universal and inextinguishable urge and as such an archetypal one at the deepest level of primary processes.

Perhaps Jung's most signal contribution to the theory and practice of psychotherapy lay in his insistence that any approach to therapy that did not attend to the individual's psychospiritual engagement with the Mystery and a certain vision of oneself both *in* and *as* this engagement, would leave the patient's problems finally unresolved because her fundamental existential situation and deepest desires had been unacknowledged and thus unaddressed.

Similarly, any system of education that ignores the ethical and cultural impulse toward a higher vision of things will fall short in nurturing the whole student in its failing to account for the student's "ultimate concerns" (Tillich, 1956). These do not simply go away in the classroom but are actually magnified in it.

This is the case because being in a classroom setting already constellates a wide range of archetypal characters and narratival symbols and motifs in and among the teacher and students—a transpersonal power circulating between its four walls with a tremendous force.

At the core of these constellations is the fact that the teacher-student relationship is archetypal. And because the presence of the archetypal realm generates a sense of spiritual significance in the individual, it is wise to draw upon it in teaching and learning to spiritualize educational processes.

For it is also true that *spirituality is itself an archetype*, an inborn human need and capacity—one which, in both the consulting room and classroom, must be honored and explored as the precondition of health and the engine of creativity.

Jung's writings call our attention to the fact that students will naturally want to explore what they feel to be the ethical implications of topics under analysis in the classroom—and will feel bored and short-changed if they are deprived the opportunity to do so. For according to Jung, the ethical domain is an archetype.

Perhaps the greatest of curriculum theorists of the 20th century, Duane Huebner, echoing the Existentialist Theologian Paul Tillich (1956), similarly asserted that we must frame our educational endeavors in "ultimate terms" (1999, p. 405), just as another great but sadly under-celebrated Curricularist, James MacDonald (1995), called for a "transcendental ideology of the curriculum" in order to help teachers and students explore the abiding issues and themes at the core of every subject matter.

There are many ways to engage in psychospiritually sensitive teaching that are pedagogically powerful, institutionally appropriate, legally permissible, and personally enriching (Brown et al., 1976; Whitmore, 1986). And as anyone who has ever had an inspiring science teacher knows, such teaching does not only occur in such areas as the humanities or arts. The social and physical sciences, too, indeed all the areas across the curriculum, offer many opportunities to engage in such spiritually generative education, which, at once inclusive and expansive, is necessarily also holistic (Mayes, 2005a, 2005b; 2016, in press)

No less than the sculptor or novelist, the math and the science teacher can draw from the psychospiritual roots of their own sense of calling into a field that is itself archetypally abundant. It is only the withering touch of an overbearing positivism that has led us to believe otherwise—turning the doing of science into merely a technical matter—the loveless memorization of formulas, not an involvement of the whole person with the sentient, pulsing, evolving organism of the universe. Like the sculptor or novelist, says Huebner, "the scientist awaits the call of the transcendent other" (Huebner, 1999, p. 408).

To be relevant and full-bodied, the curriculum must address across the spectrum of subject matter issues that are both timely and timeless, topical and archetypal. When it does so, the classroom becomes not only a place of learning about conceptual models and acquiring pragmatic skills. It also becomes a zone of Ultimacy, vibrating with the constant call of archetypal reality within us and around us—that "highest dominant" and "superordinate idea" in our hearts and minds which always possesses "a religious or philosophical" character (1985, p. 80; 1969a, p. 61f).

The great teacher thus fills an almost prophetic role for his students—the words "professor" and "prophet" being etymologically related in their root sense of "speaking forth" and "speaking out." Jung captures this beautifully:

> Whoever speaks in primordial images speaks with a thousand voices; he enthralls and overpowers, while at the same time he lifts the idea he is seeking to express out of the occasional and transitory into the realm of the ever-enduring. He transmutes our personal destiny into the destiny of mankind, and evokes in us all those beneficent forces that ever and anon have enabled humanity to find a refuge from every peril and to outlive the longest night. (1966, p. 82)

Lord Whitehead (1929) made a similar point in speaking of what he called "religious" education—but in the broadest possible sense of that term as "this perception, that the present holds within itself the complete sum of existence, backwards and forwards, that whole amplitude of time, which is eternity" (as cited in Wilber, 2012, p. 112).

No one would deny the educational importance of acquiring bodies of knowledge or acquiring certain skills. But when—as is now the case in our educational systems—such activities do not have an archetypal dimension, attempting to involve the student wherever and whenever possible at both the highest and deepest levels of his being, we might well ask with T.S. Eliot, "Where is the wisdom we have lost in knowledge? Where is the knowledge we have lost in information?"

Not only communicating knowledge and teaching skills but also honoring and building on the student's sense of ultimacy should be key to our educational endeavors. These are not antagonistic goals. They go together and indeed "both are necessary, for knowledge alone, like faith alone, is always insufficient" (1970b, p. 532).

"Teleos" in Education

Jungian psychology specifically, and depth psychology in general, reminds us that cognition is a secondary process that grows out of and never ceases to be shaped by the primary processes of the subconscious and the unconscious. Schooling that attends to this fact allows the teacher to teach and the student to learn in ways that, integral, are consistent with their whole nature.

When this is not the case, the effects on teacher and student are grievous. The teacher finds himself alienated from his work, out of touch with the archetypal sources of his professional calling, alienated from himself, his subject matter and his students. The student's cognitive processes grow increasingly distanced from her emotional and spiritual nature and needs. She becomes a house divided against itself—living in a painful internal conflict that may well cause her inner turmoil all her life and bar the realization of her full cognitive potential.

Heart, mind, and soul need each other. They are the human trinity of knowledge in passion and compassion. Jungian psychology offers unique and utile ways of bringing these elements together in educational processes.

Indeed, one of Jung's greatest themes was synthesis-and-transcendence— ongoing dialectical tension into ever-upward-tending unities. The ego and the Self, the poetic and the mathetic, the archetypally male and the female principles of *Logos* and *Eros,* the legal claims of the Great Father and the forgiving nurturance of the Great Mother, the higher vision and the reality of the Shadow, the individual and culture, normative reality and the boundary crossings of the Trickster—these are all dualities in oneself and in the world that one needs to experience, identify, and then craft into ascending syntheses in the never-ending process of individuation or wholeness.

Wholeness, not perfection.

Jung was interested in the difference in ancient Greek between the lexically very similar but semantically very different words *teleois* and *teleos*—"perfect" and "perfected," respectively. This might seem an obscure linguistic point, but for Jung it was of first importance. As Christ was the central myth of Western culture, Jung felt that one had to come to grips with the influence of that myth in the shaping of the Western psyche and to some degree of one's own. And one of the most influential—and Jung believed destructive—of Christ's utterances was what seems to be the impossible demand: "Be ye perfect!"

But the fault was not to be laid at Christ's door. Christ's words had been mistranslated from the Greek, said Jung, an accomplished student of ancient languages. Christ had not demanded that we be "perfect"—*teleois*.

Rather, suggested Jung in an alternative translation, what Christ had really enjoined was the more generous *evangel*: "Become ye perfected!" *Teleos* was the actual word used in the Greek, and it captured the message of the alchemists' mystical Christ, the *salvator macrocosmi.* His more humane gospel was of psychospiritual maturation in the roiling retort of complex experience, through dialectical stages—sometimes involving ideological death and resurrection—so that the Philosopher's Stone might finally emerge in the form of the dynamically balanced, endlessly creative human being, *the individuated man or woman.*

To promote the teacher's and student's individuation in this light has been my purpose in writing this book—a plea for education for wholeness, education for individuation.

For perfection is not possible in any case, except in very specific instances, artificial contexts, and to realize a strictly delimited objective—one that has usually been imposed from above. This is increasingly the case in U.S.

education. But the education of a student *must* be better than that because anything less than attending to the whole student easily proves injurious to him. Education rises to its full measure when it makes the whole student—the student's *individuation*—its central concern, when the student is the focus of educational processes, not the object of miseducative purposes.

In that spirit and toward that aim, I have drawn upon a Jungian psychospiritual lexicon to suggest some ways of imagining education for wholeness—a pedagogy of *Teleos* in the archetypally rich space of the classroom, and in the service of the teacher's and student's intellectual and psychospiritual growth as they relate to each other, around a living curriculum, in educational communion.

Commentary by Barbara Smith

Barbara M. Smith (M.Ed.) is an associate clinical professor at Brigham Young University, where she teaches courses and coordinates practicum experiences for teacher candidates. She has taught students (K-12) with mild to severe disabilities in various public school settings.

In our current educational climate of extreme accountability, professional educators at every level are grappling with the concepts of teaching and learning.

Many ask questions such as the following.

What does the most effective teaching look like? Do I personally have the capabilities to raise my students' performance level and how should that be measured? How can significant learning happen in just the limited instructional time I have with the students, especially since other opposing factors such as a student's home life, background, attendance, disability, motivation, conflicting priorities, readiness and maturity, desire to learn, resources, etc. are also pressing? How can I reconcile what I believe students in my class (school) should learn, with what authorities dictate my students should learn?

Likewise, Jung as a psychotherapist mined for answers to questions that were likely similar in nature, but probably different in magnitude and application—although, as Mayes points out, there is an educational dimension to therapy and a therapeutic dimension to education.

But in words that any teacher would understand, he advised teachers to pay "special attention to this delicate plant 'individuality'." So, how do educators nurture individuality—promote "education for individuation"—especially in a group setting?

A teacher in a 21st-century classroom may choose to self-evaluate his own philosophy and implementation of Jung's advice by considering the following questions.

Does my teaching practice show evidence of my belief in the sanctity of the individual and each person's search for wholeness, balance, and uniqueness? Does my curriculum allow students to make choices and progress at their own rate? In my planning, do my instructional objectives foster personal goals and gifts or more of a "corporatist education"?

Would my students agree that I value personal expression in the arts, in academics, in social situations, and in psychospiritual exploration? Do I accept various methods of demonstrating mastery of the course content? Or, do I communicate the expectation that all students will achieve (not necessarily the same as "learning," as Mayes insists) at the same level before the end of the unit?

Periodic and candid self-reflection, peer review, and student feedback can inform teachers about how well they are recognizing individual differences (or at least are *perceived* to be recognizing them—not an unimportant piece of information for a teacher to have).

English language learners include those with a language-related disability, a native language difference, immature language development, or limited academic language proficiency. Generally, ELLs appreciate teachers who plan group projects and cooperative learning activities where they don't feel pressure to speak in front of the whole class. They value opportunities to draw pictures or act out concepts instead of explaining them verbally.

In addition, fear of taking tests can be minimized when the assessment involves formats like multiple choice, matching, short answer, or better yet, demonstration, instead of essay questions—which largely gauge their expressive vocabulary and writing skills, and can misrepresent their *actual* knowledge of the content.

Regarding *intrapersonal learning*, Mayes quotes Jung, "We can know ourselves only by being rooted in an informed appreciation of our past." Mayes goes on to explain how each person can understand the traditions and narratives of his culture which lead to enlightened self-awareness.

A recent example comes from a high school senior who explored his heritage by conducting research into the incidence of certain genetic traits in his family members, recording personal interviews with grandparents and reading historical accounts of the founding of the city where the family resided for generations.

"Finding our roots," studying genealogy, and participating in family history projects are becoming popular, and also meaningful, pastimes for youth and adults. Here is one quite "mathetic" means of engaging in the "poetic" project of profound self-examination and self-realization that Mayes argues for. It is also an example of reconciling opposite modalities in the transcendent function of this student's fascinating work.

Noting that the teacher-student relationship is archetypal, and this realm generates a spiritual significance, Mayes has reminded readers that a spiritual educational process must reach into the student's psyche and create powerful impressions there. This type of learning is difficult to forget and may produce lasting changes which are integral in students. This may not be religious, but it *is* spiritual, and it can happen in a classroom—and also in the music room, a science lab, the library, or the gym.

Perhaps the greatest value of a pedagogy of *Teleos* is that it may bring to pass in any educational space a type of learning that is so deep and enduring that the student has already moved that much closer toward the goal of individuation in her larger life narrative.

NOTE

1. He did not share all of his mystical experiences, however, which were kept secret from the public eye, because he felt they would be injuriously misconstrued, but reserved others of them for a private journal, *The Red Book,* which he shared with only a few friends. It became public in 2009 in the Rubin Museum of Art in New York City. Its profound significance in how we must now (re)vision Jung the man and Jung the writer is only beginning to be appreciated.

Bibliography

Adams, M. (1996). *The multicultural imagination: "Race," color, and the unconscious*. London: Routledge.

Aichhorn, A. (1925/1951). *Wayward youth: A psychoanalytic study of delinquent children, illustrated by actual case histories*. New York: Viking Press, Bergin and Garvey.

————. (1930). *Wayward youth: A psychoanalytic study of delinquent children, illustrated by actual case histories*. New York: Viking Press.

Almon, J. (1999). From cognitive learning to creative thinking. In J. Kane (Ed.), *Education, information, and transformation: Essays on learning and thinking* (pp. 249–269). Upper Saddle River, NJ: Prentice-Hall.

Anthony, E. (1989). The psychoanalytic approach to learning theory (with more than a passing reference to Piaget). In K. Field, B. Cohler, and G. Wool (Eds.), *Learning and education: Psychoanalytic perspectives* (pp. 99–126). Madison, CT: International Universities Press, Inc.

Appel, S. (1996). *Positioning subjects: Psychoanalysis and critical educational studies*. New York: Bergin and Garvey.

Apple, M. (1990). *Ideology and curriculum*. London: Routledge.

Assagioli, R. (1973). *The act of will*. New York: The Viking Press.

Bair, D. (2003). *Jung: A biography*. Boston: Little, Brown.

Barford, D. (Ed.). (2002). *The ship of thought: Essays on psychoanalysis and learning*. London: Karnac Books.

Barnaby, K., and D'Acierno, P. (1990) (Eds.) *C.G. Jung and the humanities: Toward a hermeneutics of culture* (pp. 45–66). Princeton, NJ: Princeton University Press.

Becker, C. (1966). *The heavenly city of the eighteenth-century philosophers*. New Haven, CT: Yale University Press.

Belmonte, T. (1990). The trickster and the sacred clown: Revealing the logic of the unspeakable. In K. Barnaby and P. D'Acierno (Eds.), *C.G. Jung and the humanities: Toward a hermeneutics of culture* (pp. 45–66). Princeton, NJ: Princeton University Press.

Bender, J., and Wellerby, D. (Eds.) (1991). Chronotypes: *The construction of time.* Stanford, CA: Stanford University Press.

Berger, P. and Luckmann, T. (1967). *The social construction of reality: A treatise in the sociology of knowledge.* New York: Anchor Books.

Bernstein, B. (1996). *Pedagogy, symbolic control, and identity: Theory, research, critique.* London: Taylor and Francis.

Bettelheim, B. (1976). *The uses of enchantment: The meaning and importance of fairy tales.* New York: Random House.

Block, A. (1997). *I'm only bleeding: Education as the practice of social violence against children.* New York: Peter Lang.

Blos, P. (1940). *The adolescent personality: A study of individual behavior for the Commission on Secondary School Curriculum.* New York: D. Appleton-Century Co.

Blumer, H. (1969). *Symbolic interactionism.* Englewood Cliffs, NJ: Prentice-Hall.

Bodkin, M. (1974). *Archetypal patterns in poetry: Psychological studies of imagination.* Oxford: Oxford University Press.

Bolt, R. (1988). *A man for all seasons.* New York: French Publishing.

Bourdieu, P. (1977). Cultural reproduction. In J. Karabel and A. Halsey (Eds.), *Power and ideology in education* (pp. 487–507). New York: Oxford Press.

Bowles, S. and Gintis, H. (1976). *Schooling in capitalist America.* New York: Basic Books.

Britzman, D. (2003). *After-Education: Anna Freud, Melanie Klein, and psychoanalytic histories of learning.* Albany: State University of New York Press.

Brooke, R. (1991). *Jung and phenomenology.* London: Routledge.

Brophy, J. (1994). *Motivating students to learn.* Boston: McGraw-Hill.

Brown, J., Collins, A., and Duguid, O. (1988). Situated cognition and the culture of learning. *Educational Researcher,* 18, pp. 32–42.

Brown, G., Phillips, M., and Shapiro, S. (1976). *Getting it all together: Confluent education.* Bloomington, IN: Phi Delta Kappa Educational Foundation.

Brubacher, J. and Rudy, W. (1997). *Higher education in transition: A history of American colleges and universities.* 4th Edition. New Brunswick, NJ: Transaction Publishers.

Bruner, J. (1996). *The culture of education.* Cambridge, MA: Harvard University Press.

———. (1960). *The process of education.* New York: Vintage.

Buber, M. (1965). *I and thou.* New York: Vintage.

Buber, M. (1985). *Between man and man.* New York: Scribners.

Bullough, R. Jr. and Gitlin, A. (1995). *Becoming a student of teaching: Methodologies for exploring self and school context.* New York: Garland Publishing, Inc.

Burke, K. (1989). *On symbols and society.* J. Gusfield (Ed.), Chicago: University of Chicago Press.

Campbell, J. (1949). *The hero with a thousand faces.* Princeton, NJ: Princeton University Press.

Cassirer, E. (1965). *The philosophy of symbolic forms.* New Haven, CT: Yale University Press.

Castoriadis, C. (1991). Time and creation. In J. Bender and D. Wellerby (Eds.), *Chronotypes: The construction of time* (pp. 38–64). Stanford, CA: Stanford University Press.

Chardin, T. de. (1975). *The phenomenon of man.* New York: Perennial Library.

Charet, F.X. (1993). *Spiritualism and the foundations of C.G. Jung's philosophy.* Albany: State University of New York Press.

Chi, M.T.H., Feltovich, P.J., Glaser, R. (1986). Categorization and representation of physics problems by experts and novices. *Cognitive Science*, 5, pp. 121–152.

Chinn, C. and Brewer, W. (1993). The role of anomalous data in knowledge acquisition: A theoretical framework and implications for science instruction. *Review of Educational Research*, 63(1), pp. 1–49.

Chomsky, N. (1968). *Aspects of the theory of syntax.* Cambridge, MA: MIT Press.

Conforti, M. (1999). *Field, form, and fate: Patterns in mind, nature, and psyche.* Woodstock, CT: Spring Publications

Cohler, B. (1989). Psychoanalysis and education: Motive, meaning, and self. In K. Field, B. Cohler and G. Wool (Eds.), *Learning and Education: Psychoanalytic Perspectives* (pp. 11–84). Madison, CT: International Universities Press, Inc.

———. (1964). *The transformation of the school: Progressivism in American education, 1876–1957.* New York: Vintage Press.

Cremin, L. (1988). *American education: The metropolitan experience.* New York: Harper & Row.

De Castell, S. and Luke, A. (1983). Defining "literacy" in North American schools. *Journal of Curriculum Studies,* 15, pp. 373–389.

Devine, D. (1995). Prejudice and out-group perception. In A. Tesser (Ed.), *Advanced social psychology* (pp. 467–524). New York: McGraw-Hill.

Dewey, J. (1916). *Democracy and education.* New York: Macmillan.

Dourley, J. (1984). *The illness that we are: A Jungian critique of Christianity.* Toronto, Canada: Inner City Books.

Duschl, R. and Gitomer, D. (1991). Epistemological perspectives on conceptual change: Implications for educational practice. *National Association for Research in Science Teaching,* 9(2), pp. 839–858.

Edinger, E. (1985). *Anatomy of the psyche: Alchemical symbolism in psychotherapy.* La Salle, IN: Open Court Press.

Edinger, E. (1973). *Ego and archetype: Individuation and the religious function of the psyche.* Baltimore, MD: Penguin Press.

Eisner, E. and Vallance, E. (1985). *The educational imagination: On the design and evaluation of school programs.* New York: Macmillan.

Ekstein, R. and Motto, R. (1969). *From learning for love to love of learning: Essays on psychoanalysis and education.* New York: Brunner/Mazel.

Ekstein, R. (1969a) Psychoanalytic notes on the function of the curriculum. In R. Ekstein, and R. Motto (Eds.), From learning for love to love of learning: Essays on psychoanalysis and education (pp. 47–57). New York: Brunner/Mazel Publishers.

Eliade, M. (1974). *Shamanism: Archaic techniques of ecstasy.* Princeton, NJ: Princeton University Press.

Ellenberger, Henri F. (1970). *The discovery of the unconscious: The history and evolution of dynamic psychiatry.* New York: Basic Books.

Elson, M. (1989). The teacher as learner, the learner as teacher. In K. Field, B. Cohler, and G. Wool (Eds.), *Learning and education: Psychoanalytic perspectives.* Madison, CT: International Universities Press, Inc.

Esman, A. (Ed.). (1990). *Essential papers on transference.* New York: New York University Press.

Fairbairn, W.R.D. (1940/1992). *Psychoanalytic studies of the personality.* London: Routledge.

Fay, B. (2000). *Contemporary philosophy of social science: A multicultural approach.* Oxford: Blackwell Publishers Ltd.

Fay, B. (1986). *Critical social science: Liberation and its limits.* Ithaca, NY: Cornell University Press.

Feinstein, D. and Krippner, S. (1988). *Personal mythology: Using rituals, dreams, and imagination to discover your inner story.* Los Angeles: Jeremy P. Tarcher, Inc.

Fenichel, O. (1945). *The psychoanalytic theory of neurosis.* New York: Norton.

Ferrucci, P. (1982). *What we may be: Techniques for psychological and spiritual growth through Psychosynthesis.* Los Angeles: Jeremy Tarcher, Inc.

Field, K., Cohler, B., and Wool, G. (Eds.). (1989). *Learning and education: psycho-analytic perspectives.* Madison, CT: International Universities Press, Inc.

Foucault, M. (1980). *Power/knowledge: Selected interviews and other writings, 1972–1977.* New York: Pantheon Books.

Fowler, J. (1981). *Stages of faith: The psychology of human development and the quest for meaning.* San Francisco: Harper & Row.

Frankl, V. (1967). *Man's Search for Meaning.* New York: Washington Square Press.

Freire, P. (2001). *Pedagogy and freedom: Ethics, democracy, and civic courage.* Lanham, MD: Rowman & Littlefield.

———. (1970). *The pedagogy of the oppressed.* New York: Seabury Press.

Freud, A. (1930). *Introduction to psychoanalysis: Lectures for child analysts and teachers, 1922–1935.* New York: International Universities Press, Inc.

Frey-Rohn, L. (1974). *From Freud to Jung: A comparative study of the psychology of the unconscious.* New York: G. P. Putnam's Sons.

Frye, N. (1957). *Anatomy of criticism: Four essays.* New York: Antheneum.

Gadamer, H. (1980). *Dialogue and dialectic: Eight hermeneutical studies on Plato.* New Haven, CT: Yale University Press.

Gellert, M. (2001). *The fate of America: An inquiry into national character.* Washington, D.C.: Brassey's, Inc.

———. (1990). *The consequences of modernity.* Stanford: Stanford University Press.

Giddens, A. (2002). *Runaway world: How globalization is reshaping our lives.* London: Profile.

Giddens, A. (1990). *The consequences of modernity.* Stanford, CA: Stanford University Press.

Giroux, H. and Myrciades, K. (2001). *The corporate university and the politics of education.* Lanham, MD: Rowman & Littlefield.

Grant, C. (Ed.). (1995). *Educating for diversity: An anthology of multicultural voices* Boston: Allyn and Bacon.

Gray, R. (1996). *Archetypal explorations: An integrative approach to human behavior.* London: Routledge.

Greene, M. (1974). Cognition, consciousness, and curriculum. In W. Pinar (Ed.), *Heightened consciousness, cultural revolution, and curriculum theory* (pp. 69–83). Berkeley, CA: McCutchan Publishing.

Greenson, R. (1990). The working alliance and the transference neurosis. In A. Esman (Ed.), *Essential papers on transference* (pp. 150–171). New York: New York University Press.

Hall, A. (2002). Psychoanalytic research on learning: An appraisal and some suggestions. In D. Barford (Ed.), *The ship of thought: Essays on psychoanalysis and learning* (pp. 17–40). New York: Karnac Books.

Hall, G. S. (1904). *Adolescence: Its psychology and its relations to physiology, anthropology, sociology, sex, crime, religion and education.* New York: D. Appleton and Company.

Halliday, M. (1978). *Language as social semiotic.* London: Edward Arnold.

———. (1984). Language as code and language as behavior. In R. Fawcett, M. Halliday, & A. Makkai (Eds.). *The semiotics of culture and language.* London: Francis Pinter.

Handy, W., and Westbrook, M. (1974). (Eds.). *Twentieth century criticism: The major statements.* New York: Macmillan.

Harris, M. (1991). *Teaching and religious imagination: An essay in the theology of teaching.* San Francisco: Harper Collins.

Hartshorne, C. (1984). *Omnipotence and other theological mistakes.* Albany: State University of New York Press.

Hauke, C. (2000). *Jung and the postmodern: the interpretation of realities.* London: Routledge.

Heath, S. (1983). *Ways with words: Language, life, and work in communities and classrooms.* Cambridge, England: Cambridge University Press.

Heidegger, M. (1964). *Being and time.* New York: Harper & Row.

Heisig, J. (1979). *Imago Dei.* Philadelphia: Bucknell Press.

Henderson, J. (1991). "The Jungian interpretation of history and its educational implications." In R. Papadopoulos and G. Saayman (Eds.). *Jung in modern perspective: the master and his legacy* (pp. 245–255). Garden City Park, NY: Avery Publishing Group.

Hewitt, J. (1984). *Self and society: A symbolic interactionist social psychology.* Boston: Allyn and Bacon.

Hobsbawm, E. (1999). *Industry and empire.* London: The New Press.

Hoeller, S. (1982). *The Gnostic Jung and the seven sermons to the dead.* Wheaton, IL: Theosophical Publishing House.

Hoffer, E. (1990). *The true believer.* New York: Basic Books.

Homans, P. (1995). *Jung in context: Modernity and the making of a psychology.* Chicago: University of Chicago Press.

Houston, J. (1996). *A mythic life: Learning to live our greater story.* San Francisco: Harper Collins Publishers.

Huberman, M., Gronauer, M., Marti, J. (1989). *The lives of teachers.* J. Neufeld (Trans.). New York: Teachers College Press.

Huebner, D. (1999). *The lure of the transcendent: Collected essays by Dwayne E. Huebner.* V. Hillis (Ed.). London: Lawrence Erlbaum Associates, 1999.

Huxley, A. (1945). *The perennial philosophy.* New York: Harper.

Hyde, L. (1998). *Trickster makes this world: Mischief, myth and art.* New York: North Point Press.

Isaacs, S. (1932) *The children we teach, seven to eleven years.* London: University of London Press.

Jansz, J. and van Drunen, P. (2004). *A social history of psychology.* Oxford: Blackwell Publishing Ltd.

Jaynes, J. (2000). *The origin of consciousness in the breakdown of the bicameral mind.* New York: Houghton Mifflin.

Jersild, A. and Lazar, E. (1962). *The meaning of psychotherapy in the teacher's life and work.* New York: Bureau of Publications, Teachers College.

Jones, M., Jones, B., and Hargrove, T. (2001). The unintended consequences of high-stakes testing. Lanham, MD: Rowman & Littlefield.

Jones, M., Jones, B., and Hargrove, T. (2003). *The unintended consequences of high-stakes testing.* Lanham, MD: Rowman & Littlefield.

Jung, C.G. (1954). *The development of personality*, vol. 17. (R. F. C. Hull, Trans.). Princeton, NJ: Princeton University Press.

Jung, C.G. (1956). *Symbols of transformation: Analysis of the prelude to a case of schizophrenia*, vol. 5. (R. F. C. Hull, Trans.). Princeton, NJ: Princeton University Press.

Jung, C. (1965) *Memories, dreams, reflections.* New York: Vintage.

Jung, C.G. (1984). *Selected Letters of C.G. Jung, 1909–1961.* Princeton, NJ: Princeton University Press.

———. (1985). *The practice of psychotherapy: General problems of psychotherapy,* vol. 16. (R. F. C. Hull, Trans.). Princeton, NJ: Princeton University Press.

———. (1978). *Psychology and the East.* Princeton, NJ: Princeton University Press.

———. (1977). *The symbolic life,* vol. 18. (R. F. C. Hull, Trans.). Princeton, NJ: Princeton University Jean Paul Sartre y Press.

———. (1970a). *Mysterium coniunctionis,* vol. 14. (R. F. C. Hull, Trans.). Princeton, NJ: Princeton University Press.

———. (1970b). *Civilization in transition,* vol. 10. (R. F. C. Hull, Trans.). Princeton, NJ: Princeton University Press.

———. (1971). *Psychological types,* vol. 6. (R. F. C. Hull, Trans.). Princeton, NJ: Princeton University Press.

———. (1969a). *Structure and dynamics of the psyche,* vol. 8. (R. F. C. Hull, Trans.). Princeton, NJ: Princeton University Press.

———. (1969b). *Archetypes and the collective unconscious,* vol. 9.1. (R. F. C. Hull, Trans.). Princeton, NJ: Princeton University Press.

———. (1969c). *Aion: Researches into the phenomenology of the self,* vol. 9.2. (R. F. C. Hull, Trans.). Princeton, NJ: Princeton University Press.

———. (1968). *Alchemical studies,* vol. 13. (R. F. C. Hull, Trans.). Princeton, NJ: Princeton University Press.

———. (1967). *Two essays on analytical psychology,* vol. 7. (R. F. C. Hull, Trans.). Princeton, NJ: Princeton University Press.

————. (1966). *The spirit in man, art, and literature*, vol. 15. (R. F. C. Hull, Trans.). Princeton, NJ: Princeton University Press.

————.(1961). *Freud and psychoanalysis*, vol. 4. (R. F. C. Hull, Trans.). Princeton, NJ: Princeton University Press.

————. (1959). *The Face to Face Interview in C.G. Jung Speaking: Interviews and Encounters* (pp. 424–439). Princeton, NJ: Bollingen Paperbacks, 1977.

Jung, E. and M.L. von Franz. (1986). *The Grail Legend*. London: Coventure.

Kalsched, D. (1997). *The inner world of trauma: Archetypal defenses of the personal spirit*. London: Routledge.

Kane, J. (Ed.). (1999). *Education, information, and transformation*. Columbus, OH: Merrill/Prentice Hall.

Kant, I. (1781/1997). *The critique of pure reason*. Chicago: Hackett Publishing.

Kaufmann, W. (1975). *Existentialism from Dostoyevsky to Sartre*. New York: Penguin Books.

Kelsey, M. (1984). Jung as philosopher and theologian. In R. Papadopoulos and G. Saayman (Eds.), *Jung in modern perspective: The master and his legacy* (pp. 182–192). Lindfield, Australia: Unity Press.

Kerenyi, C. (1956). *The Trickster: A study in Native American mythology*. New York: Knopf.

Kierkegaard, S. (1969). *A Kierkegaard anthology*. R. Bretall (Ed.), Princeton, NJ: Princeton University Press.

Kirsch, J. (1995). Transference. In M. Stein (Ed.), *Jungian analysis* (pp.170–209). Chicago: Open Court Publishing Co.

Kirschner, S. (1996). *The religious and romantic origins of psychoanalysis: Individuation and integration in post-Freudian theory*. New York: Cambridge University Press.

Klein, M. (1975)/[1932]). *The psychoanalysis of children* (Trans. A. Strachey). New York: Delacorte Press.

Kliebard, H. (1986). *The struggle for the American curriculum: 1893–1958*. New York: Routledge.

Kohlberg, L. (1987). *Child psychology and childhood education: A cognitive-developmental view*. New York: Longman.

Kohut, H. (1950/1978). *The search for self: Selected writings of Heinz Kohut: 1950–1978*. Ornstein (Ed.), Madison, CT: International Universities Press.

Komar, A. and Hatzoglou, M. (2005). Internal ribosome entry sites in cellular mRNAs: The mystery of their existence. *The Journal of Biological Chemistry*, 280(25), pp. 23435–23428.

Kozol, J. (1991). *Savage inequalities: Children in American schools*. New York: Harper.

Kuhn, T. (1970). *The structure of scientific revolutions*. Chicago: University of Chicago Press.

Lauter, E., and Rupprecht, C. (1985). *Feminist archetypal theory: Interdisciplinary re-visions of Jungian thought*. Knoxville: The University of Tennessee Press.

Levinas, E. (1996). *Basic philosophical writings*. Bloomington: Indiana University Press.

Lyotard, J. (1988). *The differend*. Minneapolis: University of Minnesota Press.

Macdonald, J. (1995). *Theory as a prayerful act: The collected essays of James P. Macdonald*. New York: Peter Lang.

Main, R. (2004). *The rupture of time: Synchronicity and Jung's critique of modern Western culture*. New York: Brunner-Routledge.

Marx, K. and Engels, F. (1978). *The Marx-Engels reader*. R. Tucker (Ed.), New York: W.W. Norton & Co.

May, R. and Yalom, I. (1995). Existential psychotherapy. In R. Corsini and D. Wedding (Eds)., *Current psychotherapies* (pp. 262–292). Itasca, IL: F.E. Peacock Publishers: New York.

Mayes, C. (2016). *An introduction* to The Collected Works of C.G. Jung: *Psyche as spirit*. Lanham, MD: Rowman & Littlefield.

Mayes, C. (2009a). The psychoanalytic view of education: 1922–2002. *Journal of Curriculum Studies*, 49(1), pp. 539–567.

———. (2009b) *The hero's journey in teaching and learning: A study in Jungian pedagogy*. Madison, WI: Atwood Publishing.

———. (2007). *Inside education: depth psychology in teaching and learning*. Madison, WI: Atwood Publishing.

———. (2005a). *Jung and education: Elements of an archetypal pedagogy*. Lanham, MD: Rowman & Littlefield Education.

———. (2005b). The teacher as shaman. *Journal of Curriculum Studies*, 37(3), pp. 329–348.

———. (2004). *Seven curricular landscapes: An approach to the holistic curriculum*. Lanham, MD: University Press of America.

———. (2003). Foundations of an archetypal pedagogy. *Psychological perspectives: A semiannual journal of Jungian thought. C.G. Institute of Los Angeles*, 46, pp. 104–116.

———. (2002). Personal and archetypal aspects of transference and counter-transference in the classroom. *Encounter: Education for Meaning and Social Justice*, 15(2), pp. 34–49.

———. (2001). A transpersonal developmental model for teacher reflectivity. *Journal of Curriculum Studies*, 33(4), pp. 477–493.

———. (1999). Reflecting on the archetypes of teaching. *Teaching Education*, 10(2), pp. 3–16.

Mayes, C., Maile Cutri, R., Goslin, N., and Montero, F. (2016). *Understanding the whole student: Holistic multicultural education (2nd edition)*. Lanham, MD: Rowman & Littlefield.

Mayes, C., and Williams, E. (2012). *Nurturing the whole student: Five dimensions of teaching and learning*. Lanham, MD: Roman & Littlefield.

Mayes, C., Cutri, R., Montero, F., and Rogers, C. (2010). *Understanding the whole student: Holistic multicultural education*. Lanham, MD: Rowman & Littlefield.

Mayes, C., Blackwell-Mayes, P., and Williams, E. (2004). Messages in the sand: Sandtray therapy techniques with graduate students in an educational leadership program. *International Journal of Leadership in Education*, 7(3), pp. 257–284.

McLaren, P. (1998). *Life in schools: An introduction to critical pedagogy in the foundations of education*. (3rd edn.). New York: Longman.

McMillan, S. (2013). *A pedagogy of liminality: Kierkegaard's challenge to corporate education.* A dissertation. Department of Educational Leadership and Foundations. Provo, UT: Brigham Young University.

Miller, J. (2004). *The transcendent function: Jung's model of psychological growth through dialogue with the unconscious.* Albany: State University of New York Press.

Mocanin, R. (1986). *Jung's psychology and Tibetan Buddhism: Western and Eastern paths to the heart.* London: Wisdom Publications.

Morrow, R. and Torres, C. (1995). *Social theory and education: A critique of theories of social and cultural reproduction.* Albany: State University of New York Press.

Nagy, M. (1991). *Philosophical issues in the psychology of C.G. Jung.* Albany: State University of New York Press.

Neumann, E. (1969). *Depth psychology and a new ethic.* New York: P.G. Putnam and Sons.

Niebuhr, R. (1986). *The essential Reinhold Niebuhr: Selected essays and addresses.* R. Brown (Ed). New Haven, CT: Yale University Press.

———. (1944). *The children of light and the children of darkness: A vindication of democracy and a critique of its traditional defenders.* Chicago: University of Chicago Press.

Nieto, S. (2000). *Affirming diversity: The sociopolitical context of multicultural education.* New York: Addison, Wesley, Longman.

Noddings, N. (1995). Care and moral education. In W. Kohli (Ed.), *Critical conversations in the philosophy of education* (pp. 137–148). New York: Longman.

Noddings, N. (1985). *Caring: A feminine approach to ethics and moral education.* Berkeley: University of California Press.

Noll, R. (1994). *The Jung cult: Origins of a charismatic movement.* Princeton, N.J.: Princeton University Press.

Odajnyk, V. (1976). *Jung and politics: The political and social ideas of C. G. Jung.* New York: Harper & Row.

Otto, R. (1960). *The idea of the holy.* Middlesex, England: Penguin Books.

Owens, L. (2015). *Jung's hermeneutics of vision.* An unpublished manuscript. Salt Lake City: The Holy Gnosis of Thomas Chapel.

Palmer, M. (1995). *Freud and Jung on religion.* New York: Routledge.

Pai, Y. and Adler, S. (2001). Cultural foundations of education (3rd edition). New York: Merrill, Prentice Hall.

Pauli, W., and Jung, C.G. (2001). *Atom and archetype: The Pauli/Jung Letters, 1932–1958.* C.A. Meier (Ed.). Princeton, NJ: Princeton University Press.

Pauson, M. (1988). *Jung the philosopher: Essays in Jungian thought.* New York: Peter Lang, Inc.

Pfister, O. (1922). *Psycho-analysis in the service of education, being an introduction to psycho-analysis.* London: Henry Kimpton.

Pinar, W. (Ed.). (1975). *Curriculum theorizing: The reconceptualists.* Berkeley, CA: McCutchan Publishing.

Pinar, W., Reynolds, W., Slattery, P., Taubman, P. (Eds.). (2000). *Understanding curriculum: An introduction to the study of historical and contemporary curriculum discourses.* New York: Peter Lang.

Pintrich, P., Marx, R., and Boyle, R. (1993). Beyond cold conceptual change: The role of motivational beliefs and classroom contextual factors in the process of conceptual change. *Review of Educational Research*, 63, pp. 167–199.

Popkewitz, T. (1987). *Critical studies in teacher education.* London: The Falmer Press.

Posner, G.J., Strike, K.A., Hewson, P.W., and Gertzog, W.A. (1982). Accommodation of a scientific conception: Toward a theory of conceptual change. *Science Education*, 67(4), pp. 498–508.

Redl, F. and Wattenberg, W. (1951). *Mental hygiene in teaching.* New York: Harcourt, Brace and Company.

Renfrew, C. (2007). *The role of evolutionary theory in archaeological thought.* New York: State University of New York Press.

Richards, A. (2014). Education in the Third Reich. A lecture delivered in the Department of Educational Leadership and Foundations, Brigham Young University: Provo, Utah.

———. (1991). *Freud and philosophy: An essay in interpretation.* New Haven, CT: Yale University Press.

Ricoeur, P. (1976). Introduction. In P. Ricoeur (Ed.), *Cultures and time* (pp. 13–33). Paris: UNESCO.

Riegel, K. (1979). *Foundations of dialectical psychology.* New York: Academic Press.

Rowland, S. (2005). *Jung as a writer.* London: Routledge.

Salzberger-Wittenberg, I. (1983) *The emotional experience of learning and teaching.* London: Routledge and Kegan Paul.

Samuels, A. (2001). *Politics on the couch: Citizenship and the internal life.* London: Routledge.

———. (1997). *Jung and the post-Jungians.* London: Routledge.

———. (1991). *Psychopathology: Contemporary Jungian perspectives.* London: The Guilford Press.

Schwartz-Salant, N. And Stein, M. (1995) (Eds.), Transference/ countertransference. Wilmette, IL: Chiron Publications.

Sartre, J. (1956). *Being and Nothingness: An essay on phenomenological ontology.* New York: Philosophical Library.

Schön, D. (1987). *Educating the reflective practitioner.* San Francisco: Jossey-Bass Publishers.

Schumpeter, J. (1975). *Capitalism, socialism and democracy.* New York: Harper & Row.

Shalem, Y., and Bensusan, D. (1999). Why can't we stop believing? In S. Appel (Ed.), *Psychoanalysis and pedagogy* (pp. 27–44). London: Bergin and Garvey.

Shamdasani, S. (2005). *Jung stripped bare by his biographers, even.* London: Karnac.

———. (2003). *Jung and the making of modern psychology: The dream of a science.* Cambridge, U.K.: Cambridge University Press.

Sheldrake, R. (1981). *A new science of life: The hypothesis of formative causation.* Los Angeles: J.P. Tarcher.

Skinner, B. F. (1971). *Beyond freedom and dignity.* New York: Knopf.

———. (1956). *The technology of teaching.* New York: Appleton-Century-Croft.

Spindler, G. and Spindler, L. (1992). Cultural process and ethnography: An anthropological perspective. In M. LeCompte, W. Millroy, and J. Preissle (Eds.), *The handbook of qualitative research in education* (pp. 52–92). London: Academic Press.

Spring, J. (1976). *Educating the worker-citizen.* New York: McGraw Hill.

Stein, M. (2005). Individuation: Inner work. *Journal of Jungian Theory and practice*, 7(2), pp. 1–13.

Suzuki, D.T. (1964). *An introduction to Zen Buddhism.* New York: Grove Press, Inc.

Tarnas, R. (2006). *Cosmos and psyche: Intimations of a new world view.* New York: Viking.

Tillich, P. (1956). *The essential Tillich.* New York: Macmillan Publishing Co.

Trostli, R. (1991). Educating as an Art: The Waldorf Approach. In *New directions in education: Selections from Holistic Education Review.* R. Miller (ed.). (pp. 338–353). Brandon, VT: Holistic Education Press.

Tyack, D. (1974). *The one best system: A history of American urban education.* Cambridge, MA.: Harvard University Press.

Ulanov, A. (1999). *Religion and the spiritual in Carl Jung.* New York: Paulist Press.

Underhill, E. (1961). *Mysticism: A study in the nature and development of man's spiritual consciousness.* New York: E.P. Dutton.

Vedfelt, O. (2001). *The dimensions of dreams: From Freud and Jung to Boss, Perls, and R.E.M.—a comprehensive sourcebook.* New York: Fromm International.

———. (1984). Meaning and order: Concerning meeting points and differences between depth psychology and physics. In R. Papadopoulos and G. Saayman (Eds.), *Jung in modern perspective: The master and his legacy* (pp. 268–286). Lindfield, Australia: Unity Press.

———. (1981). *Puer aeternis.* New York: E.P. Dutton.

———. (1974). *Number and time: Reflections leading toward a unification of depth psychology and physics.* Evanston, IL: Northwestern University Press.

———. (1991). Meeting and order: Concerning meeting points and differences between depth psychology and physics. In R. Papadopoulos and G. Saayman (Eds.), *Jung in modern perspective: The master and his legacy* (pp. 268–286). Dorset, U.K.: Prism Press.

Vygotsky, L. (1986). *Mind in society: The development of psychological functions.* Cambridge, MA: Harvard University Press.

Wehr, G. (2002). *Jung and Steiner: The birth of a new psychology.* Great Barrington, MA.: Anthroposophic Press.

Welsford, E. (1935). *The fool: His social and literary history.* New York: Farrar & Reinhart, Inc.

Weston, J. (1957). *From ritual to romance.* Garden City, NY: Doubleday.

Wheelwright, P. (1974). Poetry, myth, and reality. In W. Handy and M. Westbrook (Eds.), *Twentieth century criticism: The major statements* (pp. 252–266). New York: Macmillan.

Whitehead, A. (1929). *The aims of education.* New York: Knopf.

White, M. and Epston, D. (1990). *Narrative means to therapeutic ends.* New York: W.W. Norton and Co.

Whitmore, D. (1986). *Psychosynthesis in education: A guide to the joy of learning.* Rochester, VT: Destiny Books.

Wilber, K. (2012). *The spectrum of consciousness.* Wheaton, IL: Theosophical Publishing House.

Winnicott, D.W. (1988). *Psychoanalytic explorations.* C. Winnicott, R. Shepherd, and M. Davis (Eds.). Cambridge, MA: Harvard University Press.

Winnicott, D.W. (1992). The mother-infant experience of mutuality. In C. Winnicott, R. Shepherd, and M. Davis (Eds.), *Psychoanalytic explorations* (pp. 251–260). Cambridge, MA: Harvard University Press.

Woodman, R. (2005). *Sanity, madness, transformation: The psyche in Romanticism.* Toronto: University of Toronto Press.

Wool, G. (1989). Relational aspects of learning: The learning alliance. In K. Field, B. Cohler, and G. Wool (Eds.), *Learning and education: Psychoanalytic perspectives* (pp. 747–770). Madison, CT: International Universities Press, Inc.

Zachry, C. (1940). *Emotion and conduct in adolescence. For the Commission on Secondary School Curriculum.* New York: Appleton-Century.

———. (1929). *Personality adjustments of school children, with an introduction by William Heard Kilpatrick.* New York: C. Scribner's Sons.

Zinn, H. (1990). *A people's history of the United States.* New York: Harper Perennial.

Index

Adams, Michael, 115
*Aion: Researches Into the
    Phenomenology of the Self,* 39
alchemical processes, 98, 122
alchemists:
    Christian, 139;
    spiritual, 142
*American Education: The Metropolitan
    Experience,* 58
Apocalypse, 124
Apollo, 132
archetypal:
    defenses of the personal spirit, 62;
    dialectic, 132;
    figure, 51;
    images, 3, 112;
    lens, 2;
    narrative, 51, 147;
    of the Divine, 4;
    pedagogical reflectivity, 63;
    reflectivity, 60, 77, 95;
    shadows, 113, 116, 119;
    symbols, 9, 51
archetype, 153;
    of order, 12;
    of the teacher, 60
archetypes, 1, 7, 48
Ardent Disciple, 100

behaviorism, 1, 5

Being and Nothingness, 66
Beings of Ultimacy, 111
Bhagavad Gita, 55
Blake, William, 66
Bolt, Robert, 141
Brecht, Bertolt, 68
Buber, Martin, 28, 67, 85, 110
Buddhist psychology, 7
Burke, Kenneth, 68

Campbell, Joseph, 50, 63
Camus, Albert, 121
capitalism, 149
Cloud of Unknowing, 47
cognition, 20
coincidentia oppositorum, 139
Collected Works, 6, 39, 150
collective:
    cultural conscious, 93;
    unconscious, 6, 146
collectivism, 148
community of discourse, 148
conscientizacion, 119
counter-transference, 25
Cremin, Lawrence, 14, 57, 58, 115
The Critique of Pure Reason, 42
cubist curriculum, 134
cultural:
    archetypes, 112;
    reflectivity, 125, 151

Curricularist, 153

Dark Magician, 76
de Castillijo, Irene, 60
Democracy and Education, 59
demythologized, 81
Dewey, John, 59
dominant-cultural conscious mind, 117

Eckhart, Meister, 47
Edinger, Edward, 77
education for individuation, 91
Educational Progressivism, 134
ego, 21, 155
enantiodromia, 141
Enlightenment, 41, 82
ere-pour-soi, 70
esse-:
    in-intellectu, 44;
    in-anima, 44
ethnographic detectives, 125
existential:
    beings, 4;
    theology, 28;
    worth, 109
extraversion, 106

Fairbairn, Ronald, 28, 34
Faust, 131
feeling type, 105, 111
Foucault, Michel, 57, 130
Fowler, James, 72
Friere, Paulo, 119
From Ritual to Romance, 66

Giddens, Anthony, 118
Gnosis, 48
Goethe, von Johann Wolfgang, 131
good-enough:
    mother, 33, 88, 123;
    teacher, 33
good holding environment, 123
Great Father, 155
Great Mother, 155
Greene, Maxine, 134
Ground-of-Being, 48

Heidegger, Martin, 27, 29, 85
hermeneut, 136, 137
hermeneutics of hope, 122
Hermes, 129, 130, 131, 135, 136, 138, 147
hermetic teacher, 131, 134
The Hero with a Thousand Faces, 63
hero's cycle, 50
Hero's Journey, 147
Hitler, Adolf, 116
holding environment, 32
Huebner, Duane, 114, 153

id, 21
imago Dei, 63, 76
individuation, 124, 130, 147, 156
inferior function, 103, 104, 109
introversion, 106
intuitive type
isomorphic, 82
I-Thou, 21, 29, 60, 67, 85, 95, 102, 110, 135

Jonah Complex, 63

Kalsched, Donald, 62
Kant, Immanuel, 42, 44, 49
Keats, John, 45
Kerenyl, Karl, 140
Kierkegaard, Soren, 85
Kliebard, Herbert, 148
Kohlberg, Lawrence, 72
Kohut, Heinz, 28, 31

learning:
    disabilities, 108;
    ego, 87
life narrative, 87
liminality, 138
Logos and Eros, 132, 147, 155

MacDonald, James, 153
A Man for All Seasons, 141
Maslow, Abraham, 10
massa confusa, 101
mathetic faculties, 42, 155

Mercurius duplex, 139
Mercury, 139
The Meyers-Briggs Personality Type Indicator, 107
military-industrial-educational complex, 58, 115
Milton, John, 97
mirroring transference, 31
multicultural psychoanalysis, 124
multiculturalism, 113
mysterium tremendum et fascinans, 3
mystery, 147

narcissistic wounds, 110
Nada, 47
narrative, 2
    structures, 9
Neumann, Erich, 121
Niebuhr, Reinhold, 7, 123
nigredo, 122
Noddings, Nel, 109
numinous, 3, 10

object-relations:
    psychology, 27, 28, 29;
    theorists, 146
official curriculum, 57
ontological:
    beings, 48;
    encounter, 27;
    realm, 85
Otto, Rudolf, 3

Paradise Lost, 97
Pauli, Wolfgang, 12
pedagogies of care, 30, 109
A People's History of the United States, 73
persona, 88
personal subconscious, 13
Philosopher's Stone, 101, 122, 155
poetic faculties, 43, 70, 71, 155
positive pedagogical self-object, 30
The Prelude, 45
prima materia, 100
The Process of Education, 114

projection, 11, 151
psychoanalysis, 1, 44, 145
psychoanalytic educational theory, 145
Psychological Types, 104
psychopomp, 142
psycho-:
    social identity, 4;
    spiritual beings, 48;
    spiritual identity, 4;
    spiritual lexicon, 147;
    spiritual reflectivity, 171
puer or puella, 64, 74, 94, 141, 147

Reconceptualist Movement, 114, 115
religious education, 154
Renaissance, 139
renaissance alchemy, 13
repetition compulsion, 24

salvator microcosmi, 99, 155
Salzberger-Wittenberg, Isca, 26
Samuels, Andrew, 41
Sartre, Jean Paul, 29, 66, 70
savior archetype, 11
self, 84, 155
self-object psychology, 27, 28
Senex, 66, 77
sensate type, 105
shadow, 151, 155;
    archetypes, 94;
    curriculum, 103
shamanic teacher, 133
social efficiency, 148
soul-making, 45
speculum mentis, 142
Spindler, G., 151
Spindler, L., 151
spiritus rector, 130, 133
Stages of Faith, 72
Steiner, Rudolf, 13
structuration, 118
Student Ideology Revealed: Culture in the Holistic Classroom, 113
sub specie eternitatis, 2, 48
subjective curriculum, 103

superego, 21
superior function, 104, 105
Symbols of Transformation, 5
synchronicity, 7, 8

technical rationality, 148
The Technology of Teaching, 114
teleos, 155
temenos, 48, 70, 74, 133, 135
therapeutic classroom environment, 26
thinking type, 105, 111
Thorndyke, Edward, 20, 41, 82
Tillich, Paul, 3, 10, 153
transcendent function, 83, 88, 95
transference, 24
transrational, 85
Trickster, 74, 129, 133, 140, 155
Tyack, David, 57

Ultimacy, 153
unconscious, 47
Unus Mundus, 7, 48

Verfremdungseffekt, 68, 69

Waldorf, 13
Weston, Jessie, 65
Whitehead, Lord, 154
Winnicott, D. W., 28, 33, 56, 88, 123,
    146
Wise Elder, 65, 78, 95, 101, 131, 135,
    141, 147
Wordsworth, William, 45

Zachry, Caroline, 134
Zeus, 131, 132
Zinn, Howard, 73, 115

About the Author

Clifford Mayes, PhD, PsyD, is professor of educational psychology in BYU's McKay School of Education. Considered the founder of archetypal pedagogy, Mayes has written nine other books and forty scholarly articles on the intersection of education, culture, and spirit.

www.ingramcontent.com/pod-product-compliance
Lightning Source LLC
Chambersburg PA
CBHW030652270326
41929CB00007B/320